# Restructuring Trade Agreements

# Restructuring Trade Agreements

Juscelino F. Colares
Mustafa T. Durmuş

Wolters Kluwer

*Published by:*
Kluwer Law International B.V.
PO Box 316
2400 AH Alphen aan den Rijn
The Netherlands
E-mail: international-sales@wolterskluwer.com
Website: lrus.wolterskluwer.com

*Sold and distributed by:*
Wolters Kluwer Legal & Regulatory U.S.
7201 McKinney Circle
Frederick, MD 21704
United States of America
E-mail: customer.service@wolterskluwer.com

ISBN 978-94-035-3034-5

e-Book: ISBN 978-94-035-3030-7
web-PDF: ISBN 978-94-035-3032-1

*For Susana and Vildan*

# Table of Contents

# List of Abbreviations

| | |
|---|---|
| AB | Appellate Body |
| AD | Antidumping Duty |
| AK Parti or JDP | Justice and Development Party |
| BTC | Baku-Tbilisi-Ceyhan |
| CAP | EU Common Agricultural Policy |
| CETs | Common External Tariffs |
| CU | EU-Turkey Customs Union |
| CVD | Countervailing Duty |
| DDA | Doha Development Agenda |
| DEIK | Foreign Economic Relations Board of Turkey |
| DSB | Dispute Settlement Body |
| DSU | Understanding on Rules and Procedures Governing the Settlement of Disputes |
| ECJ | European Court of Justice |
| EEC | European Economic Community |
| EFTA | European Free Trade Association |
| EU | European Union |
| FDI | Foreign Direct Investment |
| FIT | Ontario Feed-in Tariff Program |
| FTA | Free Trade Agreement |
| FTCs | Foreign Trade Companies |
| FTZ | Free Trade Zone |
| GATT | General Agreement on Tariffs and Trade |
| GCC | Gulf Cooperation Council |
| GDP | Gross Domestic Product |
| GNA | Grand National Assembly |

| | |
|---|---|
| IIP | Investment Incentive Program |
| IMF | International Monetary Fund |
| ISI | Import Substitution Industrialization |
| ITP | Iraq-Turkey Pipeline |
| LPG | liquefied petroleum gas |
| LPR | Leave-in-Place-and-Ratification Approach |
| MFN | Most Favored Nation |
| NAMA | Non-Agricultural Market Access |
| NATO | North Atlantic Treaty Organization |
| NGOs | Nongovernmental Organizations |
| OPEC | Organization of Petroleum Exporting Countries |
| QRs | Quantitative Restrictions |
| ROOs | Rules of Origin |
| RPR | Repeal-Pause-and-Ratification Approach |
| SCM | Agreement on Subsidies and Countervailing Measures |
| SCT | Special Consumption Tax |
| SMEs | Small and Mid-Sized Enterprises |
| SOEs | State-Owned Enterprises |
| SPO | State Planned Organization |
| TANAP | Trans-Anatolian Natural Gas Pipeline |
| TAP | Trans-Adriatic Pipeline |
| TIM | Turkish Exporters Assembly |
| TRIPS | Agreement on Trade-Related Aspects of Intellectual Property Rights |
| VCLT | 1969 Vienna Convention on the Law of Treaties |
| WTO | World Trade Organization |

# Introduction

## I. TREATY-MAKING AND TREATY-RESTRUCTURING CONCEPTS

Practical scholarship on international law and, particularly, on treaty-making provides thoughtful insights on the motivations that cause states to enter into international agreements.[1] States, instrumentalists posit, enter into agreements in pursuit of at least two objectives: *one*, obtaining substantive benefits from the codification of prior practices or informal understandings into a finalized bargain; *the other*, increasing the likelihood that such expected benefits materialize, by enshrining the terms of the bargain into a written instrument that both facilitates mutual compliance and has increased normative strength. Thus, expected mutual benefits, a necessary condition for treaty-making, are not enough to induce two or more states to enter into an agreement. The logic of treaty-making requires that expectations be matched with mechanisms for monitoring compliance and enforcement. In short, idealistic expectations, even when held mutually, do not turn bargains into agreements.

It is no coincidence that the history of and literature on international trade relations is rich with examples of successful negotiations and long-lasting agreements precisely because *trade* agreements focus on ensuring that parties shift their trade practices to something easily verifiable and, thus, enforceable: tariffs.[2] Of course, the argument runs in the other direction, too: the possibility of monitoring and enforcing compliance will not suffice to induce states into an agreement if the proposed bargain (e.g., tariff concessions) proves unappetizing. Treaty-negotiating and treaty-making require the simultaneity of these conditions.

*But what can be said of treaty continuity?* Should we expect a treaty to remain in place if one of the two treaty-making conditions no longer observes? In principle, one

1. *See, e.g.*, ANDREW T. GUZMAN, HOW INTERNATIONAL LAW WORKS—A RATIONAL CHOICE THEORY 119-80 (2008); JACK L. GOLDSMITH AND ERIC A. POSNER, THE LIMITS OF INTERNATIONAL LAW 83-106, 135-62 (2005).
2. *See, e.g.*, General Agreement on Tariffs and Trade, Oct. 30, 1947, 61 Stat. A-11, 55 U.N.T.S. 194, Arts. XI (prohibiting quantitative restrictions on the trade in goods) & II (binding each contracting party to its own tariff commitments) [hereinafter GATT].

would be tempted to answer in the negative, on the theory that, for instance, once expected benefits no longer accrue to one of the parties (or prove to be altogether unfounded), the treaty should perish for lack of one of its founding properties. Yet, loss of a deal's expected gains—one aspect of treaty erosion—typically occurs over a number of years. Over time, private-vested interests in treaty-continuity may become entrenched, and bureaucratic and elite preferences may oppose change, thereby raising the domestic costs of treaty-termination. One only needs to look beyond the state as a unitary actor to perceive how motivation distortions *within* governments can help explain why treaty-restructuring or termination might be politically unpalatable, even when national interest is maximizing.

Far from a challenge to rational choice theory, this observation merely highlights how states can and often settle for second-best policies. States do so, because states are *not* unitary actors. In fact, a rational choice theory of treaty continuity or treaty-renegotiation must take into account the phenomenon known (at least in the United States) as the "Administrative State"—the complex of large bureaucracies, run by career civil servants, to whom the power to administer treaties is typically delegated, and whose interests may not necessarily coincide with the state's. Thus, treaties that persist on deviating from once expected net positive benefits need not be perceived as anomalous. Rather, such treaties may be viewed as a *feature* of bureaucratic-captured policymaking processes that perpetrate bad deals from a national interest standpoint in favor of a preferred status quo. Goldsmith and Posner recognize this as global phenomenon:

> It is true that a bureaucracy charged with ensuring compliance will often insist on compliance in instances that do not serve the state's immediate interest, either because the bureaucracy is trading off relatively unimportant short-term interests for more important medium-term interests, ... or because, as is sometimes the case, bureaucratic self-aggrandizement leads to continued bureaucratic support for a treaty regime, or for bureaucratically self-serving interpretations of the treaty, even in instances that do not serve the state interest. The former case is an example of the state following its interest; *the latter is an example of agency costs that encumber all political systems.* Neither is an example of international law becoming part of a state's "internal value set" (Koh 1997), and neither prevents a state's leadership from changing course in a sufficiently important case.[3]

Remarkably, bureaucracies *themselves* are not unitary. One may see different agencies adopt opposing positions on a given treaty regime if, for example, that particular regime does not further or even creates obstacles to a given agency's mission while favoring that of the other.[4] In the context of inter-bureaucratic rivalry, these differences may be exacerbated: agencies that view a treaty regime as a *gain* are likely to perceive change in the form of treaty-renegotiation or termination with *risk aversion*, whereas agencies that perceive such regime as a *loss* may exhibit *risk-seeking* behavior and may be quite supportive of change. At a minimum, different risk preferences may

3. Goldsmith and Posner, *supra* note 1, at 104 (emphases added).
4. *Id.* (citing and reacting to Harold Hongju Koh's theory that repeated compliance with international law leads government officials to develop a "habit of complying with international law, even when doing so would not serve their government's interests").

lead agencies, political elites, and economic actors to differ on characterizations of the national interest.[5] Thus, any theory on treaty-renegotiation or restructuring must go beyond the unitary state and consider the role of such groups in resisting change, among other variables.

While a given domestic alignment may give rise to opposition to treaty-restructuring, one must also consider *external* constraints on state behavior, particularly how they can lead to keeping the status quo in regard to treaties, even in net-negative-benefit contexts. Arguably, a state is likely to bear the occasional short-term disadvantages of a bargain when it believes such forbearance furthers its overarching foreign policy goals and, thus, the national interest. This also means that states consider their options in contemplation of their *anticipated* external effects. How might other states respond to deviations from a set of commitments? How might decisions in one policy domain affect others? What particular sequence of steps would pave the way for restructuring a particular agreement while minimizing friction? These are a few questions national leaders seek to answer when contemplating the trade-offs involved in maintaining, renegotiating, or terminating agreements. Viewed in this perspective, a state's decision to keep a given net-negative benefit agreement illustrates, more likely, an assessment of its own national interest in contemplation of internal and external constraints, rather than putative deference to international treaty compliance.[6] In sum, leaders and states "pick their battles," and they do it by looking both inward and outward.

## II. ROADMAP AND SCOPE OF THE BOOK

Not including this introduction and the concluding chapter, the book contains six chapters, divided into three parts. Part I deploys rational choice concepts to develop a model of how states behave in regard to restructuring agreements. The model explains how leaders weigh internal factors (e.g., resistance from economic sectors, political elites, and the domestic bureaucracy against change) and external considerations (e.g., whether an agreement's expected positive stream of benefits has materialized or is likely to do so in the foreseeable future) before attempting to restructure a given agreement. It posits that, whether as the party considering such restructuring or the party resisting it, states tend to act within a range of behavioral patterns, not randomly. Because states exhibit behavioral regularities both when maintaining or restructuring agreements, the model we develop in Chapter 1 provides the analytical framework for analyzing the book's major illustration: the EU-Turkey Customs Union ("CU"), a trade relationship that we posit and demonstrate is ripe for restructuring.

5. For a deeper discussion on how risk preferences emerge, *see* EYAL ZAMIR AND DORON TEICHMAN, BEHAVIORAL LAW AND ECONOMICS (Oxford University Press, 2018).
6. *Contra* Harold Hongju Koh, *Why Do Nations Obey International Law*, 106 YALE L.J. 2599, 2634 (1997) (positing state deference to international commitments derives from government officials' developing a habit for obedience to international law, which leads to repeated compliance and norm internalization).

Before demonstrating why that is the case and how Turkey might restructure its trade arrangement with the European Union (EU), we first provide the background on the origins of and reasons for the CU (Part II). In Part II, we also offer an in-depth discussion of the CU's increasingly asymmetric effects against Turkey, which should prompt its government to pursue a renegotiation soon, if not in the next few years. Because of these asymmetries—particularly, the loss of trade sovereignty, a major impediment to addressing perennial trade and current account deficits, an important source of Turkey's "boom and bust" cycles—Part III applies the model developed in Chapter 1 and explains how Turkey may accomplish such restructuring both *legally* and *transactionally*.

The book concludes with a brief exposition of the main takeaways from our model and its application in the EU-Turkey context. We hope our readers will appreciate the insights we derive throughout the book, as well as learning more about Turkey—a most fascinating country—and its relationship with the European Union and other parts of the world.

# PART I State Behavior in Regard to Restructuring Agreements

## Chapter 1

# A Model of State Behavior

To help us consider the set of internal and external constraints pushing states to maintain, renegotiate, or terminate treaties, we adopt a modified version of Goldsmith and Posner's "theory of international law."[1] This seminal work provides a useful methodology for understanding the *emergence* of customary international law and treaty law. Here, rather than examining what causes sovereigns to converge on practices that give rise to customary international law and, at times, even prefer written agreements, we take *existing* agreements as the point of departure. We then ponder their fate, particularly, when the conditions leading to the signing of such agreements change over time. Because Goldsmith and Posner's methodological insights instigate clear, analytical thinking on the problem of agreement emergence, and because these insights can be adapted to the study of agreement continuity (or discontinuity), we rely on them to develop the *model* we apply throughout the book.

## I. ASSUMPTIONS AND REALITY

For the sake of simplicity, assume a two-state context. State A and State B, each, have certain capacities and interests. Their leaders can assess their *capacities* (e.g., natural resource endowments, human capital, military might, etc.) by resort to information available from national institutions. They can ascertain their countries' *interests* according to the preferences of citizens and groups, as articulated through the interplay of politics (i.e., in democracies) or by the dominance of one or a few institutions (e.g., a central party, royal family, the army, etc.).

At a given point in time, let us call it $t_0$, the initial stage from which our model evolves, States A and B agree to share a particular common *resource* (e.g., a river, a mineral resource, fisheries, etc.), or subject their relationship to some basic rules in one sector (e.g., transportation, energy, etc.), their entire economy (e.g., a common market

1. *See* Jack L. Goldsmith and Eric A. Posner, The Limits of International Law 10-13 (2005).

or trade agreement, etc.), or defense (e.g., common defense pact, arms control agreement, etc.). Time passes, and the relative power of State A increases, either because of a shock in B (e.g., a major natural calamity), or the result of a favorable turn of events in A (e.g., discovery of a rare, highly valuable resource). In a purely Hobbesian world, either change, accruing in $t_1$, means that State A would likely force its will upon State B, by taking some of B's territory; requiring tribute; overusing a shared resource; or any combination of these. In our days, State A may be subtler and merely choose to abrogate, at least partially, the bargain it struck with State B at $t_0$ (while expecting B to honor its bargain), or State A may remove a benefit that it used to render to B that, though outside the initial bargain, it no longer feels compelled to provide.

A world in which (i) States A and B have *complete information* about each other's capacities and interests ("perfect information" assumption) and (ii) parties can costlessly agree on the most efficient allocation of entitlements, with no barriers to negotiation ("zero transaction cost" or Coasean assumption) will quickly transition to a new stage, $t_2$—a time, when States A and B converge into a new accommodation. State A will be better off, obviously. That will be the case either because State A gets a bargain superior to the one it had negotiated with State B, at $t_0$, or because A is now entitled to some form of wealth transfer from B deriving from an unrelated bargain.

This is clearly *not* what happens in our world, however. Specifically, State A and State B do not have perfect information about each other's capacities and interests, and renegotiating their previous deal is clearly not costless. In fact, resentment and different perceptions on what constitutes a "fair" reallocation of entitlements (if agreement can be reached at all), *or* what the most efficient allocation might be, will often lead to complicated, protracted negotiations and, possibly, diplomatic friction. In this environment, the likelihood that states will hold overly optimistic, chauvinistic assessments of their own capacities while discounting those of other states is ever present. As discussed above, motivation distortions *within* governments may exacerbate transaction costs and degrade the quality of assessments further, making renegotiation difficult, if not impossible, for a while, and in some cases, even lead to war. For instance, financial authorities might want to minimize budgetary losses due to the economic uncertainty associated with greater diplomatic friction. Therefore, such officials may favor a quicker, peaceful adjustment (risk-averse behavior). In contrast, armed forces might see a benefit in testing the will of the other state, one whom they now perceive as relatively less capable (risk-taking behavior). Manipulation of public sentiment via traditional media, social media, and rent-seeking interests can also help intensify preexisting tendencies that depart from rational assessments. Regardless, before a final settlement emerges, the process for adjustment will be anything but smooth or optimal.

Still, despite the multiplicity of factors influencing states' mutual assessments, *their actions and responses will not be random*. An observer of international relations and international law detects patterns in how states behave and relate to each other, even in a world of imperfect information and nonzero transaction costs. Following Goldsmith and Posner's framework, the starting point of our model is the *foundational* notion that a state's behavior in regard to international commitments is a function of its pursuit of self-interested policies in contemplation of its own and its counterparties' capabilities. Of course, the focus on self-interest as the independent variable influencing observance or renegotiation (or termination) of prior commitments does not imply that states hold casual views on international law. Surely, international law matters. For states, it matters, particularly, when it affords them the means to ensure their bargains will be observed, such as when treaties contain provisions on monitoring compliance and even, in some cases, authorizing sanctions to infringing behavior (e.g., "suspension of concessions," the World Trade Organization ("WTO") term for authorized retaliation).[2] Such ordered regimes increase opportunities for cooperation and coordination, thereby helping states achieve mutually beneficial outcomes.[3]

As will be demonstrated in this chapter and throughout the book (particularly in Chapter 6), more often than not, self-interest *pushes* states to observe international law when compliance is perceived as beneficial in the long term. By contrast, when compliance is increasingly viewed as contrary to state self-interest, the likelihood of deviations from previous commitments, requests for renegotiation of particular agreements, or termination of such obligations increases. Remarkably, international law anticipates and even regulates these situations. The Vienna Convention on the Law of Treaties, discussed later in the book (Chapter 6), specifies the various ways countries can amend or terminate treaties, even when a treaty lacks modification or termination clauses.[4] That states agreed to regulate treaty-amending and treaty-termination is not surprising: it is in their very *self-interest* to reduce uncertainty by providing, *ex ante*, disciplines for these situations. Goldsmith and Posner put it best: international law "is not a check on state self-interest; it is a *product* of state self-interest."[5]

## II. HOW STATES APPROACH RESTRUCTURING AGREEMENTS

Bearing in mind these preliminary comments on risk behavior, imperfect information, positive transaction costs, and the relationship between state self-interest and international law, we extend Goldsmith and Posner's international law theory and postulate that, states tend to act in one of the four main behavioral patterns when considering whether to maintain, renegotiate, *or* terminate their international commitments. Though originally developed to explain state treaty-making behavior, these behavioral patterns or regularities—namely "Coincidence of Interest," "Coordination," "Cooperation," and "Coercion"—are just as useful to analyzing treaty-restructuring and treaty-termination.

To demonstrate this point and flesh out our extended model, recall that, originally (i.e., at $t_0$), States A and B had agreed to share a particular resource, say

2. *See* Understanding on Rules and Procedures Governing the Settlement of Disputes, Apr. 15, 1994, Marrakesh Agreement Establishing the World Trade Organization, Annex 2, 1869 U.N.T.S. 401, Art. 22(1).
3. *See* Goldsmith and Posner, *supra* note 1, at 13.
4. *See* Vienna Convention on the Law of Treaties, May 23, 1969, 1155 U.N.T.S. 331 [hereinafter VCLT], Arts. 39, 54, and 59-62.
5. *See* Goldsmith and Posner, *supra* note 1, at 13 (emphasis added).

harvesting from a nearby fishery. That agreement's fate—its continuation, renegotiation, or termination—will undergo reassessment at $t_1$, when State A, now more powerful, reassesses its options. As explained before, State A considers its choices on the existing arrangement by taking into account State B's expected responses and vice-versa. Stated in the simplest way, the behavior of States A and B in regard to the fishery agreement, our initial illustration, will fit into one of the four patterns that follow.

*Coincidence of Interest*

At $t_1$, a more powerful State A may decide against exploiting its newfound advantage over State B even if A knows B would not be able to resist A's increased catch from the fishery. This might occur, for instance, when State A already has enough of that resource and does not want to engage with B further. When the weaker State B, acting in its own self-interest, has the same outlook in regard to State A, nothing changes. When inaction results from each state's pursuit of its own self-interest—despite the change in their relative capabilities and regardless of the action of the other—we have one form of Coincidence of Interest: one that leads to keeping the agreement on fisheries intact.

Yet, Coincidence of Interest may also lead to alteration of an agreement. All one needs is changing one or more variables in the illustration. For instance, if the more powerful State A *now* believes it benefits from harvesting more fish, it might do so *unilaterally* (i.e., without engaging with B). If State B believes that it will still be able to meet its needs, despite A's catch increase, without depleting the fishery, B will tacitly acquiesce. Here, again, each state recognizes its own self-interest (e.g., more fish for A; no reduction in B's present and future catch) *independently* of what the other does. Although State A's greater extraction rate *alters* the fishery agreement, State A's and State B's interests *still* coincide: sustainability, one of the main tenets of the fishery agreement, remains assured. In this second case, Coincidence of Interest gives rise to a restructured, tacit agreement that combines State A's greater extraction with State B's lack of objection and continued compliance.[6] Because neither party directly engages with the other, this alteration never results from negotiations nor yields written changes to the existing agreement.

*Coordination*

Again, State A, though more powerful at $t_1$, may have a *second* reason for keeping the status quo. Where State A believes that casting more nets (to extract more fish) would *not* be beneficial because State B's nets might be there at the same time, State A will not push for an increase in catch. State A knows that, without agreement on who might fish when and where, nets will become entangled, and fishermen from both states will bear losses. Perceiving that the benefit from one's action depends on the action of the other,

6. *See* Restatement (Third) of the Foreign Relations Law of the United States § 102 cmt. e (1987) (noting that the "practice of states in a regional or other special grouping may create 'regional,' 'special,' or 'particular' customary law for those states inter se.").

States A and B will stick to their prior understanding to achieve their expected net yields. Thus, the agreement on fisheries remains intact. Though resembling Coincidence of Interest, coordinated action differs in the sense that one state's successful outcome *depends* directly on what the other does.

Yet, Coordination also allows for change. State A may begin harvesting more fish, either: (i) after engaging directly with State B and reaching an understanding on amending the deal (e.g., one that provides for a wider area for State A fishing nets during a particular season of the year); or (ii) when, through repeated play, both States realize they benefit from not getting their nets entangled and, thus, reach an informal understanding on time and place for casting nets (e.g., think about how truck drivers smartly come up with ways to pass each other in narrow, one-lane mountain passes when they happen upon one another). In either situation, so long as State B believes that it will still be able to meet its needs despite A's catch increase, B will acquiesce formally (i.e., in case of direct negotiations) or tacitly (i.e., in case of repeated play), and the agreement will be restructured, either de lege or de facto. Unlike with Coincidence of Interest, the *ability to observe* what the other does is essential for coordinated outcomes to emerge.

*Cooperation*

Though tempted, the more powerful State A, at $t_1$, may still decide against harvesting more from the shared fishery for a *third* reason. State A may believe that State B, in response to A's eventual catch increase, will begin harvesting more, too, resulting in depletion of the fishery. Just as State A, State B desires to avoid that result, which would make both worse off. That State A is more powerful and could possibly keep State B from overfishing (e.g., by dispatching more surveillance boat patrols) may not be enough for A. State A might incur further costs by engaging in war (in case of B's resistance) and, thereafter, by having to make sure that B does not resume overfishing. By contrast, State B recognizes that it is likely to lose the war and that overfishing would threaten its ability to both co-manage and exploit the fishery for the foreseeable future. If the fishery agreement is commensurate to their relative capacities *and interests*, the fishery agreement will be maintained by virtue of credible threats of retaliation in case of unilateral catch increases.

Of course, this assumes that both States understand "what counts as cooperation and what counts as cheating,"[7] which, in turn, depends on their ability to monitor each other's conduct around the fishery. Note that, as with the Coincidence-of-Interest and Coordination patterns, Cooperation also assumes that states have relatively *low* time preferences, meaning they care more about ensuring a stream of future benefits from an existing arrangement than realizing immediate gains by breaching it. Thus, given the present structure of capabilities and interests, both states cooperate and keep the fishery agreement as is.

Yet, cooperative interaction might also result in the restructuring of a preexisting agreement. For instance, if States A and B believe that they can each harvest more fish

7. *See* GOLDSMITH AND POSNER, *supra* note 1, at 31.

*sustainably*, though at different catch levels—say, a 10-percent increase for the more powerful State A being "matched" by a 5-percent increase for State B—they might agree to restructure their heretofore egalitarian fishery agreement. Here, both States *gain* from the new, agreed-to catch increase. Although State A might have wanted a *higher* increase, A recognizes the long-term benefit of present compromise and self-restraint in the assurance that the fishery will remain a long-term *viable* resource. Furthermore, State A might also be happy to avoid the costs of war and constantly keeping State B from overfishing should their relations remain sour, in case of B's humiliating defeat in war, or A's push for a far-one-sided, resented deal. As to State B, although its share of the catch increase is smaller relative to State A's under the restructured deal, B still benefits from a lawful catch increase under a restructured agreement that both avoids war and secures co-management and exploitation of the fishery for the foreseeable future. Again, as with Coincidence of Interest and Coordination, Cooperation can lead to agreement restructuring. Coercion, the final behavioral pattern in our modified model, is no different in this respect.

### *Coercion*

Coercion becomes appreciably more likely when a stronger state has sufficient capabilities to impose its will on the weaker state at the latter's expense. In our model, Coercion occurs when State A believes it can harvest more, while maintaining the fishery sustainable, by forcing State B to reduce its catch. State A will do so when States A and B know both that A is *stronger* than B, *and* that A can impose its will, *regardless of what State B does*. For that to occur, however, State A must be prepared and willing to punish State B, in case of resistance, and the cost of punishment for A must be *less* than what it stands to gain from the change, while being prohibitive for B. When these conditions are observed, State A's threats are *credible*; State B rationally yields to State A's advances and thereby minimizes its losses (i.e., B is capable of objectively considering its capabilities and interests); and State A maximizes its gains. In case State B resists, however—possibly as a result of underestimating A's capabilities *or will*—State A's use of force reduces A's maximum payoff, but still leaves A better off than under the status quo ex ante. Under either case, the fishery agreement undergoes restructuring by operation of the stronger State's will—a development independent from the weaker State's preference.

Note that when State A is content with its fish allocation, State A's and State B's interests coincide, and the status quo prevails. This illustrates the first type of Coincidence of Interest, discussed earlier. You may also recall that, depending on the context, Coincidence of Interest can result in restructured agreements or in no change at all. Remarkably, either outcome is possible under Coercion, too. Take the last example (i.e., State A is content with its current allocation): should the weaker State B desire to increase its fish catch, and should State A not acquiesce, the agreement will remain *unchanged*. That is the case because, *by definition*, coercive settings necessarily require that weaker states do what is contrary to their interests (i.e., if conditions were different, we would not be describing Coercion). Furthermore, because, under Coercion, the final outcome is independent from the weaker State's preference, State A and *only* State A can determine whether an agreement is preserved or restructured. That said, coerced states can *still* affect whether coercing states obtain their *maximum* payoffs. They do so by either resisting or yielding (*see* previous paragraph). Therein lies the major difference between Coincidence of Interest and Coercion: under the latter, the weaker state *can* impact—though at a significant cost—the stronger state's payoff.

The insights we extract from our model help illustrate why Coercion cannot always explain the result of asymmetric interactions in the "real world," particularly, the actions of weaker states. Historically, what "experts" viewed as instances of weaker states' "irrational" resistance may very well have been *rational* bets by such states that, in the long run, resistance would impose costs on the more powerful states (or a reduction in payoffs) that the latter might not be willing to accept. To the stronger state, then, the higher the likelihood of the weaker state's resistance *and* the lower its own cost tolerance (or appetite for reduced payoffs), the greater the appeal for Coincidence-of-Interest-, Coordination- or Cooperative-based strategies and behavior.

## III. IMPLICATIONS

Broadly speaking, States A and B will keep the fishery agreement (or any similar commitment) when the mutual gains from keeping it exceed the costs of changing it. The behavioral regularities explained above demonstrate how states evaluate the gains and costs of *keeping*, *restructuring*, or even *terminating* agreements. States take note of a number of internal and external variables—including each other's capabilities, interests, risk behavior, time preferences, resource availability (i.e., input variables)—and, then, choose whether to keep, restructure, or terminate preexisting agreements by engaging in one or some combination of the behavioral patterns modeled above. Thus, by processing these input variables through state behavior regularities, we are better positioned to understand the approach a state might take in regard to the fate of an agreement, the outcome variable.

Modeling state behavior in regard to agreements by reference to these behavioral regularities is useful in two significant ways. First, by focusing on a given agreement's *factual* context, this kind of modeling aims for descriptive relevancy, not normative evaluation, and, thus, can offer instrumental, *practical insights*. Second, by narrowing down the range of state behavior relative to an agreement in a given factual context, the model yields *predictions* as to the fate of that agreement—i.e., the model leads to testable hypotheses, and, as such, is falsifiable. At a minimum, if we model agreement outcomes (e.g., to keep, restructure, or terminate) as a function of self-interested pursuits based on input variables that are bounded by behavioral regularities, these outcomes will not be random. Specifically, changes in input variables—whether derived from emerging asymmetries (e.g., economic, military, etc.) or disruptions (e.g., major natural disasters, pandemics, immigration surges, etc.) that have long-lasting effects—*may* affect the future of a given agreement or set of commitments. Yet, as each of the four illustrated behavioral patterns demonstrates, though changes in one or more input variables may increase pressure toward agreement restructuring, the latter is neither automatic nor simple. Rather, a given net-negative-benefit agreement's fate depends on: (i) whether significant changes in input variables have occurred; (ii) whether a particular state *wants* to change such an agreement (i.e., a function of whether bureaucratic and/or interest-group preferences recognize or even trump the national interest, etc.); (iii) whether the existing agreement can accommodate the preferred amendments or revisions; and (iv) whether and *how* the states involved will pursue any significant change to that agreement—i.e., given answers to (i)-(iii), will States A and B follow behavioral pattern X, Y, or a combination thereof, and come to a restructured deal? In sum, the model we propose helps to organize thinking about agreement restructuring in a dispassionate, analytical way.

## IV. MODEL APPLICATION: THE EUROPEAN UNION-TURKEY CUSTOMS UNION

Because this model and its behavioral categories help explain and predict state behavior in regard to a given preexisting agreement impacted by exogenous change, we examine throughout the book one particular, *consequential* bilateral agreement currently under significant stress: the EU-Turkey Customs Union ("CU").[8] The CU is the trade arrangement whereby EU Members and Turkey eliminated all tariffs on each other's covered imports, while agreeing to apply common external tariffs ("CETs") to similar goods from other countries.[9] Specifically, the CU phased out tariffs and eliminated all restrictions on industrial and processed agricultural products (i.e., minerals, grains, fruits, and vegetables are not included) circulating between the European Union and Turkey.[10] Pursuant to the CU, Turkey also gradually implemented EU commercial and competition policy.[11]

Most significantly, starting in 1996, Turkey began applying EU CETs on third-country industrial imports. These tariffs were well below Turkey's original, otherwise applicable WTO commitments.[12] After fully implementing CETs, Turkey had one of the lowest levels of tariffication among developing countries.[13] In addition, Turkey implemented EU technical standards, and, pursuant to its General Agreement on Tariffs and Trade (GATT), Article XXIV obligations,[14] Turkey began negotiations and signed free trade agreements ("FTAs") with countries with which the European Union had

8. *See* Decision No. 1/95 of the EC–Turkey Association Council of 22 December 1995 on implementing the final phase of the Customs Union, 96/142/EC, Art. 4, 1996 O.J. (L 035) [hereinafter CU Decision].
9. *See id.*, Art. 13.
10. *See id.*, Arts. 2 & 4.
11. *See id.*, Arts. 12, 32, 33, 34, 35, & 37.
12. *See* WTO Secretariat, *Trade Policy Review of Turkey*, WT/TPR/S/259/Rev.1, Table III.2 (Jan. 17, 2012) (using 2011 MFN tariff data on Harmonized Schedule Chapters 25-97, which cover all industrial products).
13. *See* Chad P. Brown, *Trade Policy Flexibilities and Turkey: Tariffs, Antidumping, Safeguards and WTO Dispute Settlement*, 5 (World Bank, Policy Research Working Paper No. 6322, 2013).
14. *See* Subidey Togan & Bartlomiej Kaminski, The Foreign Trade Regime and Trade Liberalization in Turkey, in *Economic Liberalization and Turkey* 13-46, 46 (Subidey Togan ed., 2010).

previously signed FTAs.[15] Despite committing to and implementing these major legal and economic changes, Turkey, the junior member in the CU, did not secure any say in EU trade policy.[16] The general thinking among Turkey's officials, the military, and economic elites was that, despite its asymmetric terms, the CU would foster both economic growth and closer economic ties with the more developed senior partner, and, thus, lead to further economic convergence and eventual full EU membership.[17]

The creation of the CU with the European Union was one of the most significant developments for Turkey. The CU induced extra competitiveness onto Turkish manufacturing, which, benefitting from lower tariffs and existing supply chains, increased exports to the single market. The FTAs Turkey had to sign as a result of the CU also helped Turkish exporters, at least initially. Moreover, opening the Turkish economy enabled Turkey to attract more foreign direct and indirect investment. Turkish industrial products could move to Europe without any tariffs or barriers and were treated preferentially. As a result of the CU and its related developments, Turkey's exports to EU countries (not including the United Kingdom) increased more than five-fold, from $12 billion to $70 billion between 1995 and 2020, while its imports from the same group jumped from $18 billion to $73 billion in the same period.[18] Thus, in the last two decades, the European Union has been Turkey's main trade partner and biggest export destination.[19]

Yet, for reasons discussed in the early chapters of the book (in more depth, particularly, in Chapter 4), the CU has failed to live up to Turkey's membership aspirations. Political skirmishes with its senior partner have caused a deadlock in Turkey's EU accession process, and, Turkey has seen an appreciable *reduction* in its chances of becoming a full EU Member. If, politically, EU accession is not a realistic option for the near future, it stands to reason why Turkey, by keeping the CU, should continue waiving the substantial tariff discretion and trade sovereignty it could enjoy under its generous WTO schedule of concessions. A return to full trade sovereignty and to administration of its own WTO tariff schedule would give Turkey the necessary flexibility and *leverage* to negotiate more favorable terms with the European Union and other countries, as well as provide it the tools with which to address historical trade and current account deficits, well-known vectors of financial volatility and economic crises in the country.

---

15. *See* M. Sait Akman, *Turkey in the World Trading System and the WTO: Activism under Global Challenges and the EU Process*, 1(1) Afro Eurasian Studies 134, 139 (2012).
16. *See* Ufuk Alkan, *The Modernization of Turkey's Customs Union with the European Union: Reasons and Possible Outcomes*, 5-8 (Department of EU International Relations and Diplomacy Studies, EU Diplomacy Paper, Collage of Europe No. 9/2017).
17. *See id.*
18. *See* Turkish Statistical Institute, Foreign Trade Statistics, Foreign Trade by Country Group and Year, New Exports by Country Group and Year, New Imports by Country Group and Year, https://data.tuik.gov.tr/Kategori/GetKategori?p=dis-ticaret-104&dil=1%20 (last visited Mar. 16, 2021); Nurullah Altun & Hakan Yavuz, *Türkiye'nin Avrupa Birligi Ülkeleri Ile Olan Dış Ticaretinin Yapısal, Sektörel ve Ürün Grupları Itibariyle Degerlendirilmesi (1990–2009 Dönemi)*, 22 Bilgi, 13-32, 16 (2011).
19. *See id.*

Next, Part II introduces our readers to Turkey's past and current economic challenges; describes the conditions and interests that led the European Union and Turkey to establish the CU; and explains why the CU has become a net-negative-benefit trade arrangement for Turkey. Part III then discusses Turkey's limited options (Chapter 5) and explains how Turkey may make best use of them to restructure its trade relationship with the European Union—both legally and transactionally (Chapter 6). Based on their shared interests and differences, Part III also applies this chapter's model to predict the particular behavioral pattern (or combination thereof) that will prevail in that renegotiation.

# Part II Turkey, the Rationale for the Customs Union, and Related Outcomes

CHAPTER 2

# Turkey's Economic Challenges and the Experts

## I. OVERVIEW

Turkey is an upper-middle-income country with a mostly young population exceeding 80 million.[1] It is surrounded by the Black Sea, Caucasus, Middle East, Mediterranean Sea, Aegean Sea and the Balkans. This geographically unique country serves as a "bridge" between East and West and connects Northern countries (e.g., Russia) to the Middle East and Africa. In 2017, Turkey was the 17th largest economy in the world, with a gross domestic product ("GDP") of $851 billion.[2] It has a dynamic, diversified and open economy, with a large private sector.[3]

Having experienced recurring financial and economic crises throughout its history, more recent years (2001-2014) saw Turkey reach a 4.9-percent average GDP growth—impressive economic performance, despite significant global economic turbulence resulting from the 2008-2009 global recession and the 2011-2014 Eurozone crisis.[4] During this period, Turkey also addressed major structural problems in its economy (e.g., high inflation, high debt-to-GDP ratio, etc.); paid off its debts to the International Monetary Fund ("IMF"); and attracted more foreign direct investment

1. *See* International Monetary Fund, Turkey: 2017 Article IV Consultation-Press Release, Staff Report, and Statement by the Executive Director for Turkey, 17 IMF Staff Country Reports, 17/23, 1 (February 2017).
2. World Bank, Gross Domestic Product 2016, 1 (April 2017), *available at*: http://databank.world bank.org/data/download/GDP.pdf [hereinafter World Bank GDP Data].
3. *See* WTO Secretariat, *Trade Policy Review of Turkey*, WT/TPR/S/331 10-12 & 90 (Feb. 9, 2016) [hereinafter Turkey TPR 2016].
4. A. Benlialper, H. Cömert & G. Düzçay, *2002 Sonrası Türkiye Ekonomisinin Performansı: Karşılaştırmalı Bir Analiz* [*Performance of Turkey's Economy After 2002: A Comparative Analysis*], 18 (ERC Working Papers in Economics 15/04, May 2015), http://www.erc.metu.edu.tr/me nu/series15/1504.pdf.

("FDI"), about $12.8 billion per year.[5] Despite achieving better economic fundamentals and high growth rates, Turkey still faces hurdles to escape the "middle-income trap"[6] and experiences high current account and trade deficits (we explain these concepts in footnotes).[7]

Turkish foreign trade policy also underwent significant change over 90 years, since the establishment of the Republic in 1923. After decades of import substitution industrialization ("ISI")—a set of policies that heavily favored nascent domestic industries with subsidies and protection from foreign competition through high tariffs and quotas—Turkey shifted its trade policy in the early 1980s to focus on liberalization and export promotion.[8] By the mid-1990s, Turkey had integrated itself into the world economy, becoming a member of the WTO, in 1995, and entering into a customs union with the European Union, the following year.[9] As will be demonstrated throughout the book, although the CU brought significant benefits for Turkey, it amounted to Turkey's de facto surrender of trade sovereignty to the European Union. Briefly stated, the CU: (i) eliminated all trade barriers between the European Union and Turkey on industrial goods; (ii) required Turkey to submit to EU-determined CETs with respect to third-country industrial imports; (iii) bound Turkey to the EU's preferential trade regime, by which Turkey committed to signing FTAs with other EU FTA partners, having to offer them similar, though not necessarily reciprocal tariff concessions; and (iv) led to broad legal harmonization, including Turkey's adoption of EU competition policy.[10]

Entry into the WTO and, more significantly, the CU contributed to a significant transformation in Turkey's trade profile and economic outlook. In the 1995-2019 period, Turkey's exports increased from $21.6 to $171.4 billion while imports rose from

5. *See, e.g.*, Turkey TPR 2016, *supra* note 3, at 10 (stating Turkey's success in attracting FDI); Invest in Turkey, FDI in Turkey, INVEST, http://www.invest.gov.tr/en-US/investmentguide/investorsguide/Pages/FDIinTurkey.aspx (last visited Feb. 28, 2019) (stating FDI inflow figures).
6. The middle-income trap has been defined as the great degree of difficulty middle-income countries find in transitioning to economic and social conditions similar to those in more advanced economies. Typically, high-debt-to-GDP ratios and low-tech manufacturing serve, simultaneously, as economic mainstays and barriers to such advancement. *See* Izzet Tasar, Esma Gultekin & Yunus Acci, *Is Turkey in a Middle Income Trap?,* 1 J. OF APPLIED RES. IN FIN. AND ECON. 36, 41 (2015).
7. Generally, a country's "current account" captures the balance of trade transaction income (e.g., income from exports and imports of goods and services); property income (e.g., payments or receipts of royalties and other rents); and gifts, received or remitted. Because, historically, Turkey has run trade deficits that exceed net property income and gifts (despite substantial expatriate remittances from abroad), Turkey has also run perennial current account deficits. For further information on balance of payments, *see* RAJ BHALA, DICTIONARY OF INTERNATIONAL TRADE LAW 90-92 (2d ed. 2012).
8. *See* Mustafa Yıldıran, *Foreign Trade Strategy in the Existence Area of Turkey: Emerging Markets Originating from the East and the Economical Politics of New Orientations*, 15 SULEYMAN DEMIREL U. J. OF FAC. OF ECON. & ADMIN. SCI. 313 314 (2010).
9. *See* Turkey TPR 2016, *supra* note 3, at 31.
10. *See generally* Juscelino F. Colares and Mustafa Durmuş, *TURK-SWITCH: The Tariff-Leverage and Legal Case for Turkey's Shift from Customs Union to FTA with the European Union and Beyond*, 22.1 J. INT'L ECON. L. 99, 105-106 (2019) (commenting on Decision No. 1/95 of the EC-Turkey Association Council of 22 December 1995 on implementing the final phase of the Customs Union, 96/142/EC; and WTO Secretariat, *Trade Policy Review of Turkey*, PRESS/TPRB/83 (Oct. 7, 1998), *available at*: https://www.wto.org/english/tratop_e/tpr_e/tp83_e.htm [hereinafter Turkey TPR 1998]).

$35.7 to $202.7 billion.[11] However, Turkey's trade deficit, uninterrupted since 1946, also increased, dramatically, from $14 to $31 billion between 1995 and 2019.[12] Although trade became a more significant component of the economy (60 percent of GDP),[13] Turkey's share of global merchandise trade was only 0.89 percent in 2016.[14] In 2017, Turkey, the world's 17th economy,[15] was the 31st largest exporter and 21st largest importer.[16] As this book will demonstrate, further trade liberalization could help this dynamic, strategically located middle-income country increase its share of global merchandise trade and, thereby, reduce its perennial trade deficits, which hover around 4.1 percent of GDP (2019).[17] Yet, because the CU—the arrangement under which Turkey surrendered its trade sovereignty—is inherently incompatible with any autonomous pursuit of greater trade liberalization, the reader would benefit from understanding why Turkey chose to waive its trade sovereignty in the first place. This chapter begins answering this question by explaining how Turkey experts have historically understood the major levers in Turkey's trade policy.

## II. TRADE POLICY AND THE EXPERTS

Turkish foreign trade policy has been the subject of much historical and economic analysis. Typically, scholars have looked at the relationship between historical-political-economic developments (e.g., Westernization, macroeconomic crises, world events, military intervention, national security, foreign policy, etc.) and trade policy in one direction, i.e., from the first to the latter. For instance, Kirişçi (2009), Babacan (2010), and Akman (2012) portray pre-1980 Turkish trade policy as a mere result of historical, economic, and political processes.[18] Trade policy would begin being viewed as a driver of other processes only after 1980, when major shifts in Turkey's economy took place (discussed in Chapter 3).[19] Kirişçi and Kaptanoğlu (2011) illustrate this shift by stating that "becoming a 'trading state' … ha[d] an important impact on Turkey's

11. *See* Appendix I.
12. *Id.*
13. *See* Turkey TPR 2016, *supra* note 3, at 10.
14. *See* Turkiye Ihracatcilar Meclisi [Turkish Exporters Assembly], Ekonomi ve Dis Ticaret Raporu 2017 [Economy and Foreign Trade Report, 2017], 9 https://www.tim.org.tr/files/downloads/Raporlar/T%C4%B0M_Ekonomi_Raporu_2017.pdf [hereinafter TIM Report].
15. *See* World Bank GDP Data, *supra* note 2.
16. *See Turkey*, World Trade Organization, *available at*: http://stat.wto.org/CountryProfiles/TR_e.htm (last visited May 2, 2019) [hereinafter Turkey WTO Trade Profile, 2017].
17. *See* Appendix I; Turkey WTO Trade Profile, 2017, *supra* note 16 (providing data on Turkey's GDP and other trade-related statistics). Note that, according to the latter source, Turkey has a service surplus (2.4 percent of GDP), which significantly helps to reduce its overall trade and current account deficits.
18. *See* Kemal Kirişçi, *The Transformation of Turkish Foreign Policy: The Rise of the Trading State*, 40 New Perspectives on Turkey 29, 43-46 (2009); Mehmet Babacan, *Whither Axis Shift: A Perspective from Turkey's Foreign Trade*, 4, SETA Policy Report 6-19 (2010); Sait Akman, *Turkey in the World Trading System and the WTO: Activism Under Global Challenges and the EU Process*, 1 Afro Eurasian Studies 134, 141 (2012). *See also* discussion in Chapter 3 and accompanying references of these authors.
19. *See id.*

domestic politics as well as foreign policy."[20] Section A, below, briefly outlines the literature on Turkey's trade policy *prior* to 1980. Section B demonstrates the literature's *shift* to describing trade policy as a driver of broader developments after 1980.

### A. Literature on Turkey's Pre-1980 Foreign Trade

Krueger and Aktan (1992), Aktan (1993), Togan and Kaminski (2010), Oran (2011), and others unanimously agree that, from 1923 to 1980, Turkey consistently followed inward-oriented economic policies, except for a brief four-year period (1950-1953).[21] As discussed in detail in Chapter 3, the early years of the Republic of Turkey saw a country focused on Westernization, national security, and domestic industrialization. During the 1923-1980 period, domestic industry, if existing, tended to be largely inefficient, so trade could not be a priority—except in a defensive, protectionist sense. In fact, despite a trade-favorable, geostrategic location and improving socioeconomic profile, Turkey's trade-to-GDP ratio in this period was only 13.56 percent.[22] In light of Turkey's limited industrial development, it is understandable how the view of trade as dependent on exogenous policies and events became entrenched in the literature.[23]

With the establishment of the Republic in 1923, Ataturk began modernizing Turkey (again, these developments are discussed in depth in Chapter 3). According to Rittenberg (1998), modernization was always defined as "Westernization" of the country.[24] Economic independence became the main goal of Ataturk's Westernization project.[25] The founding leader wanted to create national industries and fashion a business elite to protect Turkey's economic interests.[26] External constraints—particularly, the Lausanne Peace Treaty's compulsory *laissez-faire* terms and lack of a trained Turkish business elite—made it mostly impossible for the country to implement the self-reliant trade policies Ataturk desired, until 1929.[27] As Amelung (1988) and Oran (2011) explain, only upon termination of the Lausanne Treaty's trade constraints and the beginning of the Great Depression, did Turkey see the emergence

20. Kemal Kirişçi & Neslihan Kaptanoglu, *The Politics of Trade and Turkish Foreign Policy*, 47:5 Middle Eastern Studies 705, 705 (2011).
21. *See* Anne O. Krueger & Okan H. Aktan, Swimming Against the Tide: Turkish Trade Reform in the 1980s 1 (1992); Coşkun C. Aktan, *Turkey: From Inward-Oriented Etatism to Outward-Looking Liberal Strategy*, 17-19 Turkish Public Admin. Annual, 67 (1993); Subidey Togan & Bartlomiej Kaminski, The Foreign Trade Regime and Trade Liberalization in Turkey, *in Economic Liberalization and Turkey* 13 (Subidey Togan ed., 2010); Baskin Oran, Turk Dis Politikasi [Turkish Foreign Policy] 38-46 (2011).
22. Calculation was made by the book's authors according to the numbers provided by Oran. *See* Oran, *supra* note 21, at 243, 389, 487, & 662.
23. *See* Babacan, *supra* note 18, at 6-19.
24. *See* Libby Rittenberg, The Political Economy of Turkey in the Post-Soviet Era: Going West and Looking East? 38 (1998).
25. *See* Oran, *supra* note 21, at 244.
26. *See id.*
27. Amelung Torsten, *The Political Economy of Import Substitution and Consequent Trade Liberalization: The Case of Turkey* 12-14 (Kiel Working Paper, No. 330, 1988), https://www.econstor.eu/bitstream/10419/47120/1/25568407X.pdf (last visited Jun. 7, 2021).

of Etatism,[28] government-directed intervention that came to be identified with ISI and other protectionist policies.[29] According to Oran (2011), the successful application of Etatism provided Turkey "relative autonomy," which helped the country achieve trade surpluses until 1946.[30]

The post-World War II (WWII) period saw Turkey make some adjustments to its Westernization project. As Hale (1981), Oran (2011), Saygin and Çimen (2013) explain,[31] Turkey's national security concerns led to its entry into the *Pax Americana* and membership in the institutions that undergirded it (i.e., IMF, GATT, North Atlantic Treaty Organization ("NATO"), etc.).[32] Saygin and Çimen (2013) posit that, alignment with the Western Block meant accepting free-trade doctrines, abandoning heavy ISI, and relaxing protections on imports, which resulted in an import boom in the exceptional four-year, free-trade period (1950-1953).[33] Because exports could not offset imports in those years, Turkey ran trade deficits and had balance-of-payment problems, Oran (2011) explains.[34]

However, a return to protectionism in 1954 did not solve these structural problems, either. Currency bottlenecks, mainly the result of rising, out-of-control trade and current account deficits, made the Turkish economy heavily dependent on continuous foreign aid and debt refinancing. Dependence on external financing contributed to a sharp, destabilizing boom-and-bust business cycles. From 1954, the end of the free-trade period, to 1959, Turkey's Gross National Product ("GNP")—a measure of the total domestic and foreign output that includes only *residents* of a country and thus deducts transfers to abroad of income by foreign residents[35]—rose from $8.28 to $22.72 billion,[36] an average 29 percent annual growth rate. Yet, the boom would not be long lived. Deteriorating trade and current account deficits increased an already high foreign debt,[37] whose servicing led to hard-currency shortages that, in turn, brought a massive currency devaluation and sharp recession. In 1960, GNP collapsed to $7.55 billion,[38] nullifying much of the gains achieved during the boom years. Amidst economic chaos, social and political instability increased, contributing to the military takeover of May 1960.[39]

28. Etatism is "a systematic attempt at a rapid and state-led industrialization and structural transformation." SADIK ÜNAY, NEOLIBERAL GLOBALIZATION AND INSTITUTIONAL REFORM: THE POLITICAL ECONOMY OF DEVELOPMENT AND PLANNING IN TURKEY 39 (2006). Etatism and its effects will be broadly discussed in Chapter 3.
29. *See* Torsten, *supra* note 27, at 15; ORAN, *supra* note 21, at 256-257.
30. *See* ORAN, *supra* note 21, at 256-257.
31. *See* WILLIAM HALE, POLITICAL AND ECONOMIC DEVELOPMENT OF MODERN TURKEY 54 (1981); HASAN SAYGIN & MURAT ÇIMEN, TURKISH ECONOMIC POLICIES AND EXTERNAL DEPENDENCY 56 (2013); ORAN, *supra* note 21, at 40.
32. Soviet Union was a significant threat for Turkey at that time. *See* ORAN, *supra* note 21, at 40.
33. *See* SAYGIN & ÇIMEN, *supra* note 31, at 6.
34. *See* ORAN, *supra* note 21, at 487-491.
35. *See* 3 THE NEW PALGRAVE: A DICTIONARY OF ECONOMICS 590-592 (1996).
36. *See* SAYGIN & ÇIMEN, *supra* note 31, at 65.
37. *See id.*, at 66-68.
38. *See id.*, at 65.
39. *See* Torsten, *supra* note 27, at 18-20.

Left-leaning authors examined the influence of external factors on Turkey's policy choices in the following decade. Oran (2011) suggested that the collapse of the Bretton Woods system and the decrease in U.S. "hegemonic power" in the 1960s and early 1970s[40] "enabled" countries like Turkey to apply relatively independent foreign and economic policies in the following decades.[41] More plausibly, Amelung (1988) theorized that the political stability provided by the Turkish military facilitated the relaunch of the government's ISI strategy, which heavily relied on continuous economic planning and close trade management through 1980.[42]

Yet, the wider literature on the pre-1980 period also viewed external events as impacting Turkey's policies. For instance, Celasun and Rodrik (1989) indicate that the 1973 global oil crisis dramatically increased accumulation of debt among many developing countries, Turkey not being an exception.[43] As such, like other less-developed countries that could not finance a growing debt burden, Turkey saw the need to alter its course, switching, eventually, to export-led growth in 1980. Surely, the late 1970s/early 1980s Debt Crisis significantly weighed on Turkey's shift away from ISI. The trade and financial liberalization that occurred in the next decade would not only transform Turkey's economy but also influence the literature's views on the role of trade policy: post-1980, trade policy slowly came to be viewed as an independent driver of historical-political developments.

## B. Trade Policy Takes the Front Seat: Turkey Becomes a Trading State

Torsten (1988), Celasun and Rodrik (1989), Baysan and Blitzer (1990), Krueger and Aktan (1992), Kirişçi (2009), Togan and Kaminski (2010), and Babacan (2010) share the view that, starting in 1980, Turkey's trade policy shifted outward.[44] Still, to them, this development owed to the Washington Consensus, a set of market-friendly and trade-liberalizing policy "packages," advanced by the Washington, DC-based, World Bank and IMF.[45] Saygin and Çimen (2011) argue that Turkey's policy shift to the Washington Consensus—taken to combat inflation and reduce foreign debt—fundamentally altered Turkey's trade policy.[46] At the time, only a rise in export

40. *See* Oran, *supra* note 21, at 657-660.
41. *See id.*
42. *See* Torsten, *supra* note 27, at 20-22.
43. *See* Merih Celasun & Dani Rodrik, *Trade Regime and an Anatomy of Export Performance*, Volume Title: Developing Country Debt and Economic Performance, 3 Country Studies—Indonesia, Korea, Philippines, Turkey 716, 718 (1989), *available at*: http://www.nber.org/chapters/c9063.pdf.
44. *See* Torsten, *supra* note 27, at 29; Celasun & Rodrik, *supra* note 43, at 719; Tercan Baysan & Charles Blitzer, Turkey's Trade Liberalization in the 1980s and Prospects for Its Sustainability, *in The Political Economy of Turkey: Debt, Adjustment and Sustainability* 9 (Aricanli Tosun and Rodrik Dani eds., 1990); Krueger & Aktan, *supra* note 21; Togan & Kaminski, *supra* note 21, at 14; Kirişçi, *supra* note 18, at 38-43; Babacan, *supra* note 18, at 7-19.
45. Some of the main items in the "consensus" are: (i) financial discipline; (ii) market-set interest rates; (iii) competitive foreign exchange regimes; (iv) liberalization of foreign capital; (v) privatization of the SOEs; (vi) freer foreign trade regime; and (vii) deregulation. *See* Saygin & Çimen, *supra* note 31, at 6.
46. *See id.*, at 14; Babacan, *supra* note 18, at 7.

incomes could help Turkey finance its public deficit and reduce its trade deficit—two major weaknesses contributing to Turkey's economic instability.[47]

Throughout the 1980s and early 1990s, Turkey also gradually liberalized its financial system.[48] Higher interest rates (i.e., up to 100 percent per year) attracted foreign money, resulting in short-term, mostly speculative, capital inflows.[49] According to Demir (2004), financial liberalization made the Turkish economy weaker and more exposed to currency shocks, which triggered financial and economic crises, thereafter.[50]

Önder (2008), Kirişçi (2009), and Davutoğlu (2011) explain that finding new export markets became a central objective for Turkey after 1980.[51] Turkey slightly shifted its priorities from national security to economic priorities via creation of new trade partnerships in its neighborhood.[52] The collapse of the Soviet Union (1991) also helped Turkey achieve this objective.[53] The more independent Turkic Republics (e.g., Azerbaijan, Kazakhstan, Kyrgyzstan, Turkmenistan and Uzbekistan), with which Turkey has strong historical, cultural, and linguistic ties, were ideal grounds for trade expansion, a strategy Turkey pursued with some success.[54]

The formation of a customs union with the European Union in 1996, as Akman (2012) explains, resulted from "Turkey's [historical] ambition" to become a member of the European Union.[55] According to Voigt (2008), Kirişçi (2009), and Akman (2012), the creation of the CU helped Turkey reform its economy, increased FDI inflows and restored domestic industry's competitiveness.[56] Voigt (2008) and Macovei (2009) also explain that, with the CU, Turkey improved its technology, which helped it shift to more technology-intensive production.[57]

Yet, as Akman (2012) and Bown (2013) posit, Turkey's simultaneous undertakings of the CU and WTO membership made trade more complex, less subject to government control.[58] Exposed to the wider play of market forces, Turkey's trade and

47. *See* Togan & Kaminski, *supra* note 21, at 14.
48. Firat Demir, *A Failure Story: Politics and Financial Liberalization in Turkey, Revisiting the Revolving Door Hypothesis,* 32:5 World Development 851, 853 (2004).
49. *See id.*
50. *See id.*
51. *See* Nilgün Önder, *The Turkish Project of Globalization and New Regionalism* 7 Alternatives: Turkish Journal of International Relations 86, 97-8 (2008); Kirişçi, *supra* note 18, at 43-44; Ahmet Davutoglu, Stratejik Derinlik [Strategic Depth] 522 (109th ed. 2011).
52. *See* Kirişçi, *supra* note 18, at 43.
53. *See* Önder, *supra* note 51; Davutoglu, *supra* note 51.
54. *See* Önder, *supra* note 51, at 98.
55. *See* Akman, *supra* note 18, at 138.
56. *See* Suzanne Voigt, The Customs Union Between Turkey and the EU: How Did It Affect Turkey? 59-60 (2008); Kirişçi, *supra* note 18, at 39-44; also Akman, *supra* note 18, at 144.
57. *See* Voigt, *supra* note 56, at 42; Mihai Macovei, *Growth and Economic Crises in Turkey: Leaving Behind a Turbulent Past?* 10 (Economic Papers 386, Economic and Financial Affairs Directorate-General of the European Commission, 2009).
58. *See* Sait Akman, Dynamics of the European Union's Trade Strategy: Drawing Conclusions for Relations with Turkey, 15-31, Paper presented in UACES Exchanging Ideas on Europe 2012 "Old Borders—New Frontiers," Passau, Germany (Sept. 3-5, 2012) (cited with permission); Chad P. Bown, *Trade Policy Flexibilities and Turkey: Tariffs, Antidumping, Safeguards and WTO Dispute Settlement,* 3-5 (World Bank, Policy Research Working Paper No. 6322, 2013).

account deficits between 1995 and 2001 would lead to a formidable economic crisis that precipitated major political transformations in 2002. Following the rise of (then-)Prime Minister Erdoğan (2002), Krueger (2011) explains, the Turkish economy underwent significant transformation (e.g., privatization of state-owned enterprises ("SOEs"), tightened monetary policy, fiscal discipline, etc.).[59] According to Bakkalci and Argin (2013), the adoption of the EU *Acquis Communautaire* further decreased the government's role in the economy.[60] For instance, to meet the Maastricht Criteria,[61] Turkey abandoned currency devaluations, and the lira became a free-floating currency after 2001.[62] The influx of foreign capital and application of market-oriented policies allowed exporters to enjoy the benefits of freer trade under the CU and WTO systems, which soon increased Turkey's share of trade in goods and services as a portion of GDP.[63] Yet, entry into the CU and the WTO and adoption of the *Acquis* significantly reduced Turkey's ability to use discretionary policies (e.g., devaluations, massive export subsidies, etc.), often relied on in the past.[64]

While attributing Turkey's restored, economic "self-confidence" to greater macroeconomic stability and liberalized trade, scholars agree that a large portion of Turkey's trade policy—and surely Turkey's trade sovereignty in regard to industrial goods—is under EU control.[65] Under the CU, Turkey is bound to adopt EU trade policy (e.g., EU-set CETS, EU's preferential trade regime, etc.), without having a say in the EU decision-making process.[66] As a non-EU Member, Turkey is denied a seat in EU FTA negotiations.[67] Worse, as Akman (2012) indicates, the European Union encourages its FTA-negotiating partners to start separate FTA negotiations with Turkey only *after* the European Union has concluded negotiations.[68] For this reason, the recent years saw a marked increase in the EU-Turkey power asymmetry, particularly as the European

59. Anne O. Krueger, *Economic Policy Reform in Brazil and Turkey*, 11 (Stanford Center for International Development, Working Paper No. 445, 2011).
60. Can Bakkalci & Nilüfer Argin, *Turk Dıs Ticareti ve Ekonomi Politikaları Arasındaki Nedensellik Iliskileri* [The Relationship Between Turkey's Trade and its Economy Policies], 11 YÖNETIM BILIMLERI DERGISI 49, 68 (2013).
61. "The Maastricht criteria [are] formulated with the purpose of helping member states to ensure fiscal and monetary discipline ... [and] to join the common currency, Euro." Member States and candidates are to meet certain criteria such as: (i) low government deficit; (ii) low government debt; (iii) low inflation rates; (iv) low interest rates; and (v) no devaluation. Halit Burç Aka & Bilge Gürsoy, *Turkey's Objective of Full Membership in the EU with Reference to Maastricht Criteria*, ATATURK UNIVERSITESI J. ECON. ADMIN. SCIEN. 271, 274 (2014).
62. Krueger, *supra* note 59, at 9.
63. *See* Turkey TPR 2016, *supra* note 3, at 10.
64. *See* Togan & Kaminski, *supra* note 21, at 29-31.
65. *See* Akman, *supra* note 58, at 19.
66. It is important to note that the European Court of Justice ("ECJ") decided on May 16, 2017 that an FTA agreement's provision, creating an investor-state dispute settlement system via arbitration has to be approved not only by the EU Commission and Parliament but also by each Member State. This decision clearly shows that each Member State should have its consent before such binding provisions, limiting the Member State's sovereignty enter into force. *See* Opinion C-2/15, Opinion pursuant to Article 218(11) TFEU, ECJ, 2017 ECLI:EU:C:2017:376. If Turkey was a member of the European Union, Turkey would not only influence the terms of any FTAs during the negotiations in the European Commission, but it would also veto it even after such an agreement concluded.
67. *See* Akman, *supra* note 58, at 19.
68. *See id.*, at 19-20.

Union shifted toward establishing more bilateral FTAs in response to the failure of multilateral negotiations.[69] Turkey, which applies EU-set CETs, has also had to follow the same path, pursuing negotiations with EU FTA partners under less than ideal circumstances.[70] Thus, while trade policy has taken on a much more significant role in Turkey's economy and daily life, most commentators recognize its cost: Turkey's lost autonomy to *direct* its own course.

In conclusion, this book contributes to the rich literature on Turkey's trade policy by, among other things, highlighting that, despite its best efforts to follow the European Union along the market liberalization path, Turkey has been significantly handicapped because of its passive status under the CU. As previewed, Turkey must conform to the tariff and market access concessions the European Union has already negotiated with its growing number of FTA partners. In other words, by the time Turkey comes to the table, its leverage has already been negotiated away. Thus, in order to truly leverage the power of trade, Turkey must look beyond the CU.

69. *See id.*, at 13-14.
70. *See* Decision No. 1/95 of the EC-Turkey Association Council of 22 December 1995 on implementing the final phase of the Customs Union, 96/142/EC, Arts. 12, 13, 14, 15, & 16, 1996 O.J. (L 035).

CHAPTER 3

# Trade Policy: Foundation to the New Millennium

## I. OVERVIEW

This chapter provides a detailed discussion of the evolution of Turkey's foreign trade policy from 1923 to 2001. It examines developments in Turkey's economic and political history and explains the forces that compelled Turkey's economic choices, particularly the decision to surrender sovereignty in trade policy by entering the EU-Turkey CU. This chapter also analyzes Turkey's current legal trade framework (i.e., its memberships in the WTO and CU); and prepares the reader for a deeper discussion of Turkey's current foreign trade priorities and challenges, which we take up in the following chapter (Chapter 4).

Since the establishment of the Republic of Turkey in 1923, Turkish trade policy experienced two major periods.[1] The first period, 1923-1980, was marked by the deployment of inward-oriented policies.[2] Inward-oriented policies seek to restrict imports and to encourage domestic import substitution in an "attempt to increase productivity and living standards."[3] These policies are typically characterized by focusing on the domestic economy and applying high tariffs and import restrictions.[4] With application of inward-oriented policies, Turkey addressed its early economic challenges by fostering agriculture; and establishing and protecting its infant industries, so they could meet domestic demand. These policies achieved some measure of

1. *See* Subidey Togan & Bartlomiej Kaminski, The Foreign Trade Regime and Trade Liberalization in Turkey, *in Economic Liberalization and Turkey* 13, 13 (Subidey Togan ed., 2010).
2. *See* Fikret Şenses, An Assessment of the Pattern of Turkish Manufactured Export Growth in the 1980s and Its Prospects, *in The Political Economy of Turkey: Debt, Adjustment and Sustainability* 60-77, 60 (Aricanli Tosun and Rodrik Dani, eds., 1990).
3. GREGORY N. MANKIW, PRINCIPLES OF ECONOMICS 567 (5th ed. 2009).
4. *See* Colin I. Bradford, William H. Branson, Patterns of Trade and Structural Change, *in Trade and Structural Change in Pacific Asia*, 3, 17-21 (University of Chicago Press, 1987), *available at*: http://www.nber.org/chapters/c6914.pdf.

success soon after their adoption in the 1930s, and in the 1960s, when they were last introduced.[5]

By the late 1970s, inward-oriented policies could no longer be maintained. The rapid increase in the price of oil rose the prices of Turkey's prized imports—imported semi-finished goods and machinery[6]—and also led to a world recession, hurting the economy on both ends. The continued misallocation of SOEs resources for electoral purposes made the application of inward-oriented policies unsustainable.[7] The mid- to late-1970s also saw Turkey face a balance-of-payment crisis and high inflation rates, which increased social and political tension. To solve major macroeconomic problems, Turkey was forced to quit inward-oriented policies and accept pro-market reforms in 1980.[8]

Turkish foreign trade policy enters a new period in 1980 with the application of policies that focused on export promotion and trade liberalization.[9] The country deployed export promotion by devaluating its currency and using fiscal and financial subsidies to provide more incentives for Turkish exports.[10] To liberalize foreign trade, Turkey reduced nominal tariff rates, relaxed bureaucratic controls over imports,[11] and abolished quantitative restrictions and quota systems gradually, starting in 1983.[12] By deploying outward-oriented policies, Turkey aimed to reduce its balance-of-payment deficit and to combat inflation. Policymakers also aimed "to foster competition."[13] They turned to international trade as a tool for promoting greater competitiveness in the domestic market.[14]

These outward-oriented policies caused dramatic improvements in Turkish exports and led to high growth rates throughout the 1980s. The composition of Turkish exports also changed for manufactured goods.[15] Rodrik characterized the profound transformation from inward-oriented to outward-oriented policies as "a success story" for other developing countries.[16] Turkey used pro-market reforms to help integrate its industry into the world economy, a process which it completed by "meeting the requirements of membership in the [WTO] and [by its] close association with the

5. *See* Baskin Oran, Turk Dis Politikasi [Turkish Foreign Policy] 38-41 & 661-665 (2011).
6. *See* Togan & Kaminski, *supra* note 1, at 14.
7. *See id.*
8. *See id.*
9. *See id.*, at 15.
10. *See* Coşkun Can Aktan, *Turkey: From Inward-Oriented Etatism to Outward-Looking Liberal Strategy*, 9:1 Dokuz Eylül University I.I.B.F. Dergisi 41, 54-70 (1994).
11. *See* Utku Utkulu & Durmuş Özdemir, *Does Trade Liberalization Cause a Long Run Economic Growth in Turkey*, 14 (2004), *available at*: https://www.researchgate.net/publication/5145477_Does_Trade_Liberalization_Cause_a_Long_Run_Economic_Growth_in_Turkey.
12. *See* Amelung Torsten, *The Political Economy of Import Substitution and Consequent Trade Liberalization: The Case of Turkey* 29 (Kiel Working Paper, No. 330, 1988), https://www.econstor.eu/bitstream/10419/47120/1/25568407X.pdf (last visited Jun. 7, 2021).
13. Togan & Kaminski, *supra* note 1, at 15.
14. *See id.*
15. *See* Utkulu & Özdemir, *supra* note 11, at 15.
16. *Id.*, at 14.

European Union... ."[17] Turkey became an "original member" of the WTO in 1995 and entered into the CU with the European Union in 1996.[18]

The two latter developments significantly changed the structure of the Turkish economy and its foreign trade policy.[19] To meet WTO requirements, Turkey amended its legislation in intellectual property, safeguards, antidumping and countervailing duty measures.[20] To meet the CU requirements, Turkey adopted EU laws and regulations, such as EU competition law and started to apply CETs. These EU-set tariffs on industrial products are among the lowest charged by a developing country.[21] Although the CU liberalized Turkey's trade practices dramatically in the last two decades, the country remains an active user of temporary trade barriers, mostly antidumping and safeguard measures.[22]

What follows is a detailed account of the two major policy regimes Turkey followed throughout much of its history: (i) *inward*-oriented policies (1923-1980); and (ii) *outward*-oriented policies (1980-2001). Although Turkey remains committed to the trade and financial liberalization model pursued since 1980, we reserve discussion of trade policy for the last two decades to Chapter 4.

## II. FIRST PERIOD: INWARD-ORIENTED POLICIES (1923-1980)

Turkey was a mostly closed economy between 1923 and 1980. During this period, Turkey's top priority was to create a *national* economy that would accomplish three goals: (1) balance the budget; (2) reduce inflation; and (3) avoid, or at least control, trade deficits.[23] A predominantly agricultural economy at the end of Ottoman Empire, the new Republic of Turkey (1923) would soon rely on ISI to create and protect its nascent domestic industry. This policy remained in place until 1980. Knowledge of this period of Turkey's economic history is useful to understanding Turkey's president-day trade challenges.

### A. The Fall of the Ottoman Empire and the Creation of the Republic of Turkey

By losing World War I ("WWI"), the Ottoman Empire lost most of its territories, including Saudi Arabia, Yemen, Libya, Syria, and Iraq. Its remaining territories were

17. Togan & Kaminski, *supra* note 1, at 13.
18. *Id.*
19. *See* Nilüfer Argin & A. Can Bakkalci, Türkiye'nin Diş Ticaret Tarihi [The History of Turkish Foreign Trade] 424 (2011).
20. *See* Togan & Kaminski, *supra* note 1, at 15.
21. *See id.*, at 13.
22. *See id.*
23. These three goals are Atatürk's economy policy objectives, yet they can be generalized for the whole first period. For more information, *see* Hasan Saygin & Murat Çimen, Turkish Economic Policies and External Dependency 48 (2013).

also occupied by Western Powers (i.e., WWI "Allies"),[24] who, evidently, were not welcomed by the Turks.[25] With the occupation of Istanbul (the capital at that time), Sultan Mehmet Vahdettin's ability to govern the country was crippled. As a last resort, Sultan Vahdettin sent Mustafa Kemal (later Atatürk), one of the promising generals in the Ottoman Empire's Army, to Anatolia to organize the Turks for a Turkish War of Independence (1919).[26]

After organizing many "Congresses,"[27] namely, assemblies aimed at increasing popular awareness in Anatolia against the occupying powers, Atatürk, with the help of the military and local elites, opened a new parliament, the Grand National Assembly ("GNA"), in Ankara in 1920.[28] Atatürk was elected president of the GNA.[29] Although the two governments, one in Istanbul, the other in Ankara, were in a collision course, they largely cooperated during the War of Independence. With Istanbul under occupation, soon, it became clear that the Ankara Government was the only *functioning* government of, by, and for the Turks.[30] The GNA, whose rising legitimacy came from the popular vote, took its legislative function seriously. It wrote a constitution, levied taxes, raised a military, and, strategically, took control of and managed to hold Anatolia until 1922.[31] The GNA's military success prompted the Allies to invite GNA leaders to take part in the Lausanne Peace Conference of 1922.

Originally, the Allies invited both Istanbul and Ankara Governments to negotiate the permanent peace.[32] However, the Ankara Government persistently objected to the attendance and legitimacy of the Istanbul delegation, because the Sultan had not participated in the War of Independence.[33] Thus, the GNA enacted a law abolishing the Sultanate in November 1922. Following the resignation of the Sultan and his Istanbul Government, the Sultan left to exile in Italy. Thus, the Ankara delegation became the only Turkish representative to attend the Lausanne Peace Conference.[34] After protracted negotiations, the parties signed the Lausanne Peace Treaty in 1923.[35] The most important outcome of the Treaty was the official recognition, by the Allies, of the Ankara Government as the sole, legitimate representative of Turkey.[36] Soon after the signature of the Treaty and becoming an independent country, Turkey emerged as the Republic of Turkey, on October 29, 1923.

---

24. The occupations: British Army, Mosul in 1918; Italian Army, Antalya and Kusadasi in 1919; French Army, the Southwest of Anatolia in 1919; Greek Army, Izmir 1919; and Istanbul by British Army in 1920.
25. *See* ORAN, *supra* note 5, at 110-112.
26. *See* ERIC J. ZURCHER, TURKEY: A MODERN HISTORY 143 (1993).
27. The three biggest Congresses which were organized by Atatürk were known as Erzurum, Amasya, and Sivas Congresses. *See id.*, at 151.
28. *See* MAX WESTON THORNBURG, TURKEY: AN ECONOMIC APPRAISAL 16 (1949).
29. *See* ZURCHER, *supra* note 26, at 151.
30. *See id.*
31. *See* GÜLTEN KAZGAN, TANZIMATTAN 21. YUZYILA TURKIYE ECONOMISI [TURKISH ECONOMY FROM TANZIMAT TO 21TH CENTURY] 38 (5th ed. 2013).
32. *See* ORAN, *supra* note 5, at 215.
33. *See id.*
34. *See id.*, at 216.
35. *See* ZURCHER, *supra* note 26, at 162.
36. *See* Torsten, *supra* note 12, at 13.

## B. Atatürk's Economic Reforms and Trade Policy (1923-1938)

With the proclamation of the Republic, Atatürk became Turkey's first president.[37] He stayed in power until his death, in 1938. Early on, Atatürk faced numerous political, social, and economic challenges. For example, the Ottoman Empire and its dynasty were gone, yet many of its traditional institutions remained. The literacy rate was 11 percent in the early years of the Republic, and 12 years of war (i.e., including the War in the Balkans, the WWI, the War of Independence) had weakened its mostly agricultural economy.[38] Thus, Atatürk and his colleagues from the reformist wing of the military-bureaucratic elite of the Ottoman Empire had to shape the foundations of the nascent Republic.

Atatürk's primary objective was the modernization of Turkey, which, to him, required Westernization, institutionalization, and nationalization. Yet, Westernization had been a goal since the last century of the Ottoman Empire.[39] Although Turkey fought against Western countries during the WWI and the War of Independence, there was a consensus among the country's founders that Western high standards for law and governing institutions were to be emulated.[40] Turkey made political, legal, and educational reforms, such as abolishing the Caliphate, borrowing Italy's and Switzerland's Criminal and Civil Code, respectively, and adopting the Latin alphabet, which was viewed as a significant focal point for public policy.

Institutionalization, the second objective, was defined as requiring the adoption of *secular* governmental institutions and practices, a change deemed essential for the replacement of traditional, Ottoman-era institutions that had proven ineffective.[41] For instance, Atatürk abolished all independent religious institutions like dervish lodges. Instead, he established the Presidency of Religious Affairs, with centralization of power in mind.[42] The third idea was nationalization.[43] After the collapse of the Ottoman Empire and the loss of Arabian and Balkan territories, Turkey's main population was mostly Muslim-Turk. Therefore, Muslim-Turkish nationalization was viewed as inevitable to unite the new Republic. Pursuant to an agreement Turkey signed with Greece after the War of Independence, Turkey exchanged its non-Muslim, Greek population (outside of Istanbul) with the Muslim-Turk population then living in Greek territory.

Besides people, major businesses held by foreign corporations (e.g., railroads, ports, mining, water, electricity, coal and gas, and telecommunication utilities) were nationalized by the late 1920s.[44] To consolidate modernization and, thereby, to strengthen and shape Turkey as an independent state, Atatürk implemented additional

37. *See* Zurcher, *supra* note 26, at 167.
38. *See id.*, at 165 & 189.
39. *See* Libby Rittenberg, The Political Economy of Turkey in the Post-Soviet Era: Going West and Looking East? 38 (1998).
40. Huseyin Sahin, Turkiye Economisi [Turkish Economy] 22 (2014).
41. *See* Jacob M. Landau, Atatürk and the Modernization of Turkey 57 (1984).
42. *See* Zurcher, *supra* note 26, at 187.
43. *See* Landau, *supra* note 41, at 46.
44. *See* Kazgan, *supra* note 31, at 41-51. For a detailed analysis of the Greece-Turkey forced migration, *see* Oran, *supra* note 5, at 329-334.

economic reforms. The following subsections discuss his government's economic policy, reforms, and trade policy.

### 1. *Reforms*

Immediately after the War of Independence, but before signing the Lausanne Peace Treaty, Atatürk assembled an "Economy Congress" in Izmir in 1923 to discuss the prospective economy policies for Turkey.[45] In his opening speech, Atatürk summarized the reasons for the collapse of the Ottoman Empire and emphasized the importance of economic sovereignty:

> If Turkish history is analyzed, it will be observed that the reasons for [its] decline and collapse are linked to economic problems. ... No matter how great the political and military victories are, without ... economic victory, they cannot be long lasting. ... The objective of our war years at present is full independence. And full independence is only possible with financial independence. For full independence ... national sovereignty should be strengthened with *economic sovereignty*.[46]

Atatürk and his colleagues' arguments for greater economic autonomy won support in the Izmir Congress,[47] which also discussed the government's role in the economy, adopting a mixed-economy model.[48] While this model seemed to recognize the private sector's primacy in the economy, it envisaged too large a role for government intervention by adopting a typical developing country maxim: "the task of the state begins where the activity of private enterprise[] ends."[49] So authorized, the government would indeed "take an active part" in the Turkish economy.[50] Among other Izmir Congress-approved policies were: (i) support for private entrepreneurs, domestic production, and industrialization; (ii) prohibition of luxury imports; (iii) regulation of foreign capital inflows (i.e., all of which subject to a "national interest" assessment); (iv) nationalization of all foreign-owned monopolies; (v) abolition of religion-imposed tithe taxes on land; and (vi) passage of a tariff schedule aimed at protecting domestic-producing industry.[51] These proposals envisaged the creation of a "national economy," largely administered by the new institutions of the nascent Republic.[52]

Yet, the financial commitments made under the Lausanne Peace Treaty operated as a key constraint on such policies. Two provisions, in particular, impaired their

---

45. Izmir Economy Congress composed of 1,100 delegates which represented farmers, traders, industrialists and laborers. *See* William Hale, Political and Economic Development of Modern Turkey 35 (1981).
46. *See* Saygin & Çimen, *supra* note 23, at 48 (emphasis added).
47. *See* Aktan, *supra* note 10, at 43-44.
48. *See id.*, at 44.
49. *Id.*
50. *Id.*
51. Abdullah Takım & Ensar Yilmaz, *Economy Policy During Atatürk's Era in Turkey*, 4 African J. of Business Management 549, 551 (2010).
52. *Id.*, at 552.

aims.[53] First, Turkey took on a significant portion of Ottoman Empire foreign debt, a financial burden that would not be fully repaid until 1954.[54] Second, Turkey agreed to maintain low tariffs for five years on Allied-country imports (discussed in Section II.B.2), the WWI victors.[55]

Under these constrains, Turkey, at least initially, sought to foster agriculture by abolishing the 10 percent flat tax on land, establishing agricultural cooperatives, and enlarging the Ziraat Bankasi's (Agricultural Bank) activities to improve agricultural production.[56] Thanks to agriculture, the annual GDP-growth rate reached 13.3 percent between 1923 and 1929.[57] To further industrialization, Atatürk established İşbank (Business Bank) and Sanayi ve Maadin Bankasi (Industry and Mining Bank) to finance and assist private industry and "to manage and finance state-owned industrial establishments," respectively.[58] Turkey also promulgated a law encouraging domestic industrialization.[59] Under this statute, the government exempted tariffs on machinery, construction materials, and other capital goods for enterprises.[60] Thus, Turkey began to see the birth of basic, processing industries, including sugar-refineries, cotton and wool mills, tanneries, and cement plants.[61]

### 2. *Trade Policy*

In the late Ottoman Empire and even during the war years, the Sultan's government ran a liberal trade policy, with low tariffs and no quantitative restrictions.[62] No foreign exchange controls were in place, "so the value of Turkish lira was determined solely by free market."[63] In short, the government had no control of over national accounts and the balance of payments. Obviously, this situation was anathema to Atatürk's desired "nationalized" economy, with its focus on domestic industrialization, export growth, and trade management. Of course, application of protectionist trade policy tools and tighter control over currency fluctuations would have killed off the old liberal order.[64] Yet, because of its Lausanne Peace Treaty commitments, Turkey could not invoke its sovereignty to change tariffs nor to impose import restrictions on the Allies for five more years (i.e., until 1929). Thus, throughout this period, Turkey followed the 1916 Ottoman customs rate for goods imported from England, France, Italy, Japan, Greece,

53. *See* ORAN, *supra* note 5, at 231 & 244.
54. *See* ZURCHER, *supra* note 26 at 162-165.
55. *See id.*, at 162-165.
56. *See* THORNBURG, *supra* note 28, at 23.
57. *See* Torsten, *supra* note 12, at 14.
58. *See* THORNBURG, *supra* note 28, at 23.
59. *See* MÜKERREM HIÇ, TURKISH ECONOMY AND POLITICS 2 (2009).
60. *See* HALE, *supra* note 45, at 43.
61. *See* THORNBURG, *supra* note 28, at 23.
62. *See* LANDAU, *supra* note 41, at 161.
63. *Id.*
64. *See* SAYGIN & ÇIMEN, *supra* note 23, at 51.

Yugoslavia, and Romania.[65] This trade constraint became known as "compulsory laissez-faire."[66]

Despite these constraints on policymaking, Atatürk had other tools at his disposal. Besides abolishing the land tax, the government gave public lands to entrepreneurs for free and granted financial and fiscal subsidies to support industry.[67] In this environment, constant devaluations of the lira would have helped decrease imports and increase exports. Devoid of a central bank, and thus unable to control exchange rates, the value of the lira was completely market-determined. Although the lira underwent a slight devaluation between 1923 and 1929, such devaluation was not steep enough to influence the trade deficit.[68]

Therefore, because of externally imposed trade constraints and an inability to adjust to foreign exchange appreciation, Turkey ran uninterrupted foreign trade deficits between 1923 and 1929. The export-to-import ratio was 73.6 percent in this period.[69] The foreign trade deficit actually peaked in 1929. The near expiration of the Lausanne Treaty's *compulsory laissez-faire* system led the public to expect tariff increases. This expectation led to a sharp increase in short-term import volumes.[70] Worse news would follow: because of the Great Depression, Turkish agricultural and mine-based exports decreased initially about 15 percent and, then, collapsed in 1931.[71] The end of the Lausanne Peace Treaty's trade constraints had come too late. Although the government would adopt a new tariff schedule (e.g., tariffs climbed to 40 percent *ad valorem* ("a.v.") in 1929) and gain some control over its trade deficit, the policies adopted to cope with the global economic crisis did little to help—in fact, some even hurt—Turkey in the next few years.[72]

### 3. *The Effects of the Great Depression and Forced ISI (1930-1938)*

The Great Depression brought a major reduction in world trade, as most countries attempted to adjust to deflation and decreasing exports at the same time.[73] Turkey was not immune to this crisis, of course.[74] Although a minor player in trade, the average trade-to-GNP ratio for the 1923-1929 period was a far from negligible 14.56 percent.[75] Despite government assistance in the form of fiscal and financial subsidies, the mostly urban private sector had been unable to make a significant contribution to reducing the trade deficit, hovering at 2.1 and 3.3 percent of GNP in 1928 and 1929, respectively.[76]

65. *Id.*, at 49.
66. Torsten, *supra* note 12, at 12.
67. *See* Hıç, *supra* note 59.
68. *See* Hale, *supra* note 45, at 48-49.
69. Saygın & Çimen, *supra* note 23, at 56.
70. *Id.*, at 56-59.
71. *See id.*
72. *See* Hale, *supra* note 45, at 43.
73. *See* Torsten, *supra* note 12, at 14.
74. *See* Oran, *supra* note 5, at 244.
75. *See id.*
76. *See* Aktan, *supra* note 10, at 45-46. Some of the measures Atatürk's Government took to respond to a deteriorating economy made matters worse. For instance, the government increased or

Facing a foreign currency shortfall and lacking monetary sovereignty (i.e., lira devaluation was not an option) in a deteriorating economic environment, Turkey, unable to honor the old Ottoman debt coming due in 1929, declared a moratorium.[77]

Still unable to secure international funding, the Turkish Government decided to intervene in the economy to "ensure the welfare of the nation and the prosperity of the state"[78] by adopting collectivist policies under the term "Etatism." Rejecting socialism, Atatürk described "Etatism" as "a system peculiar to Turkey [that] ... evolved from [relying] on ... the private activity of the individual ... [to] plac[ing] on the state [the] responsibility for ... do[ing] quickly [what has] not been done throughout centuries in [the] Turkish motherland ... ."[79] This view became Atatürk's response to both the Great Depression and the inability of Turkish private enterprise to modernize the country's economic infrastructure at a faster pace.

Atatürk made industrialization a primary focus mainly because Turkey was an importer of even basic consumer goods. With scarcer access to hard currency and foreign financing, Turkey had to substitute basic consumer imports with domestic products. The government, then, became responsible for economic planning and created SOEs to implement its plans.[80] The launch of the First Five-Year Industrial Plan ("FFYIP") made Turkey the first (formally) nonsocialist, developing country to set up a planned economy.[81] According to the FFYIP, SOEs were to establish textile, chemical, sugar, building materials, coal, iron and steel, and paper and cellulose industries.[82] The FFYIP (1933-1937) seemed successful: Turkey was able to transform domestically available raw materials into the textile, iron and steel, cement, and tobacco products.[83]

## 4. *Trade Policy after the Great Depression (1930-1938)*

Turkey ran a highly protective trade policy following the Great Depression. Besides maintaining pre-Depression tariffs—already high (i.e., up to 40 percent a.v.) for all imports except certain medical and capital goods[84]—the Parliament, once freed from Lausanne Treaty strictures, enacted import restrictions and introduced a broad spectrum quota system,[85] in 1931.[86] Having regained monetary sovereignty, the Republic established its first central bank in 1930, which, following a restrictive foreign exchange regime, enabled the government to tightly monitor and constrain the flow of

enacted new taxes on the agricultural sector during a major recession, leading to a cycle of increasing rural indebtment that harmed small farmers and the peasantry the most. *See* Cem Emrence, *Turkey in Economic Crisis (1927-1930): A Panoramic Vision*, 39:4 MIDDLE EASTERN STUDIES 67, 68-70 (2003).

77. *See* KAZGAN, *supra* note 31, at 52 and DIETMAR ROTHERMUND, THE GLOBAL IMPACT OF THE GREAT DEPRESSION 1929-1939, 75 (2002).
78. Aktan, *supra* note 10, at 46.
79. Aktan, *supra* note 10, at 47 (citations omitted).
80. *See* Torsten, *supra* note 12, at 14.
81. *See* SAYGIN & ÇIMEN, *supra* note 23, at 49.
82. *See* Aktan, *supra* note 10, at 48-49; SAYGIN & ÇIMEN, *supra* note 23, at 53-54.
83. *Id.*, at 53.
84. HALE, *supra* note 45, at 43.
85. *See id.*, at 72.
86. This quota system stayed in force until 1980.

imports.[87] Specifically, importation of goods was conditional on raising export incomes, the latter generating the required hard currency to finance imports. These protective and restrictive policies were essential to and did support the application of ISI.

Turkish foreign trade was also managed by a set of "clearing and compensation" agreements, common in that period.[88] Clearing agreements are bilateral trade agreements based on bartering goods and products without the use of foreign currency.[89] Typically established as short-term arrangements, these agreements are managed through clearing offices, under which all bilateral trade is undertaken.[90] Such offices calculate the balance of exports and imports at the end of each year.[91] If there is an imbalance between exports and imports, the deficit country pays off the balance in gold or convertible foreign currency.[92] Struggling to obtain hard currency, Turkey relied heavily on this clearing and compensation mechanism.

Turkey signed clearing agreements with its European trade partners, more so, particularly, with Germany. Turkey and Germany had had strong ties in the 19th century and had been partners in WWI. Later on, particularly in the 1930s, Nazi-Germany would pay Turkish agricultural and mining commodities favorable prices,[93] which allowed Turkey to import machines and other industrial products.[94] Ultimately, Turkish foreign trade became dependent on Germany. For instance, Germany had a 50-percent share of Turkish exports, while Turkey sourced 45 percent of its imports from Germany.[95] To reduce its dependency on Germany, Turkey also signed clearing agreements with England and France, in 1936 and 1937, respectively.[96] Regardless, by the late 1930s, 85 percent of Turkey's trade was done through clearing and compensation agreements.[97]

Despite recovering monetary sovereignty and running a protectionist trade policy, Turkey, unlike other countries, could not devalue its currency in the 1930-1938 period. Still carrying Ottoman Empire debt, perennially short in foreign reserves, and under the straight-jacket of clearing and compensation commitments, Turkey had to follow a restrictive currency regime that left no room for devaluations.[98] In this protected, though constrained policy environment, Turkey would still manage to foster nascent industries, based largely on redirecting revenues sourced from austerity measures and heavy taxation of the population on the countryside. Turkish-owned cotton and wool, iron and steel, paper, ceramic, glass, cement, and semi-coke

87. *See* KAZGAN, *supra* note 31, at 52.
88. Torsten, *supra* note 12, at 15.
89. The Clearing and Compensation Agreements, based on bartering goods, were popular and had to be used at that time. It is because, after the breakdown of the gold standard, there were no internationally accepted balances for capital transfers. *See* ORAN, *supra* note 5, at 305.
90. *See id.*
91. *See id.*
92. *See id.*, at 305.
93. *See id.*, at 304.
94. *See id.*
95. *See id.*, at 305.
96. *See id.*
97. *See* HALE, *supra* note 45, at 72.
98. *See id.*, at 73.

industries emerged in this period.[99] Trade increased from $140 million to $233 million between 1930 and 1938.[100] Thanks to protectionism and other command-and-control policies, Turkey generated a notable foreign trade surplus. This surplus allowed Turkey to begin paying the Ottoman-period debt.[101] Despite contractionary taxation and tight monetary policy, the Turkish economy grew at about 7.7 percent a year in the 1930-1938 period.[102] The World War II ("WWII") would force a neutral Turkey to shift into a wartime economy.

## C. WWII and Trade Policy (1939-1950)

### 1. *The War Economy (1939-1945)*

The new war economy would overlap with the Second Five-Year Industrial Plan ("SFYIP") (1938-1942). Its architects had envisaged this as a period for strengthening heavy industries (e.g., "mining, electricity power, machinery and equipment and cement") and processing industries, such as sugar mills.[103] The start of WWII delayed government officials' "best" plans. Although neutral until 1945, threatened by the Soviet Union, Turkey had to be ready for war. Accordingly, the government allocated national resources and mobilized over one million people[104] to shore up national defense.[105] The Parliament passed the National Protection Law ("NPL") in 1940 giving the government even more power to control the economy.[106] Industrialization plans were also revised due to a reduced global supply of capital goods.[107] If government command-and-control policies already had a strong grip on trade policy, implementation of the NPL turned trade into a *complete* state monopoly.[108] Whereas, before WWII, the government could limit imports by imposing quotas and increasing tariffs, the NPL gave it a mandate to control all exports, as well. The government would soon levy export taxes to collect revenue for military expenses.[109]

During the war years, the world price of agricultural products increased over 600 percent.[110] However, Turkey, an agriculture-based economy, did not benefit, initially, from favorable commodity prices. At war, Germany, France, and England—the main actors in WWII—could not import more Turkish foodstuffs.[111] Even if they could, Turkey's national mobilization, which had shifted labor away from the countryside,

99. *See id.*, at 57.
100. *See* HALE, *supra* note 45, at 73.
101. *See* Takım & Yilmaz, *supra* note 51, at 552.
102. *See* Appendix I; Torsten, *supra* note 12, at 15.
103. *See* Aktan, *supra* note 10, at 49-50.
104. *See* ORAN, *supra* note 5, at 388.
105. Aktan, *supra* note 10, at 62.
106. *See* Torsten, *supra* note 12, at 15.
107. SAHIN, *supra* note 40, at 72.
108. *Id.*, at 81.
109. SAHIN, *supra* note 40, at 81.
110. *Id.*, at 83.
111. *See id.*

meant decreased agricultural production.[112] The industrialized powers could not supply the machines and intermediate goods Turkey needed, either. Many of their productive facilities had been converted to help in the war effort. That Turkey's government levied taxes on exports did not help the outflow of Turkish goods, either.[113] All these policies combined to produce a sharp drop in trade levels. Despite an unofficial premium exchange rate for exporters, which incentivized and did contribute to a rise in exports after 1941,[114] the government insisted on not officially devaluating the lira.[115] This meant the government maintained tight control over trade flows, which led to trade surpluses in the war period: the export-import ratio was 136.5 percent between 1939 and 1945.[116] The foreign trade surplus enabled the government to pay the balance of the Ottoman-period debt and increased the treasury's gold and foreign exchange reserves.[117] Turkey seemed finally positioned to benefit from greater economic autonomy.

### 2. *The Post-War Period (1945-1950)*

After WWII, Turkey had to change trade and economic policies to respond to internal pressure and a changed external environment. Domestically, overregulation of the economy, particularly during WWII, had increased inflation, black markets, and corruption—all often associated with "wartime profiteering."[118] The merchant class became richer, creating resentment among farmers, industrialists, and consumers.[119] Ultimately, this domestic tension pushed the government to begin liberalizing the economy. Popular dissatisfaction also resulted in the establishment of the Democrat Party, an opponent of Etatism.[120] Internationally, Turkey wanted to: (i) continue its Westernization project; and (ii) avoid isolation by its giant-northeastern neighbor, the Soviet Union, which threatened Turkey during WWII. Hence, Turkey became a member of Western organizations, such as the IMF (1947), the World Bank (1947), and the Council of Europe (1949).[121]

Turkey also applied for financial assistance under programs administered under the Truman Doctrine[122] and the Marshall Plan.[123] Yet, such financial assistance came

112. *See* HALE, *supra* note 45, at 74.
113. *See* SAHIN, *supra* note 40, at 82.
114. *See* HALE, *supra* note 45, at 73.
115. *See* SAHIN, *supra* note 40, at 82.
116. SAYGIN & ÇIMEN, *supra* note 23, at 63.
117. *See* Torsten, *supra* note 12, at 16.
118. HALE *supra* note 45, at 60.
119. *See id.*
120. *See* Torsten, *supra* note 12, at 16.
121. ARGIN & BAKKALCI, *supra* note 19, at 383.
122. According to the U.S. President, Harry S. Truman: "the USA should and would help defend 'free nations' whose existence was threatened by foreign pressure or by militant minorities inside their borders." The Truman Doctrine can be summarized as to support so-called free nations, financially and militarily, against the big threat, the Soviet Union. *See* ZURCHER, *supra* note 26, at 209.
123. The aim of the Marshal Plan was to restructure the Europe destroyed during the WWII. *See id.*, at 209.

with conditions.[124] Max Thornburg, an American Government Advisor in that period, posited (correctly) that agriculture was Turkey's comparative advantage.[125] As such, Turkey needed to abandon its state-run ISI policies.[126] Thornburg also criticized Turkish iron and steel mills in Karabük, finding them inefficient and wasteful.[127] To Thornburg and other Western experts, Turkey should focus on achieving gains from agricultural efficiency and raw material specialization to serve markets in Europe and the developed world.[128]

At this important juncture, Turkey had to make a decision. If, on one hand, its leaders wanted to continue on the path to heavy industrialization;[129] on the other, they wanted to belong the Western Club and take part of the Marshall Plan and Truman Doctrine. The latter choice would mean a return to economic orthodoxy and expanding agricultural production, which, by creating wealth on the countryside, would decrease resentment among farmers, who had born the burden of heavy taxation since 1929.[130] Thus, economic efficiency provided the "technical rationale" for Turkey's partial deviation from ISI policies. Turkey did maintain heavy investment in some heavy industries, but, shifted some of its focus to strengthening agriculture.

Soon after WWII, Turkey adopted pro-market and free-trade doctrines cautiously and slowly.[131] In 1946, for the first time since its foundation, yet just before becoming a member of the IMF and the World Bank, which restricted members' currency devaluations to 10 percent maximum (i.e., without a special waiver),[132] Turkey devaluated its currency from 1.30 to 2.80 lira-to-dollar. This massive devaluation contributed to only a small increase in Turkish exports, however. That was the case because, during WWII, Turkey had applied, informally, a dual exchange rate system that varied between 1.80 and 1.90 lira-to-dollar for exporters and importers, respectively.[133] That is, in real terms, the lira's first official devaluation, though sizable, was not as large as it looked in the post-WWII period. Notably, the fact that Turkey's economy was not as debilitated as Europe's, its biggest trading partner, reduced opportunities for Turkish exports, while priming it to absorb more of Europe's imports.

The Turkish import regime, heretofore too restrictive due to a war-economy mentality, slowly gave away after WWII. Following the devaluation of 1946, Turkey partially liberalized its imports by removing quotas and restrictions. As a result, imports increased by more than 100 percent in 1947.[134] This increase can be seen as a recovery from the low level of imports during the WWII. Consequently, the increase in

124. ORAN, *supra* note 5, at 487.
125. *See* SADIK UNAY, NEOLIBERAL GLOBALIZATION AND INSTITUTIONAL REFORM: THE POLITICAL ECONOMY OF DEVELOPMENT AND PLANNING IN TURKEY 90-93 (2006).
126. *See* THORNBURG, *supra* note 28, at 222-226.
127. SAHIN, *supra* note 40, at 89; THORNBURG, *supra* note 28, at 24; *see* HALE, *supra* note 45, at 81.
128. *See* ORAN, *supra* note 5, at 487.
129. *See* SAHIN, *supra* note 40, at 90.
130. *See, e.g.*, Emrence, *supra* note 76, at 68-69 (explaining why taxes levied on livestock had doubled in 1929).
131. SAYGIN & ÇIMEN, *supra* note 23, at 60.
132. *See* SAHIN, *supra* note 40, at 83.
133. HALE, *supra* note 45, at 73.
134. *Id.*

imports was higher than the increase in exports, and Turkey soon had a significant foreign trade deficit, the first since 1930.[135] Such deficits have continued, uninterrupted, since 1947.[136] In return, Turkey began receiving U.S. financial aid and credits under the Truman Doctrine and Marshall Plan. This assistance helped Turkey finance its trade deficit.[137]

Allied with the Western Block, Turkey had to engage in democratic reforms. Turkey's first *free* election was held in May 1950. The Republican People's Party ("RPP"), Atatürk's party and in power since 1923, lost the election, and, as a result, control of Parliament and government. The Democrat Party, campaigning under the "Enough!" slogan, benefitted from a new wave of popular support and captured 408 seats out of 492 in the Parliament.[138] The 1950 election results showed that the Turkish people wanted change, giving the Democrat Party a mandate to begin moving Turkey away from the collectivist policies of past governments.

## D. Democrat Party Trade Policy (1950-1960)

### 1. *The Initial Liberalization Attempt (1950-1953)*

Once in power, the Democrat Party continued Turkey's Westernization project, signing the GATT (1951) and entering the NATO (1952).[139] To foster a market economy and implement free trade, the Democrat Party rejected planning and bureaucratic procedures, vowed to privatize SOEs, and enacted legislation encouraging foreign investment.[140] It also prioritized agriculture to benefit from U.S. financial and technical assistance and to maintain voter support in a mostly agricultural nation.[141] The Democrat Party agreed to support light industries (e.g., sugar and textile mills, etc.) on the belief that Turkey should become an agriculture and raw material supplier for Europe.[142] The plan was to sharply increase agricultural and mining exports. Should this plan work out, export income would skyrocket; trade surpluses would return; and Turkey's balance-of-payments troubles would be over. Accordingly, the government reduced tariffs, liberalizing trade on approximately 65 percent of all imports, between 1950 and 1952.[143]

More favorable agricultural prices (e.g., particularly cotton) resulting from the Korean War (1950-1953), good weather conditions, and mechanization efforts—which benefitted from Marshall Plan assistance—led Turkey to attain a notable export

135. *See* Saygin & Çimen, *supra* note 23, at 63.
136. *See* Appendix I.
137. *See* Sahin, *supra* note 40, at 88.
138. *See* Zurcher, *supra* note 26, at 217-221.
139. *See id.*, at 235.
140. Torsten, *supra* note 12, at 17.
141. *See* Zurcher, *supra* note 26, at 224.
142. Saygin & Çimen, *supra* note 23, at 64.
143. Abdullah Takım, *Demokrat Parti Döneminde Uygulanan Ekonomi Politikalari ve Sonuçlari* [Economic Policies Applied During Democrat Party Rule], 67:2 Ankara Universitesi, SBF Dergisi 157, 174 (2012).

performance until 1953.[144] In this period, Turkish exports rose from $263 to $396 million.[145] However, increased export income also pushed domestic demand upward, causing an unprecedented import boom.[146] Turkish imports doubled, increasing from $285 to $532 million, in the same period.[147] Thus, despite improved export performance, Turkey's foreign trade deficit actually increased. To finance this deficit, Turkey used its own reserves, commercial credits, and U.S.-based financial assistance and credits.[148]

### 2. *Unplanned Intervention in the Economy (1954-1959)*

Starting in 1954, agricultural exports dropped because of domestic crop failure and decreased global demand. Lower foodstuff supplies pressured prices, leading to more inflation.[149] Yet, lower export income did not reduce Turkey's appetite for imports, so the trade deficit increased further. Because U.S. financial assistance was not enough to fill the balance-of-payments gap, and because Turkey could not attract more foreign investment, the country ran out of hard currency. With an aggravated balance-of-payment problem, the Democrat Party's plans for liberalization came to a halt.[150] The Democrat Party never truly liberalized Turkey's currency exchange system. Lacking the disciplining effect of free-floating rates, the government had little the incentive to maintain fiscal discipline and also allowed its trade deficit to increase.

To avoid hard-currency bottlenecks, which also resulted from administered, fixed exchange rates, Democrats pivoted away from their earlier commitment to freer markets and less government management of the economy. In 1956, Parliament reenacted the National Protection Law, empowering the government to intervene in the economy.[151] The government established more SOEs, all financed by Central Bank loans.[152] This period saw Turkey establishing its Machinery and Chemical Industry, Iron and Steel Industry, Turkish Cement Industry, Turkish Coal Enterprises, and the State Supply Office—all government SOEs.[153] ISI was creeping back.

Significantly, the Democrat Party imposed selective trade barriers on quite arbitrary criteria (e.g., higher tariffs on high-income consumer goods),[154] put in place an import-licensing system,[155] increased customs tariffs, and severely curtailed access to foreign exchange.[156] Yet, the government still did not officially devalue the lira. As

144. ORAN, *supra* note 5, at 487-488.
145. *See* Appendix I; SAYGIN & ÇIMEN, *supra* note 23, at 63-67.
146. Torsten, *supra* note 12, at 17.
147. *See* Appendix I; SAYGIN & ÇIMEN, *supra* note 23, at, 63-67.
148. *See* HALE, *supra* note 45, at 104.
149. *See* Torsten, *supra* note 12, at 18.
150. *Id.*
151. *See* ZURCHER, *supra* note 26, at 231.
152. ANNE O. KRUEGER, FOREIGN TRADE REGIMES AND ECONOMIC DEVELOPMENT: TURKEY 7 (1974).
153. Aktan, *supra* note 10, at 51-52.
154. Torsten, *supra* note 12, at 18.
155. KRUEGER, *supra* note 152, at 20.
156. SAHIN, *supra* note 40, at 97.

always, "devaluation was regarded as a very dirty word, to be avoided at all costs."[157] Nevertheless, Turkey used *sub rosa* devaluation methods, including the imposition a dual exchange rate system: one for exports, one for imports. The main purposes of this system were: (i) to mitigate the effect of an overvalued lira for exporters; and (ii) to tightly manage the volume of imports.[158] However, an overvalued lira and a weather-influenced decline in agricultural production harmed exports. In sum, between 1955 and 1958, the return to protectionism did help decrease imports, emboldening plans for ever more government-directed industrialization.[159]

While foreign exchange controls restricted the importation of capital goods and semi-finished products, high tariffs and ad hoc quotas on high-income consumer goods provided a great advantage to domestic producers.[160] The domestic industry lived, again, under protection from outside competition, a de facto ISI. While this policy favored domestic production, it also limited export growth by restricting capital- and intermediate-good imports and, thus, more efficient production. At least in the initial years, these policies brought a measure of dynamism into domestic business life and encouraged some entrepreneurial spirit.[161] Indeed, with less competition, nascent domestic industrial sectors flourished, including processed foodstuffs, cigarettes, mining, textiles, iron and steel, cement, and copper industries.[162] By the end of the 1950s, Turkey had largely become self-sufficient in essential consumer goods.[163] Through a winding route, the first phase of ISI had been completed.

Yet, predictably, over-protection led to little innovation, and a stagnant export sector would ensure Turkey's trade balance remained negative. By late 1957, Turkey's uninterrupted trade deficit pushed the foreign debt beyond $1 billion, or about three times 1957 exports.[164] This led to another foreign debt crisis, which, combined with stagnation and inflation, resulted in a 1958 loan agreement with the IMF.[165] With the IMF stabilization package in place, the Democrat Party increased SOE-product prices, imposed more taxes, and restricted the domestic money supply to control inflation.[166] Policy-wise, the Democrat Party had become nearly indistinguishable from the RPP, whom they had displaced from power. The Democrats also officially devaluated the lira from 2.80 to 9 lira-dollars.[167] This over 300-percent devaluation, the first devaluation since 1946, forced Turkey to renegotiate its foreign debt. The United States and the IMF assembled a credit assistance package worth around $359 million.[168]

157. HALE, *supra* note 45, at 106.
158. *See* HALE, *supra* note 45, at 106.
159. SAYGIN & ÇIMEN, *supra* note 23, at 67.
160. *See* ANNE O. KRUEGER & OKAN H. AKTAN, SWIMMING AGAINST THE TIDE: TURKISH TRADE REFORM IN THE 1980s 16 (1992).
161. *See* HALE, *supra* note 45, at 111.
162. *See* Takım, *supra* note 143, at 169; *see also* HALE, *supra* note 45, at 192.
163. SAHIN, *supra* note 40, at 104.
164. HALE, *supra* note 45, at 106.
165. Torsten, *supra* note 12, at 19.
166. ORAN, *supra* note 5, at 490.
167. *Id.*
168. HALE, *supra* note 45, at 107.

This rescue package would become ineffective in a mere two years, however. True, the devalued lira helped increase Turkish exports from $274 to $320 million between 1958 and 1960.[169] But Turkish imports *also* increased from $315 to $468 million in that period.[170] This occurred because the new inflow of money helped finance more imports of intermediate and capital goods in furtherance of the very ISI policies the government pursued.[171] Clearly, devaluation, by itself, was not a panacea. The newly received IMF and U.S. credits were exhausted within two years, which resulted in expanding trade deficits and balance-of-payment problems.

The inability to stabilize macroeconomic fundamentals (e.g., inflation, public debt, trade and current account deficits, foreign debt, etc.) led to student demonstrations, rioting, and military unrest. Experts on Turkey posit that the military took over the country in 1960 to deflate political and social tension.[172] The military government formed a tribunal to prosecute the former leaders of the Democrat Party.[173] Following a brief trial in 1961, the military regime hanged three ministers, including Prime Minister Adnan Menderes, himself the target of rather conclusory charges of corruption and murder.[174]

## E. Full Deployment of ISI and Trade Policy (1960-1980)

### 1. *Planned ISI (1960-1973)*

#### a. *Industrial Policy and Managed Trade*

Following the military coup in 1960, the authoritarian-Etatist-military and bureaucratic elites came to power again. The military wrote a new constitution, which allowed it to shape and control economic and social policies. It also approved a state-directed planned economy and established the State Planned Organization ("SPO") in 1960.[175] The SPO was responsible for preparing and deploying five-year development plans.[176] The main objectives of development plans were to: (i) maintain high and sustainable growth; (ii) ensure a balanced foreign trade; and (iii) further industrialization with the private sector.[177]

With the planned ISI in full force, Turkey entered a second phase of command-and-control industrialization, now aimed at domestic production of durable goods and semi-finished products. As in the 1930s, the government created heavy industries

169. SAYGIN & ÇIMEN, *supra* note 23, at 67.
170. *See* Appendix I; *id.*
171. *See id.*
172. ZURCHER, *supra* note 26, at 241.
173. *Id.*, at 247.
174. *See id.*, at 248 (indicating that Prime Minister Menderes's murder charge involved his alleged role in facilitating his mistress's abortion).
175. *See* HALE, *supra* note 45, at 141.
176. *See* SAHIN, *supra* note 40, at 123.
177. *See id.*, at 125-128.

through SOEs, which were also tasked with producing intermediate goods.[178] The role of the private sector was to take advantage of the planned ISI. Private economic actors began purchasing SOE-produced intermediate goods at below-market prices and started to produce durable consumer goods.[179] To create domestic demand for these durable goods, Turkey kept wages higher, which inevitably caused high inflation rates between 1960 and 1980.[180]

As in earlier times, to implement ISI, Turkey deployed a highly restrictive import regime; created foreign exchange shortage; and promoted export incentives. Under the import quota system, published annually in the *Official Gazette*,[181] the government established three lists: (i) a "Liberalization" List; (ii) a Quota List; and (iii) a Commodity List that specified materials that could only be imported under bilateral agreements.[182] Importation of goods in neither of these lists was banned.[183] The Liberalization List was broken down into two lists: a Free-Import List (List I) consisting of raw materials and spare parts; and a Restricted List (List II), which included semi-processed and capital goods.[184] The Quota List merely itemized commodities for which there was not enough domestic production, which could be imported on an as-needed basis.[185]

Pursuant to standard ISI plans, as soon as domestic production of an imported good began, the imported good would be shifted from the Liberalization List to the Quota List. After domestic production of the imported good was sufficient enough for internal demand, the imported good was removed from the Quota List, as well.[186] In sum, if an imported product was successfully replaced with a domestic product, importation of the foreign product would no longer be allowed.[187]

To strengthen its annual import program, Turkey also used an import-licensing system.[188] Import licenses for goods itemized in the Liberalization List (e.g., raw materials, capital goods, etc.) were not subject to too much delay because those goods were essential for domestic production. Yet, obtaining import licenses for goods that were in the Quota List could take months.[189] Obviously, the main goal of this licensing system was to provide extra protection to the domestic industry and avoid trade deficits.

In addition to the application of a protectionist import regime, Turkey also deployed a restrictive foreign exchange policy.[190] Importers who had applied and received import licenses had to wait up to eight months to obtain foreign currency from

178. *Id.*, at 127.
179. *See* Torsten, *supra* note 12, at 22.
180. *See* ORAN, *supra* note 5, at 663.
181. Torsten, *supra* note 12, at 19.
182. Togan & Kaminski, *supra* note 1, at 13.
183. *Id.*
184. *See id.*, at 14.
185. *Id.*
186. *Id.*
187. *Id.*
188. HALE, *supra* note 45, at 237.
189. *Id.*
190. KRUEGER & AKTAN, *supra* note 160, at 21.

the Central Bank.[191] This foreign exchange regime allowed Turkey to control its balance of payments, which made importation quite cumbersome, if not impractical. As is invariably the case, these rules were premised on "best" intentions: they were meant to protect nascent industries and avoid foreign currency bottlenecks. In practice, however, they would lead to the protection of inefficient industries, higher domestic prices, and other effects often ignored by government experts and rent-seeking industrialists.

On the export side, Turkey created a variety of incentives for exporters. All exporters were able to use government-subsidized credits with low interest rates.[192] The government also bestowed extra subsidies on nontraditional (i.e., industrial) exporters. These exporters were entitled to rebates on their taxes (e.g., personal and corporate income taxes, etc.).[193] These nontraditional exporters could also easily obtain import licenses for importation of raw materials, capital goods and intermediate products, and if their imported goods were inputs for exports, such imported inputs were also exempted from tariffs.[194]

In general, Turkey avoided using foreign inputs in the first period of ISI (particularly, in the 1930s).[195] By contrast, Turkey would use significant amounts of imported intermediate and investment goods in its second stage of ISI (producing durable goods and semi-finished products), which increased import volumes. By value, imports increased from $468 million to $947 million between 1960 and 1970, while exports increased from $320 million to $588 million in the same period.[196] Thus, Turkey still ran foreign trade deficits and kept facing balance-of-payment problems.[197]

### b. *The 1970 Devaluation and Rising Monetary Inflows*

To tackle the balance-of-payment issue and finance more imports under ISI, Turkey needed to increase exports. The best method was to devaluate the lira, so that Turkish products would become cheaper in world markets. In 1970, with IMF approval, Turkey devaluated its currency for the third time: one dollar went from 9 to 14.85 liras—a 66 percent devaluation.[198] This devaluation did increase exports (e.g., processed foodstuffs and textiles), but, again, it did not decrease imports. With the increase in exports and imports, Turkish trade volumes and trade deficits *doubled* in just three years (i.e., 1970-1973), despite a substantial devaluation.[199]

Arguably, the rise in imports derived from increases in intermediate and capital goods imports, which had been suppressed under ISI policies.[200] According to Rodrik

191. *Id.*, at 23.
192. Hale, *supra* note 45, at 237.
193. *Id.*
194. *Id.*
195. Oran, *supra* note 5, at 611.
196. *See* Appendix I; Torsten, *supra* note 12, at 26.
197. Oran, *supra* note 5, at 662.
198. *Id.*, at 663; *see also* Hale, *supra* note 45, at 262; Appendix I.
199. Saygin & Çimen, *supra* note 23, at 73.
200. Hale, *supra* note 45, at, 230.

and Celasun, the increase in imports following those huge devaluations had to do with black-market effects: devaluations equalized formal and black-market exchange rates, which led to an increase in legal imports.[201] We also posit that, with every devaluation, Turkish financial assets held abroad in strong currencies flowed back to the country to benefit from heavily discounted nontradables (e.g., real estate, etc.), helping increase demand for other imported goods (e.g., intermediate and investment goods), as well. This indirect, capital-account effect also explains, at least partly, the paradox of why lira devaluations tend to be followed by actual rises in imports and trade deficits.

In the 1970s, Turkey, unexpectedly, found a new foreign money supplier: Turkish workers. Turkish *émigrés* had started working abroad, particularly in Germany, since the late 1960s. By 1973, Turkish remittances from abroad added up to $1.13 billion—enough to solve the Turkish balance-of-payment problem.[202] Turkey had a current account surplus for the first time since 1946.[203] Thus, the planned ISI strategy could only work because Turkey ended up also exporting workers, another nontrivial application of the law of unintended consequences.

After 1973, however, Turkey, like many developing countries, was affected by the global oil crisis. Turkey, whose main goal was to save foreign currency with ISI, saw itself forced to part away with dollars, now needed to pay a significantly higher oil bill. This development aggravated the suboptimality of ISI.

### *2. The Oil Crisis and the Rise in Foreign Debt (1973-1979)*

After 1973, Turkey faced numerous external crises, which increased inflation; stagnation; trade deficits; balance-of-payment troubles; and, consequently, its foreign debt. Starting in 1973, the Organization of Petroleum Exporting Countries ("OPEC") increased oil prices, which affected Turkish import costs in two different ways. First, Turkey's oil import bill increased dramatically—Turkey is heavily dependent on oil imports.[204] Second, Turkey's continued application of ISI—which relied on heavy importation of intermediate and investment goods, whose prices spiked due to the oil price hike—amplified this effect.[205]

Despite the escalation in global oil prices, Turkey did not allow internal oil prices to reflect world market prices. Turkey wanted to continue ISI by importing more oil, investment and intermediate goods.[206] As a result, Turkish industry was able to grow,[207] and the manufacturing sector's share of GDP surpassed that of agriculture.[208]

201. *See* Merih Celasun & Dani Rodrik, *Trade Regime and an Anatomy of Export Performance*, Volume Title: Developing Country Debt and Economic Performance, 3 COUNTRY STUDIES—INDONESIA, KOREA, PHILIPPINES, TURKEY 716, 718 (1989), *available at*: http://www.nber.org/chapters/c9063.pdf.
202. Note that, at that time, the Turkish foreign trade deficit was $769 million (X: $1.31 and M: $2.08 billion). *See* Torsten, *supra* note 12, at 26.
203. HALE, *supra* note 45, at 231.
204. *See* KAZGAN, *supra* note 31, at 85.
205. *See id.*
206. *See* KAZGAN, *supra* note 31, at 85-86.
207. *See id.*
208. *See* HALE, *supra* note 45, at 117.

Yet, continued pursuit of such an industrial policy and a rising demand for imports only aggravated Turkey's balance of payments. Turkish industrial exports could not help finance increasing import bills. Quite simply, the domestic industry, overprotected since 1954, had little incentive to produce high-quality products to compete in world markets. The overvaluation of the lira was another obstacle: Turkish products remained expensive in global markets.[209]

Although Turkey devalued the lira every year, these constant devaluations became easily ineffective.[210] As Anne O. Krueger explains, inflation rates—invariably higher than devaluation rates—make export activity unprofitable.[211] Arguably, if devaluation rates could be kept above inflation rates, Turkish exports would increase more, which would help finance Turkish foreign trade deficits. Yet, because ISI was essentially premised on saving foreign exchange and preserving domestic captive markets, devaluations lagged inflation *by design* and, thus, could not provide domestic industry a real incentive to become more competitive.

Eventually, increasing trade deficits could not be compensated for by Turkish expatriates' remittances any longer. Turkey faced a balance-of-payment crisis again after 1973.[212] To finance its foreign debt and keep its economy working (i.e., importing oil, intermediate and investment goods), Turkey had to find hard currency abroad. The best option, at that time, was borrowing petrodollars, then flowing into the international banking system, from OPEC-member countries. Developing countries were the key destinations for this money, because they needed to buy capital and intermediate goods to further their ISI policies.[213] Developing countries, including Turkey, borrowed heavily from international banks, thus bypassing IMF controls. Such borrowing sharply increased imports of intermediate and capital goods.[214] In 1977, imports exceeded $5.7 billion, while exports were $1.7 billion.[215] The export-import rate became only 30.2 percent; the foreign trade deficit rose to $4 billion; and the foreign debt exceeded $10 billion.[216] Suleyman Demirel, then Prime Minister, summarized Turkey's frantic currency bottleneck, thusly: "Turkey is in desperate need to get [even] 70 cents."[217]

In 1978 and 1979, the IMF recommended Turkey to substantially devaluate the lira; increase SOE-product prices; and implement structural economic reforms (e.g., adopt a flexible exchange rate system, privatize natural monopolies, etc.).[218] Accordingly, Turkey devaluated the lira from 19.25 to 25 per US dollar in 1978, and, from there

209. Oran, *supra* note 5, at 664.
210. Krueger & Aktan, *supra* note 160, at 21.
211. *Id.*, at 28.
212. At the same time, because of Turkey's Cyprus Peace Operation in 1974, the U.S. declared an arms embargo, and the Europe applied an implicit embargo, which decreased the financial assistance that Turkey received. *See* Kazgan, *supra* note 31, at 85.
213. *Id.*, at 86.
214. Oran, *supra* note 5, at 668.
215. *See* Appendix I; Saygin & Çimen, *supra* note 23, at 72.
216. *See* Appendix I; Saygin & Çimen, *supra* note 23, at 72.
217. Oran, *supra* note 5, at 668.
218. Hale, *supra* note 45, at 243.

to 47 lira per US dollar in 1979.[219] The government also increased prices of SOEs' products, but refused making other structural changes to the economy. Ultimately, these measures "were rapidly outdated" due to high inflation rates, exceeding 50 percent per year.[220] Dissatisfied with the efforts of the Turkish Government, the IMF did not approve additional loan packages.[221]

To extract itself from balance-of-payment/hard-currency shortage troubles, the government began searching for additional sources of financing, but failed to secure any loans. Indeed, the World Bank and other international banks had begun coordinating lending policy with the IMF. Foreign lending became subject to the approval of the IMF, which required market reforms, trade liberalization, etc.[222] The government resisted these economic reforms, believing that obtaining the support of government coalitions for the recommended hard decisions (e.g., privatizing SOEs, floating the lira, cutting public spending, etc.) would be impossible. Indeed, no party was willing to risk its popularity by adopting austerity measures, and politicians, perhaps more than any other profession, respond to incentives. The multiple coalition governments of that period opted to delay solving a problem they knew other governments would have to address later, only at their own—and the public's—cost.

Further complicating matters, OPEC countries increased oil prices, again, in 1979 and 1980. The cumulative 150-percent rise in oil prices doubled the Turkish trade deficit.[223] The economy, which "had [already] been in a state of crisis for three years," further deteriorated.[224] Inflation exceeded 100 percent per year; factories were closing; and domestic production fell because of difficulties in securing guarantees for necessary oil, capital- and intermediate-good imports.[225] Turkey and its political elites could no longer delay the need to consider structural changes, including ISI abrogation and adoption of pro-market reforms.

### *3. ISI Expiration (1980)*

Facing a deteriorating economic outlook and to get started on debt negotiations with the IMF and World Bank, Turkey finally committed to engaging in structural economic reforms. On January 24, 1980, the government launched the Stabilization Package ("1980 Package"), which abolished ISI, liberalized the import regime, and fostered exports.[226] Because the government's primary objectives were to combat inflation and pay Turkey's foreign debt, which required more reliance on market mechanisms, free-trade initiatives were adopted to modernize the economy.[227] This policy change

219. *Id.*, at 262.
220. Krueger & Aktan, *supra* note 160, at 26.
221. *See* Kazgan, *supra* note 31, at 94-97.
222. *See id.*, at 97.
223. *See* Saygin & Çimen, *supra* note 23, at 72.
224. Krueger & Aktan, *supra* note 160, at 33.
225. *Id.*
226. *Id.*, at 40.
227. Togan & Kaminski, *supra* note 1.

would be later referred to as the "Washington Consensus."[228] Thus, with the Package in place, Turkey was able to negotiate its foreign debt and sign stand-by loan agreements with the IMF and World Bank.[229]

Remarkably, with the 1980 Package, Turkey parted with inward-oriented industrialization, a set of policies that had been in place since the mid-1920s. Despite currency bottlenecks, economic crises, debt renegotiations, periodic IMF stabilization measures (e.g., 1958, 1970, 1978-1979, and 1980), huge inflation, and devaluation rates, Turkey created a national industry and fostered domestic-controlled agricultural and mining production. Turkish industry, now able to produce and/or assemble different kinds of durable consumer goods and machinery (e.g., autos, trucks, diesel locomotives, household appliances, etc.),[230] could supply the domestic demand on processed food, drinks and tobacco; textiles and clothing; and cement and cement products.[231] It could also supply over 80 percent of the domestic demand on plastic and rubber products, chemicals and petroleum products (e.g., detergents and tires), iron and steel products, and vehicles.[232] By 1980, domestic machinery production could meet up to 63.6 percent of domestic demand.[233]

Agricultural and mining production also improved in the 1923-1980 period. Massive government assistance directed mechanization; irrigation; and land reform, all contributed to greater agricultural production (e.g., cereals, legumes and industrial crops, etc.).[234] Under the guidance of Etibank, mineral production in coal, lignite, crude oil, iron ore, chromite, baron minerals, and copper—largely used in the domestic industry—also increased.[235] Thus, by 1980, with the contribution of imported intermediate and investment goods, Turkey had become largely self-sufficient. Inward-looking ISI policies had accomplished the mission. One wonders whether an alternative, more market-friendly path could have accomplished *more* for Turkey, in less time.

## III. THE POST-1980 PERIOD: THE SWITCH TO OUTWARD-ORIENTED POLICIES

Despite being motivated by sheer economic necessity, the switch from inward- to outward-oriented policies was widely supported by the private sector.[236] Able to meet most of internal demand, domestic producers began looking for different export destinations. Increasing exports to oil-exporting countries that had become wealthier after 1973 was an obvious choice. These countries were also unindustrialized and dependent on the importation of even basic consumer products.[237] Turkey's private

228. For more on the Washington Consensus, *see* Chapter 2, Section II.B and associated footnotes.
229. *See* Torsten, *supra* note 12, at 28.
230. *See* HALE, *supra* note 45, at 192.
231. *Id.*, at 194.
232. *Id.*
233. *See id.*
234. *See* HALE, *supra* note 45, at 174-182.
235. *See id.*, at 194.
236. KAZGAN, *supra* note 31, at 98.
237. *Id.*, at 97.

sector quickly became an important supplier to these neighbors.[238] In sum, after abandoning ISI (i.e., 1923-1980), Turkey switched to an outward-oriented trade policy based on three fundamental principles: (1) export promotion; (2) trade liberalization; and (3) financial deregulation. The new trade orientation would finally allow Turkey to modernize its currency regime: one that would lead to full lira convertibility.[239]

To foster exports, Turkey applied flexible exchange rates and implemented economy-wide export incentives. It slowly liberalized its import regime, thereby introducing competition to various sectors of the economy.[240] These measures would help Turkey bring domestic prices into closer alignment with international prices, enabling its industries to join global supply chains. This new period also saw Turkey become an "original member" of the WTO (1995) and form a customs union with the European Community (later the European Union) (1996). These two turning points—trade liberalization and further integration with Europe—would improve Turkish foreign trade performance, even as they also limited government control over trade policy. Exports and imports increased dramatically after 1980, making the trade sector a bigger part of Turkey's economy.[241] With trade amounting to around 60 percent of Turkey's GDP,[242] Turkey would become a genuine "trading state."[243]

Subsection A, below, discusses the gradual liberalization that took place between 1980 and 1994. Subsection B then analyzes Turkey's integration into the world economy (i.e., joining the WTO and signing the CU with the European Union) and discusses the 2001 economic crisis, which led to the rise of Recep Tayyip Erdoğan (2001), whose policies will be discussed in detail in Chapter 4.

## A. Export Promotion, Gradual Trade and Financial Liberalization (1980-1994)

As hinted above (Section II.E.2), the late 1970s coalition governments were not willing to make the structural changes Turkey needed and delayed reform as long as they could.[244] Macroeconomic mismanagement begat an economic crisis that eventually led to political violence and military unrest.[245] As a last resort, with the approval of the

238. *Id.*
239. *See* SAYGIN & ÇIMEN, *supra* note 23, at 13-21; *see also* Dani Rodrik, Some Policy Dilemmas in Turkish Macroeconomic Management, *in The Political Economy of Turkey: Debt, Adjustment and Sustainability* 183-198 (Aricanli Tosun and Rodrik Dani eds., 1990).
240. Togan & Kaminski, *supra* note 1.
241. *See* WTO Secretariat, *Trade Policy Review of Turkey*, WT/TPR/S/331, 10 (Feb. 9, 2016) [hereinafter Turkey TPR 2016].
242. *Id.*
243. *See id.*; Kemal Kirişçi, *Turkey and the Transatlantic Trade and Investment Partnership Boosting the Model Partnership with the United States*, 10 (Center on the United States and Europe at Brookings, Turkey Project Policy Paper, No. 2, September 2013), *available at*: https://www.brookings.edu/wp-content/uploads/2016/06/Turkey-and-the-Transatlantic-Trade-and-Investment-Partnership.pdf.
244. *See* Tercan Baysan & Charles Blitzer, *Turkey's Trade Liberalization in the 1980s and Prospects for its Sustainability, in The Political Economy of Turkey: Debt, Adjustment and Sustainability* 9-36, 9 (Tosun Aricanli and Dani Rodrik eds., 1990).
245. *Id.*

military, the government announced a set of economic measures (e.g., huge devaluation, privatization plan, etc.) on January 24, 1980.[246] However, implementation of these measures could not calm tensions down. Pro-market and unpopular, these measures were opposed by pro-Etatism advocates, resulting in increasing student demonstrations and political violence.[247] Amid such instability, the military overthrew the government on September 12, 1980, shot down the Parliament, and closed all political parties.[248]

As expected, military force made it easier to successfully implement the needed economic reforms.[249] The military also gave wide economic authority to the Package's drafter, Turgut Özal, a former planning bureaucrat at SPO with Word Bank experience.[250] Özal, in charge of economic policy for two years, resigned from the military government in 1982 to create the "Motherland Party." His party would win the majority of seats in Parliament in 1983, making him the Prime Minister.[251] Özal successfully governed Turkey, particularly its economy, from 1980 until his death, in 1993.

### 1. *Implementation of the Stabilization Package (1980-1989)*

The Özal-designed, 1980 Package constituted a major change of course for Turkey in the direction of pro-market policies.[252] Besides combatting inflation, it sought to control the trade deficit and address Turkey's foreign debt.[253] In pursuit of these goals, the government enacted the following regulations: (i) a more flexible exchange rate system; (ii) more efficient export-promotion measures; (iii) gradual import liberalization, by abolishing quotas and decreasing tariff rates; (iv) creation of a new external debt management system; (v) imposition of monetary controls and anti-inflation measures to decrease inflation; (vi) deregulation of interest rates; (vii) encouragement of privatization; and (viii) overhaul of SOE system.[254] Ultimately, Turkish economy policy (i.e., particularly industrialization policy) changed drastically with the application of these measures, which we discuss below.

#### a. *Export-Promotion Tools (1980-1989)*

The twin goals of decreasing the trade deficit and foreign debt required a rapid increase in exports. Accordingly, Turkey applied a variety of policy tools to promote exports.[255] Some ISI-era export incentives were already in place (e.g., tax rebates, credits with low

246. Saygin & Çimen, *supra* note 23, at 14.
247. Zurcher, *supra* note 26, at 268.
248. *Id.*, at 278.
249. Steven Webb, Turkey: Democratization and Adjustment from Above, *in State and Market: The Political Economy of Turkey in Comparative Perspective* 323-373, 348 (Ziya Öniş ed., 1999).
250. *See* Zurcher, *supra* note 26, at 282.
251. *See id.*
252. Saygin & Çimen, *supra* note 23, at 13.
253. *See* Togan & Kaminski, *supra* note 1.
254. Baysan & Blitzer, *supra* note 244, at 10.
255. Togan & Kaminski, *supra* note 1.

interest rates, tariff exemption for exportable goods' inputs, etc.). All were ineffective because of persistent overvaluation of the lira and the complete absorption of domestic production by domestic demand. As such, domestic production could only expand with further major and risky capital investments, which were not attractive to domestic businesses at the time.[256] After 1980, Turkey reshaped its export-promotion system by adding *more* incentives (e.g., foreign exchange retention rights, free trade zones, etc.). This time, however, wage suppression dampened domestic demand while an aggressive exchange rate policy favored export production[257]—both of which amounted to a massive transfer of wealth from consumers to the export sector.

Turkey also opted for a permanently undervalued currency in this period. Earlier in 1980, Turkey devalued the lira from 47 to 70, and later in the year, to 91 per US dollar.[258] Starting in 1981, the exchange rate was adjusted on a *daily* basis.[259] Constant devaluations would lead to increased and accelerating inflation rates, however. Annual inflation rates exceeded 40 percent between 1981 and 1988, bringing Turkey to a devaluation-inflation spiral, particularly after the mid-1980s.[260] To support the export sector, Turkey would keep devaluing the lira at higher rates than inflation. By the end of 1988, the nominal value of the dollar reached ₺1,816.[261] In real terms (i.e., accounting for inflation), the lira depreciated 40 percent between 1984 and 1988.[262] Devaluation had become a preferred tool for bolstering Turkish exports.

In addition to an aggressive exchange rate policy, Turkey simplified administrative procedures on exports after 1980. SPO, Turkey's central-planning agency, became responsible for all export-promotion measures, decreasing bureaucratic layers and delays in distributing export incentives.[263] As in the 1970s, the government offered export credits with low interest rates, which, in light of the contemporaneous accelerating inflation, amounted to a sizable, non-actionable (at the time), export subsidy.[264] For example, in 1980, the market interest rate reached 44.1 percent, while the effective interest rate for exporters was only 25 percent.[265] This trend persisted until 1989, with some attenuation in the tail-end years, due to subsequent restrictions imposed by the GATT Subsidy Code.[266]

The 1980 reforms introduced a new export incentive: the right to retain foreign currencies.[267] Prior to 1980, exporters had to surrender export incomes in foreign exchange to the Central Bank.[268] Starting in 1980, exporters were permitted to retain up

256. *See* Krueger & Aktan, *supra* note 160, at 71.
257. Nilgün Önder, *The Turkish Project of Globalization and New Regionalism*, 7 Alternatives: Turkish J. of Int'l Relations 86, 90 (Summer & Fall 2008).
258. *See* Sahin, *supra* note 40, at 196 & 438.
259. Baysan & Blitzer, *supra* note 244, at 11.
260. *See* Kazgan, *supra* note 31, at 119-121.
261. Sahin, *supra* note 40, at 438.
262. *Id.*, at 198.
263. Krueger & Aktan, *supra* note 160, at 76.
264. *See id.*, at 78.
265. *Id.*, at 80-81.
266. *Id.*
267. *Id.*, at 82.
268. *Id.*

to 30 percent of their export earnings in foreign currency.[269] Obviously, the right to keep at least part of export earnings in hard currency created quite a windfall for exporters in an environment where huge devaluations (and, thus, inflation) were taking place. Other incentives were: (i) provision of special foreign exchange allocations to producers whose exports had been growing rapidly;[270] and (ii) granting rebates of customs duties on all imported inputs upon exportation of finished goods (i.e., "duty drawback").[271]

Turkey, like South Korea and Japan (each, since the 1960s), began encouraging the establishment of big foreign trade companies ("FTCs") to accelerate exports.[272] Starting in 1982, FTCs with higher export volumes got higher rebates.[273] For example, FTCs, whose exports exceeded $2 million, "were entitled to a six-percent rebate."[274] Where exports exceeded $10 million, the exporter would be "entitled to a 12-percent rebate" on corporate taxes.[275] FTCs with exports exceeding $30 million were also entitled to an additional 10-percent tax rebate.[276]

Finally, Turkey enacted a Free-Trade Zone ("FTZ") Law (1985) to encourage more FDI.[277] Free-Trade Zones were industrial zones within the country, yet outside its customs territory. They were designed to accelerate export-oriented investments and bestow "domestic" production with specific incentives (e.g., exemption of all custom duties and tariffs, exemption of corporate taxes, etc.).[278] Although FTZs could not attract domestic and foreign investments in the 1980s, they became very attractive among domestic and foreign investors following lira convertibility in 1989.[279] Again, these policies significantly transferred wealth from Turkish taxpayers to the exporting sector of the economy.

With the above-mentioned export incentives in place, Turkish exports increased over fourfold between 1980 and 1989.[280] Exports jumped from $2.9 billion to $11.6 billion in the same period.[281] Nevertheless, export growth momentum would slow down after 1987. Having signed the GATT subsidies code in 1984, which required Turkey to abolish some export incentives by 1989,[282] Turkey gradually and systematically lowered export assistance (e.g., tax rebates, etc.), phasing them out completely by the end of 1989.[283]

269. *Id.*
270. *Id.*, at 83-84.
271. *Id.*
272. *See* Cigdem Balim, the Political Economy of Export-Oriented Industrialization in Turkey, *in State and Market: The Political Economy of Turkey in Comparative Perspective* 435-453, 441 (Ziya Öniş ed., 1999).
273. *See* Krueger & Aktan, *supra* note 160, at 78.
274. *Id.*, at 86.
275. Krueger & Aktan, *supra* note 160, at 86.
276. *Id.*
277. Aktan, *supra* note 10, at 68.
278. *See* Krueger & Aktan, *supra* note 160, at 230.
279. Kazgan, *supra* note 31, at 136.
280. *See* Appendix I.
281. *See id*; Saygin & Çimen, *supra* note 23, at 19 &72; Saygin & Çimen, *supra* note 23, at 19.
282. Krueger & Aktan, *supra* note 160, at 247.
283. *Id.*, at 78.

### b. *Gradual Import Liberalization (1980-1989)*

As discussed in regard to the first period, the Turkish import regime was extremely protective until 1980. Historically, the government bureaucracies administered "positive" lists that itemized importable commodities in annual import programs (e.g., liberalization lists and quota lists, etc.), applied an import-licensing system, and restricted access to foreign exchange. After the 1980 Package, Turkey liberalized its import regime slowly by eliminating quota lists[284] and import licensing (for some commodities);[285] reducing the stamp duty from 25 to 1 percent; and simplifying import procedures.[286]

The 1984 Import Program operated the most radical change in Turkey's import regime. Importation of goods other than deemed, *non-importable* commodities became much more straightforward.[287] The new import program contained three different lists: (1) the Prohibited List, covering 219 goods, most of which were consumer goods (e.g., foodstuffs; textiles; ceramic; porcelain; firearms; narcotics; etc.), whose importation was banned; (2) the Approval List, identifying 369 intermediate goods (e.g., iron and steel wires, aluminum extrusions, etc.), the importation of which required licenses; and (3) the Fund List, which focused mainly on luxury goods that could be imported upon pre-payment of specific levies.[288] Remarkably, in contrast to the previous listing approach, "negative" listing greatly simplified importation of goods: imports were presumably allowed, unless a particular good was expressly identified in the negative list.[289] This new Import Program liberalized around 60 percent of all imports.[290]

Turkey would liberalize its import regime further in the following years. In 1988, Turkey reduced the number of items in the Prohibited List to three (i.e., firearms, ammunition, and narcotics).[291] By 1989, Turkey also reduced the Approval List (i.e., list of goods subject to import licenses) significantly, from 369 to 16 classes of goods.[292] Adding to the three tariff classifications in the Prohibited List, only 19 classifications remained subject to quantitative restrictions (QRs) in Turkey's import regime.[293]

The 1988-1989 period also saw Turkey revising its taxation system (e.g., levying a 10-percent value-added tax in 1985, among other changes) and replacing hundreds of QRs with tariffs and other fees (e.g., stamp duty on imports, surcharges, etc.).[294] Initially, Turkey reduced its tariff rates for all intermediate and capital goods.[295] Turkey did impose a special levy on luxury imports under the "Popular Housing Fund,"[296]

284. Webb, *supra* note 249, at 349.
285. *See* Utkulu & Özdemir, *supra* note 11, at 11-20.
286. Baysan & Blitzer, *supra* note 244, at 15.
287. *Id.*
288. *Id.*, at 15-17.
289. *See id.*, at 17.
290. *Id.*
291. Baysan & Blitzer, *supra* note 244, at 22.
292. Aktan, *supra* note 10, at 64.
293. *See id.*
294. *Id.*
295. *See* Baysan & Blitzer, *supra* note 244, at 17, 20, 21, & 22.
296. *Id.*, at 22.

however, and increased tariffs on consumer goods, particularly on durables.[297] Baysan and Blitzer report that, with new taxes and rises in tariffs on consumer goods, nominal protection on domestically produced consumer goods increased, despite the elimination of hundreds of QRs.[298] Overall, the government *lowered* tariff rates: tariffs were set at or below 50 percent.[299]

As a result of Turkey's gradual import regime liberalization, imports doubled from $7.9 to $15.7 billion between 1980 and 1989.[300] We provide below an analysis of how this system of export incentives and gradual import liberalization affected Turkey's trade composition and macroeconomic performance.

### c. *Trade and Macroeconomic Performance Between 1980 and 1989*

As explained above, grants of export incentives resulted in an export boom, which boosted confidence in the economy.[301] Such confidence helped Turkey liberalize its import regime, leading to a rise in imports, particularly, intermediate and capital goods.[302] Imports grew an average 11 percent annually, while exports climbed to a 16.6 percent annual increase in the 1980-1989 period.[303] Thus, the export-import ratio rose from 0.36 to 0.73, which helped restore the country's creditworthiness.[304]

Prior to 1980, Turkey exported largely agricultural and mining products, mainly to OECD countries.[305] After turning to outward-oriented growth, Turkish exports not only increased more than fourfold but also changed in composition and reached new markets. Notably, the composition of exports changed in favor of industrial products. With the help of export subsidies, the share of industrial exports to total exports rose from 30 to 78 percent, between 1980 and 1989.[306] Specifically, labor-intensive industries (e.g., textiles and clothing, etc.) accounted for 45 percent of industrial exports; scale-intensive industries (e.g., iron and steel, etc.) came in second with around 23 percent; and resource-intensive industries (e.g., processed food, beverages and tobacco, etc.) contributed to about 17.2 of total industrial exports in 1987.[307]

Standard economic doctrine would predict that, following trade liberalization, old and inefficient ISI industries "would be swept away," because of intensifying competition.[308] However, as Rodrik explains, the post-1980 Turkish export boom was largely driven by *mature* ISI industries (e.g., textile, clothing, iron and steel, process

297. *Id.*, at 20.
298. *Id.*, at 17.
299. Krueger & Aktan, *supra* note 160, at 234.
300. *See* Appendix I; Saygin & Çimen, *supra* note 23, at 19.
301. Celasun & Rodrik, *supra* note 201, at 718-721.
302. *Id.*
303. *See* Appendix I; Krueger & Aktan, *supra* note 160, at 202-205.
304. *See* Appendix I.
305. *See* Krueger & Aktan, *supra* note 160, at 5-33; Sahin, *supra* note 40, at 302-303 & 419-421.
306. Krueger & Aktan, *supra* note 160, at 150.
307. *Id.*, at 154.
308. Dani Rodrik, *Notes on Trade and Industrialization Policy, in Turkey and Elsewhere*, 32 METU Studies in Development 259, 260 (2005).

foodstuff and tobacco, etc.), which operated within the domain of Turkey's comparative advantage.[309] As suggested before, while Turkey seemed to finally enjoy the benefits of industrialization, the question of whether ISI should get much credit for improved export performance remains very much open. Turkey's newfound export prowess was definitely associated with its robust export assistance program, but could hardly have materialized in the absence of broader globalization trends.

Indeed, the export-led growth strategy also helped exporters find new markets. Turkey increased its exports to Middle Eastern and North African countries in this period.[310] The Iran-Iraq War also played an important role at the time.[311] Following the cessation of Persian-Arab hostilities, however, OECD countries would again become top destinations for Turkish exports (e.g., 62 percent of all exports in 1989).[312] Turkey realized, then, the benefits of export market diversification.

The bestowal of subsidies, application of aggressive exchange rate policies, and lower domestic demand increased Turkey's underutilized industrial capacity, resulting in an unprecedented export boom (e.g., particularly between 1980-1987).[313] However, after 1987, Turkish export growth slowed down due to the effects of 1987 financial crisis in US markets, continued abuse of export subsidies for solely rent-seeking purposes, and implementation of new GATT export subsidy disciplines.[314]

Regardless, foreign trade became an important part of Turkey's GDP (25.7 percent) by 1989.[315] Although exports rose fourfold, a doubling in imports would leave Turkey with trade deficits in this period.[316] Yet, by increasing exports, Turkey restored its creditworthiness, allowing it to finance imports with foreign borrowing, which made Turkey the fifth most indebted developing country in 1987.[317] The foreign debt-to-GDP ratio reached 50 percent in the late 1980s.[318] Turkey was able to service its foreign debt because of extra income from trade in services (e.g., tourism, transportation, etc.) and Turkish expatriate remittances.[319] Notably, Turkey's current account balance was positive in 1988 and 1989.[320]

### 2. *Effects of Lira Convertibility and Financial Liberalization (1989-1994)*

In the late 1980s and early 1990s, the trend among developing countries was to liberalize and deregulate financial flows to attract foreign investment.[321] Turkey, a

309. *See id.*, at 262-264.
310. Celasun & Rodrik, *supra* note 201, at 718-721.
311. *Id.*
312. KRUEGER & AKTAN, *supra* note 160, at 157.
313. Celasun & Rodrik, *supra* note 201, at 718 and 724.
314. *See* Balim, *supra* note 272, at 441.
315. *See* SAYGIN & ÇIMEN, *supra* note 23, at 16 and 19.
316. *See* Appendix I.
317. SAHIN, *supra* note 40, at 199.
318. *See* SAYGIN & ÇIMEN, *supra* note 23, at 18.
319. SAHIN, *supra* note 40, at 199.
320. *Id.*
321. *See* SAYGIN & ÇIMEN, *supra* note 23, at 2-11.

"debt-ridden state,"[322] with a slowing export sector, was also flirting with stagflation.[323] Turkish policymakers' response was similar to other developing countries' (e.g., Argentina, Brazil, Mexico, etc.). Decree No. 32 on "Protecting the Value of the Turkish Lira" liberalized "foreign exchange transactions and capital movements," making the lira *fully* convertible.[324] With the liberalization of capital flows, "the sustainability of large trade and [current account] deficits became possible ... ."[325] Volatility, illustrated by sudden, deep capital outflows, often resulting in a currency collapse, would become the ultimate market discipline to indebted countries.[326]

Turkey, not unlike its peers in the developing world, offered high interest rates to attract foreign money, so market-set interest rates in lira increased gradually to 100 percent.[327] Thus, Turkey became an attractive destination for short-term, hot money inflows.[328] The increasing volume of foreign exchange in the domestic market reduced the demand for foreign exchange, so the lira actually appreciated after 1989.

The government also used lira appreciation to help control rising inflation in this period.[329] Inflation was rising because of labor union's greater bargaining leverage.[330] In the late 1980s and early 1990s, wage earners would again receive significant wage increases, which pressured inflation rates upward (averaging around 77 percent per year).[331] However, lira appreciation, which helped contain inflation, adversely affected the overall trade balance, through higher consumption. Higher wages, a stronger lira, and increasing foreign currency inflows led, naturally, to rising imports and a deterioration of the trade deficit. Thus, between 1989 and 1993, imports increased, by value, from $15.7 to $29.4 billion—an 87.2 percent rise.[332]

To help check imports, the Parliament enacted Law No. 3577 on Prevention of Unfair Competition on Imports, in 1989, which authorized the government to impose antidumping ("AD") and countervailing ("CVD") duties.[333] Turkey soon initiated AD and CVD investigations in textiles and iron and steel imports. By 1994, over 144 AD and CVD investigations had been launched.[334] As Karacaovali explained, the overvaluation

322. Umit Cizre Sakallioglu & Erinç Yeldan, *Politics, Society and Financial Liberalization: Turkey in the 1990s*, 31 DEVELOPMENT AND CHANGE 481, 481 (2000), *available at*: http://repository.bilkent.edu.tr/bitstream/handle/11693/25077/bilkent-research-paper.pdf?sequence=1&isAllowed=y.
323. SAHIN, *supra* note 40, at 207.
324. SAYGIN & ÇIMEN, *supra* note 23, at 20.
325. Firat Demir, *A Failure Story: Politics and Financial Liberalization in Turkey, Revisiting the Revolving Door Hypothesis*, 32-5 WORLD DEVELOPMENT 851, 853 (2004).
326. The Asian Crisis of 1998 in Indonesia, Thailand, and Malaysia is an example.
327. *See* Demir, *supra* note 325.
328. *See* Önder, *supra* note 257, at 90.
329. *See* Webb, *supra* note 249, at 444.
330. Note that after 1980, the military forces applied wage suppression. *Id.*, at 443.
331. *See* SAYGIN & ÇIMEN, *supra* note 23, at 16-22.
332. *See* Appendix I.
333. WTO Secretariat, *Trade Policy Review of Turkey*, PRESS/TPRB/83 (Oct. 7, 1998), *available at*: https://www.wto.org/english/tratop_e/tpr_e/tp83_e.htm [hereinafter Turkey TPR 1998].
334. Baybars Karacaovali, *Turkey: Temporary Trade Barriers as Resistance to Trade Liberalization with the European Union?*, 6 (Fordham University Department of Economics Discussion Paper No. 2011-02, May 12, 2011), *available at*: https://papers.ssrn.com/sol3/papers.cfm?abstract_id=1839644.

of the lira, which exposed domestic industries, prompted the government to offer protection for its "nascent industries."[335] According to the WTO Trade Policy Review of 1998, Turkey ranked sixth among users of AD measures between 1989 and 1996.[336] Aggressive implementation of AD measures helped imports decrease from $29.4 to $23.27 billion between 1993 and 1994.[337]

On the export side, lira appreciation made Turkish exports less competitive abroad. The U.S.-imposed economic embargo on Iraq, starting in 1990, did not help Turkey, either.[338] Growing reliance on financial liberalization and currency appreciation made investment in manufacturing industries an unfeasible proposition. Manufacturing companies became heavily engaged in buying financial assets, which, at that time, was profitable.[339] Unlike in the 1980s, however, Turkey's more complex, more exposed, and more indebted economy did not attract further investment. Thus, rapid increases in real production and exports were not in the cards.[340] Although imports decreased and exports increased (to $18.1 billion in 1994), the latter were not enough to offset the first, so Turkey carried trade deficits throughout the 1989-1994 period.[341]

Following financial liberalization, the Turkish economy became more dependent on short-term financial inflows, like other developing Asian and South American countries. Turkish public and private debt increased, which led to greater need for external financing and further increases in money inflows. Privatization of SOEs was not successful and did not help Turkey reduce its debt burden. The economy started showing signs of "overheating"—through higher inflation rates, increasing trade and current account deficits, stagflation, etc.—so, increasingly risk-averse, foreign capital began leaving the country, at alarming rates.[342] Therefore, in 1994, Turkey's economy faced "a severe recession"[343] and financial crisis, which was partly addressed by successive IMF "rescue packages" in years to come.[344]

Despite periodical crises, Turkey largely accomplished its trade and financial liberalization goals, which required removing QRs, decreasing tariff rates, fostering exports, and allowing foreign capital into Turkey between 1980-1994. After experiencing major liberalization, Turkey was ready to integrate itself into global markets, a point to which we now turn.

335. *Id.*
336. Turkey TPR 1998, *supra* note 333.
337. *See* Appendix I.
338. *See* M. Sait Akman, *Turkey in the World Trading System and the WTO: Activism Under Global Challenges and the EU Process*, 1:1 Afro Eurasian Studies 134, 138 (2012).
339. Önder, *supra* note 257, at 96.
340. Textiles and clothing, iron and steel and processed foodstuff accounted for 67.5 per cent of Turkey's total industrial exports. *See* Webb, *supra* note 249, at 451.
341. Exports increased from $11.6 to $18.1 billion between 1989 and 1994. *See* Appendix I.
342. Utkulu & Özdemir, *supra* note 11, at 15-16.
343. Turkey TPR 1998, *supra* note 333.
344. Demir, *supra* note 325.

## B. Turkey Integrates into the World Economy (1995-2001)

Application of export-led growth, liberalization of imports, and deregulation of capital movements allowed Turkey to: (i) leverage its WTO membership to become more integrated into the world economy; and (ii) turn to the European Union, its biggest trade partner, to remove trade restrictions and tariffs for *all industrial goods* in a new customs union. These arrangements have significantly affected the Turkish economy for the past 25 years.

### 1. *WTO Membership*

A party to the GATT, under the Torquay Protocol since 1951,[345] Turkey had participated in all trade-negotiation rounds (e.g., signing and ratifying the GATT Subsidy and Antidumping codes.) before the Uruguay Round.[346] Turkey signed the Uruguay Round Agreements and "Marrakesh Protocol to the General Agreement on Tariffs and Trade 1994," which created the WTO,[347] and thus became one of its original members.

WTO membership came with new commitments on tariff reduction, QR elimination, greater openness in agricultural and services trade, etc.[348] Turkey bound itself to a 29-percent tariff reduction in industrial goods,[349] committed to abolishing tariffs on information technology products,[350] and, in agriculture, bound its tariffs at 100 percent, promising constant tariff reductions in the following ten years and agreeing to reduce export subsidies under the Agreement on Agriculture.[351]

Turkey also amended its existing legislation on CVD and AD measures and brought its export incentive system in line with the Agreement on Subsidies and Countervailing Measures.[352] Without delay, Turkey began implementing the Agreement on Technical Barriers to Trade in 1995.[353] Moreover, Turkey amended its legislation on "industrial and intellectual property rights" (e.g., patents, trademarks, industrial design, etc.) in the same year.[354] According to the 1998 Trade Policy Review, Turkey became the first developing country to amend its legislation to comply with the Agreement on Trade-Related Aspects of Intellectual Property Rights ("TRIPS") Agreement.[355]

One of the most important outcomes of the Uruguay Round negotiations was the creation of the Dispute Settlement Body ("DSB"), pursuant to the Understanding on

345. Turkey TPR 1998, *supra* note 333.
346. *Id.*
347. *Id.*
348. *See id.*
349. *Id.*
350. *Id.*
351. *Id.*
352. *Id.*
353. *Id.*
354. *Id.*
355. *Id.*

Rules and Procedures Governing the Settlement of Disputes ("DSU").[356] With the creation of binding dispute settlement, Members could bring to the DSB any dispute arising out of the implementation of the "negotiated agreements."[357] Turkey would first avail itself of this system in 1996, although not willingly, when it appeared as Respondent in *Turkey–Restrictions on Imports of Textile and Clothing Products*.[358] As of February 6, 2021, Turkey has also been involved in six cases as Complainant, 12 cases as Respondent, and 102 cases as Third Party.[359]

In sum, as a member of the WTO, Turkey accepted free trade disciplines (e.g., elimination of QRs; granting most-favored nation and national treatment principles to foreign goods, etc.) and implemented trade commitments under different subject-matter WTO agreements.[360] It also furthered its free trade policy objectives by signing the CU Decision with the European Union in 1996. With the creation of the CU, the Turkish economy became much more open.

### 2. *Creation of the EU-Turkey Customs Union*

After becoming an original member of the WTO and as it implemented its new WTO requirements, Turkey signed a 1995 Customs Union Decision (the "Decision") with the European Union, which entered into force the following year.[361] With the creation of the CU, not only tariffs and restrictions were removed for *all* industrial goods between the parties, but Turkey also agreed to adopt CETs and trade policies as determined by the European Union.[362] To better understand the scope, purpose, and nature of the CU, the following subsection discusses the historical relationship between Turkey and the European Union. In the subsequent subsection, we provide an analysis of both parties' commitments under the CU Decision. Chapter 6 offers a thorough explanation of why the unreformed, increasingly asymmetric CU is no longer in the interest of Turkey and should be replaced with a new FTA.

#### *a. EU-Turkey Relations Prior to the CU*

As mentioned above (Section II.D.1), the post-WWII period saw Turkey continue its Westernization project, by joining major Western organizations (e.g., the Council of

356. Understanding on Rules and Procedures Governing the Settlement of Disputes Art. 2, Apr. 15, 1994, Marrakesh Agreement Establishing the Word Trade Organization, Annex 2, 1869 U.N.T.S. 401 [hereinafter DSU].
357. Juscelino F. Colares, *The Limits of WTO adjudication: Is Compliance the Problem?*, 14 J. of Int'l Econ. L. 403, 403 (2011).
358. *See* Appellate Body Report, Turkey—Restrictions on Imports of Textile and Clothing Products, WT/DS/34/AB/R (Oct. 22, 1999) (Complainant: India).
359. World Trade Organization, Member Information, Turkey and the WTO, https://www.wto.org/english/thewto_e/countries_e/turkey_e.htm (last visited Feb. 6, 2021).
360. Turkey TPR 1998, *supra* note 333.
361. Akman, *supra* note 338, at 138.
362. *Id.*, at 139.

Europe, IMF, World Bank, NATO, OECD, etc.).[363] Right after the creation of the European Economic Community ("EEC") by the 1957 Treaty of Rome,[364] Turkey applied for an associate membership in the EEC in 1959.[365] Ultimately, with the signature of the Ankara Agreement in 1963 (also known as the Association Agreement), Turkey became an associate member of the EEC.[366]

Pursuant to the Ankara Agreement, the parties agreed to strengthen their trade and economic relations.[367] The EEC would provide assistance (financial and otherwise)[368] to improve the Turkish economic development for its full integration into the ECC.[369] Turkey also agreed, in the long term, to create a customs union and to seek full membership in the EEC. In regard to the future CU, the Agreement set forth three stages: (1) a Preparation Stage; (2) a Transition Stage; and (3) a Final Stage.[370] Article 28 of the Agreement also emphasized that "[a]s soon as [Turkey accomplishes its economic development following the final stage], the Contracting Parties shall examine the possibility of the accession of Turkey to the Community."[371] Significantly, the Agreement contemplated Turkey becoming a full member of the EEC in an *undetermined* future.

During the Preparatory Stage (1964-1973), the EEC provided financial assistance and unilateral concessions for some Turkish agricultural products (e.g., hazelnuts, tobacco, dried figs, etc.), yet Turkey was not bound to any commitments.[372] A Transition Stage was contemplated in the Additional Protocol to the Agreement, which went into effect in 1973.[373] Under the Protocol, the EEC would immediately remove all QRs and tariffs on Turkish industrial products—except for textiles and clothing. In return, Turkey agreed to reduce and eliminate QRs and customs duties in a twenty-two-year period.[374] Free movement for labor would also begin in 1986.[375] Ultimately, at the end of this Transition Stage, the parties were to create a customs union for industrial products, in 1995.[376]

---

363. *See* Beken Saatçioglu, *Turkey-EU Relations from the 1960s to 2012: A Critical Overview, in Turkey's Accession to the European Union: Political and Economic Challenges* 3-24, 3 (Belgin Akçay & Bahri Yılmaz eds., 2013).
364. The history of the European Union, 1945–1959, A Peaceful Europe—The Beginnings of Cooperation, *available at*: https://europa.eu/european-union/about-eu/history_en (last visited Feb. 7, 2019).
365. Togan & Kaminski, *supra* note 1, at 15.
366. Saatçioglu, *supra* note 363, at 4.
367. *See* Agreement Establishing an Association between the European Economic Community and Turkey of September 12, 1963, 1964 J.O. (L 217), Art. 2, also *available at*: https://eur-lex.europa.eu/resource.html?uri=cellar:f8e2f9f4-75c8-4f62-ae3f-b86ca5842eee.0008.02/DOC_2&format=PDF [hereinafter Ankara Agreement or Agreement].
368. *See* Togan & Kaminski, *supra* note 1, at 15.
369. *See* Ankara Agreement, Art. 2, *supra* note 367.
370. *Id.*
371. *See* Ankara Agreement, Art. 28, *supra* note 367.
372. *See* Christina Hartler & Sam Laird, *The EU Model and Turkey a Case for Thanksgiving*, 33 J. World Trade 147, 147 (1999).
373. Saatçioglu, *supra* note 363, at 4.
374. *Id.*
375. Togan & Kaminski, *supra* note 1, at 16.
376. Saatçioglu, *supra* note 363, at 4.

The Transition Stage would not see full implementation, however. The oil crisis of 1973 caused a global recession, which led the EEC to stop providing financial assistance to Turkey.[377] The EEC also imposed quotas on textile and clothing products from Turkey and lowered its concessions for Turkish industrial exports.[378] Furthermore, the EEC announced it would not establish free movement of labor with Turkey.[379] The 1974 Turkish military intervention in Cyprus and the economic hardships that hit the country in the mid-1970s made closer ties with the EEC much harder to accomplish.[380] After the 1980 military coup, the EEC "froze ties with Turkey," alleging concerns with human rights violations under military rule.[381]

Encouraged by the major trade liberalization and an export boom of the 1980s and believing these developments had changed its fortune,[382] Turkey applied for full membership to the Community in 1987 and pursued tariff reductions under the Additional Protocol.[383] In 1988, Turkey also proclaimed its intention to fulfill provisions under the Protocol and sought the creation of a customs union.[384] The Community, however, rejected Turkey's membership application claiming that the EEC was not ready to accept any new member before major reforms on "the European Internal architecture," resulting from the Single Act[385] of 1986.[386] A 1989 EEC Commission opinion explained the main reasons for rejecting Turkey's application, thusly: Turkey "has a greater geographical area and will eventually have a bigger population than any Community Member State[,] and its general level of development is substantially lower than the European average."[387]

Remarkably, two years later, in the aftermath of the Soviet Union's collapse, the EEC deemed consideration of Eastern and Central European Countries' applications for entry into the Single Market as a "moral duty," thus expanding the scope of its enlargement program. Turkey's membership application remained "pending."[388] Thus, it became obvious that Turkey's full EEC membership was not in the cards for the

377. *Id.*
378. *Id.*
379. *Id.*
380. *Id.*, at 5.
381. Note that the Community was accepting Greece, Spain, and Portugal, which were also "formerly authoritarian countries" like Turkey was at that time. Saatçioglu, *supra* note 363, at 5.
382. AHMET DAVUTOGLU, STRATEJIK DERINLIK [STRATEGIC DEEPNESS] 511 (2016).
383. *See* Togan & Kaminski, *supra* note 1, at 16.
384. *Id.*
385. Note that "[t]he Single European Act (Single Act)' is a treaty through which the European Community (Community) seeks to achieve European unity .... The Single Act sets forth several means of achieving European unity: the establishment of a large market without internal frontiers by 1992; the involvement of the Community in new fields ... the development of a unified economic and monetary policy; a strengthening of economic and social cohesion; and the coordination of actions relating to the environment and foreign policy." Kathryn Good, *Institutional Reform Under the Single European Act*, 3:1 AM. U. INT'L. L. REV. 299, 299-300 (1988).
386. *See* Togan & Kaminski, *supra* note 1, at 16.
387. Commission of the European Communities, COMMISSION OPINION ON TURKEY'S REQUEST FOR ACCESSION TO THE COMMUNITY, Sec (89), 2290, Final/2, 4 (1989), *available at*: http://aei.pitt.ed u/4475/1/4475.pdf.
388. Saatçioglu, *supra* note 363, at 6.

near future. Nonetheless, the EEC wanted to advance its economic relations with Turkey,[389] and Turkey viewed the creation of the long-promised customs union as an important step toward eventual, full membership. In a 1995 Association Council meeting, the EEC and Turkey signed Decision No. 1/95 of the EC-Turkey Association Council on Implementing the Final Phase of the Customs Union (96/142/EC).[390] With this Decision, the Parties agreed to the creation of the CU, which would enter into force in 1996.

### *b. Scope of and Commitments under the CU Decision*

The creation of the CU with the EEC (and its successor, the European Union) was one of the most significant economic developments for Turkey.[391] The CU induced competitiveness to the Turkish manufacturing industry and opened new export markets for Turkish products.[392] While the parties agreed, bilaterally, to abolish all restrictions and tariffs on industrial goods, Turkey, the junior party, took on more commitments. Both parties bound themselves to phase out tariffs and eliminate all restrictions on industrial goods with the exception of European Coal and Steel Community's products.[393] While no commitments were made regarding agricultural products, processed agricultural foodstuffs *were* included in the CU scope.[394] The Decision also required Turkey to implement "identical" commercial and competition policies with the European Union.[395] Accordingly, Turkey adopted EU competition law and EU rules on protection of intellectual and industrial property rights; established a Competition Board and Patent Office; and started to apply EU technical standards.[396] This vastly reduced technical barriers to trade between parties.[397]

Starting in 1996, Turkey would apply EU CETs—substantially lower tariffs than Turkey's WTO commitments—against third-country industrial imports.[398] While Turkey sought temporary protection for "sensitive" products (e.g., certain types of passenger cars, furniture, iron and steel wires, etc.), these extra tariff protections were completely phased out by 2001.[399] With the implementation of CETs, Turkey had the *lowest* levels of tariffication among middle-income countries.[400] In addition, within five years (i.e., until 2001), Turkey agreed to adopt all "FTAs" the European Union had

389. *See* Togan & Kaminski, *supra* note 1, at 17.
390. *See* Decision No. 1/95 of the EC-Turkey Association Council of 22 December 1995 on implementing the final phase of the Customs Union, 96/142/EC, Art. 4, 1996 O.J. (L 035) [hereinafter CU Decision or Decision].
391. *See* Turkey TPR 1998, *supra* note 333.
392. Akman, *supra* note 338, at 139.
393. Togan & Kaminski, *supra* note 1, at 17.
394. Turkey TPR 1998, *supra* note 333.
395. *Id.*
396. Togan & Kaminski, *supra* note 1, at 46.
397. *Id.*
398. *See* Akman, *supra* note 338, at 139.
399. *See* Hartler & Laird, *supra* note 372, at 148.
400. Togan & Kaminski, *supra* note 1, at 13.

signed with third countries.[401] Turkey, then, began negotiations and signed FTAs with European Free Trade Association ("EFTA") countries (i.e., Iceland, Lichtenstein, Norway, and Switzerland), Israel, Macedonia, Croatia, Bosnia-Herzegovina, Egypt, the Palestinian Authority, Tunisia, Morocco, Syria, Albania, and Georgia.[402] Thus, as the junior party in the CU, Turkey bound itself to apply EU trade policy without actively participating in the EU trade policy- and decision-making processes.

As far trade-remedy disciplines are concerned, the Additional Protocol of 1970 and the Decision of 1995 allowed both parties to apply AD, CVD, and safeguard measures against each other and third countries.[403] Initially, both parties were active trade remedy users, but distinguished themselves by initiating investigations for different classes of products.[404] For instance, Turkey and the European Union investigated 329 and 336 different products between 1995-2011, respectively.[405] That only 6 products were investigated by both Turkey and the European Union in the same year demonstrates the two Parties applied trade remedies quite differently.[406] Remarkably, Turkey and the European Union initiated AD investigations *against* each other.[407] Between 1995 and 2001, only 3 percent of Turkish AD investigations targeted EU products, while 9 percent of EU AD investigations targeted Turkish products.[408] When Turkey applied AD and CVD measures, the typical targeted country would be a *specific* EU Member, not the entire Block. So, divergence on AD and CVD disciplines created "implicit" incentives for non-targeted, presumably more efficient EU Members to export to Turkey.[409]

Finally, the Decision provided a settlement system for disputes arising out of the implementation of the CU.[410] Any dispute could be brought to the Association Council, formed by representatives from both parties.[411] Article 61 of the Decision also provided that "if the Association Council fails to settle a dispute relating to the scope or duration of protection measures taken[,] ... either Party may refer the dispute to [binding] arbitration[.]"[412] Although the Decision does not bar either party from suing each other before the WTO DSB, both parties refrained from pursuing direct litigation against each other in the DSB, until 2019 (a topic Chapter 5 discusses in depth).[413] Recently, the European Union filed its first DSB direct case (i.e., not as a Third-Party Litigant)

401. Akman, *supra* note 338, at 139.
402. *Id.*
403. Suzanne Voigt, The Customs Union Between Turkey and the EU: How Did It Affect Turkey? 5 (2008).
404. *See* World Bank, Evaluation of the EU-TURKEY Customs Union, at 41, Report No. 85830-TR (Mar. 28, 2014), http://www.worldbank.org/content/dam/Worldbank/document/eca/turkey/tr-eu-customs-union-eng.pdf [hereinafter the World Bank Report].
405. *Id.*
406. *Id.*
407. *See* WTO Secretariat, *Trade Policy Review of Turkey*, WT/TPR/S/125, 49 (Dec. 19, 2003).
408. World Bank Report, *supra* note 404, at 41-43.
409. *Id.*, at 42.
410. *See* CU Decision, *supra* note 390, Art. 61.
411. *Id.*
412. *Id.*
413. *See* Meltem Saribeyoglu, Uluslararasi Ticaret Hukuku Açisindan Dunya Ticaret Orgutu, Gümrük Birligi ve Turkiye [World Trade Organization, Customs Union and Turkey in Light of International Trade Law] 277 (2010).

alleging the WTO-inconsistency of Turkey's localization and technology transfer requirements for certain pharmaceutical products (2019), and Turkey sued the European Union directly, also for the first time, alleging EU measures on Turkish steel products were in violation of safeguards disciplines (2020).[414]

Creation of the CU significantly altered the course of Turkey's trade policy (mostly for good) and greatly impacted its economy.[415] These liberalizing changes came through: (i) application of CETs to third countries; (ii) granting of duty-free treatment to EU industrial products; (iii) eradication of QRs on EU products; and (iv) adoption of the EU preferential trade regime.[416] Turkish industry faced more competition and became unprotected.[417] As a result, temporary trade measures (e.g., imposition of AD, CVD, and safeguard remedies) have become tools of first resort. Furthermore, granting tariff exemption to EU industrial products and applying low-level, EU tariff rates to third countries led to substantial revenue losses.[418] Clearly, some—though certainly not all—CU-related outcomes adversely affected Turkey's foreign trade balance and budget. Yet, the CU also brought great opportunities for Turkey's businesses, including new, zero-tariff markets in Europe. The preferential trade agreements Turkey had to sign as a result of the CU also resulted in new concessions for Turkish exporters. Moreover, opening the Turkish economy further enabled Turkey to attract more foreign direct and indirect investment. Turkish industrial products could now move to Europe without any tariffs or barriers and were treated preferentially.

Evidently, Turkey also remained bound to its WTO trade commitments, which meant it had to implement its CU commitments, in parallel.[419] And Turkey did bring itself into compliance with both undertakings.[420] However, some of the commitments Turkey undertook pursuant to the CU clashed with its WTO commitments. Turkey ended up as a Respondent in a WTO dispute—*Turkey–Textiles*—[421] which we discuss in Chapter 5. More importantly, as a result of these two trade arrangements, Turkey became a much more open and, thus, efficient economy. Next, we demonstrate, specifically, how joining the WTO and CU impacted Turkey's trade and macroeconomic performance between 1995 and 2001.

---

414. *See Turkey—Certain Measures concerning the Production, Importation and Marketing of Pharmaceutical Products*, WTO Doc. WT/DS583 (Panel Composed on Mar. 17, 2020) (Complainant: European Union); *European Union—Safeguard Measures on Certain Steel Products*, WTO Doc. WT/DS595 (Panel Composed on Sept. 30, 2020) (Complainant: Turkey).
415. *See* Akman, *supra* note 338, at 140.
416. *See* World Bank, *Economic Implication for Turkey of a Customs Union with the European Union* 1 (Policy Research Working Paper, 1599, The World Bank International Economics Department, International Trade Division, 1996).
417. Togan & Kaminski, *supra* note 1, at 13.
418. *See* Onur Bülbül & Aslı Orhan, *Beyond Turkey–EU Customs Union: Predictions for Key Regulatory Issues in a Potential Turkey–U.S. FTA Following TTIP* 9 GLOBAL TRADE AND CUSTOMS J. 444, 445 (2014).
419. Turkey TPR 1998, *supra* note 333.
420. *Id.*
421. *See* Appellate Body Report, *Turkey — Restrictions on Imports of Textile and Clothing Products*, WTO Doc. WT/DS34/AB/R (Oct. 22, 1999) (Complainant: India).

### 3. *Crisis and the Rise of Erdoğan (1995-2001)*

Turkey experienced financial and economic crises as it opened up and integrated itself into the world economy.[422] Crises and their tough economic remedies throughout the 1990s and early 2000s made it hard for exporters to enjoy, fully, the benefits of trade liberalization.[423] In the mid- to late 1990s, the country struggled to recover from the 1994 currency crisis (discussed above in Section III.A.2). Chronic problems, such as high inflation, large budget deficits, a volatile, unregulated financial sector, among others, remained unsolved.[424] Moreover, implementation of CU commitments brought tariff revenue losses and increasing imports, which led to increased budget and trade deficits. Economic and financial crises in Asia (1997) and Russia (1998) also adversely affected the Turkish economy.[425] Furthermore, in 1999, two major earthquakes hit the heart of Turkish industry (i.e., the Marmara Region), harming economic activity in the most productive sector of the economy. Turkey's GDP fell by 3.4 percent that year.[426]

To combat inflation and restore growth, the government resumed controlling exchange rates in 1999.[427] Although inflation slightly decreased, currency management led to further lira appreciation, resulting in private-sector, preemptive dollarization, in anticipation of a potential devaluation.[428] Meanwhile, imports increased to $54 billion, while exports rose to only $27 billion, in 2000.[429] Thus, the export-import ratio decreased to only 51 percent.[430] More importantly, the three-party coalition government could not agree on a solution to Turkey's chronic macroeconomic problems, namely high inflation and high dependence on foreign financing. In short, a real economic crisis was brewing.

Indeed, the most significant crisis in Turkish economic history hit in 2001, when Turkish President Ahmet Necdet Sezer and Prime Minister Bülent Ecevit clashed in a national security meeting over the conduct of an investigation on high-level corruption in the bureaucracy.[431] As soon as the clash became public, public trust eroded, and a new economic crisis erupted. Foreign money left the country, quickly consuming the Central Bank's foreign exchange reserves, overnight interest rates jumped to 1,000 percent, and unemployment skyrocketed.[432] The value of the dollar increased from

422. By liberalizing its financial sector, creating a CU with the European Union, and becoming a member of the WTO.
423. Akman, *supra* note 338, at 138-141.
424. Sahin, *supra* note 40, at 238-239.
425. The country's dollar reserves dropped about $7 billion within a couple of months in 1998. *See* Sahin, *supra* note 40, at 236.
426. *Id.*, at 236.
427. Turkey would abandon to control the exchange rate in 2001. *See* Anne O. Krueger, *Economic Policy Reform in Brazil and Turkey* 6 (Stanford Center for International Development, Working Paper No. 445, 2011).
428. *Id.*, at 9.
429. *See* Appendix I.
430. *See id.*
431. Krueger, *supra* note 427, at 9.
432. *Id.*, at 11; *see also* Sahin, *supra* note 40, at 247-248.

₺670,000 to ₺1,689,000.[433] Private savings evaporated, and the people, again, paid, the price.

Soon after, the government brought Kemal Derviş, a well-known World Bank expert, to Turkey to sort out the economy.[434] Derviş introduced the "Transition Program for Strengthening the Economy," a package of measures aimed at reducing inflation, managing foreign debt, and maintaining Turkey's export-led economic growth.[435] To achieve these goals, the Program called for structural changes, ranging from reforms to the financial sector, fiscal system, and exchange rate regime, to an ambitious privatization drive.[436] Although the three-party-coalition government began implementing the Program immediately, the Parliament decided to hold a snap election in November 2002.

At the polls, each party in the three-party coalition came short of the 10-percent threshold for representation in the Parliament and, thus, left the Parliament and government entirely. The Justice and Development Party ("AK Parti" or "JDP") won the majority of seats. JDP's founding leader, Recep Tayyip Erdoğan, former Mayor of Istanbul and recent political prisoner,[437] rose to Prime Minister, following a number of legislative maneuvers in 2003. Erdoğan has ruled Turkey since then, becoming President in 2014. The key decision-maker in Turkey, Erdoğan has shaped Turkey's politics, economy, and trade policy. The following chapter discusses Turkey's trade policy objectives, tools, and challenges under the rule of the Erdoğan-led JDP.

---

433. Sahin, *supra* note 40, at 247 & 438.
434. Krueger, *supra* note 427, at 11.
435. *Id.*
436. *See* Sahin, *supra* note 40, at 251.
437. While participating in a political gathering, then Istanbul Mayor Recep Tayyip Erdogan read a poem later deemed to be against the secular principles of the Republic of Turkey by Turkish courts, resulting in his political ouster and imprisonment, for nine months. *See* Deborah Sontag, *The Erdogan Experiment*, NY Times / Archives (May 11, 2003), https://www.nytimes.com/2003/05/11/magazine/the-erdogan-experiment.html.

CHAPTER 4

# Trade Policy in the New Millennium

## I. OVERVIEW

In this chapter, we discuss Turkey's trade policy under the rule of Prime-Minister-then-President Recep Tayyip Erdoğan since 2002. We seek to identify Turkey's trade policy goals and evaluate the tools that Turkey has deployed to achieving those goals. We will also look into Turkey's trade policy challenges and performance through 2019. Our ultimate goal is to evaluate the extent to which Turkey's trade policy objectives have been secured by the different trade policy tools it has deployed. Among these tools, trade litigation in the WTO will be analyzed, though separately, in the next chapter (Chapter 5).

After rising to power, successive JDP governments followed the Derviş' Program, discussed in Chapter 3.[1] Execution of this Program helped Erdoğan and the JDP succeed in restabilizing the economy (e.g., decreasing inflation to single digits,[2] SOE privatizations, etc.).[3] According to Anne Krueger, the Turkish six-year economic performance following the crisis of 2001 "was impressive by any standard."[4] Turkey's GDP grew an average 6.9 percent in the 2002-2007 period.[5] Although the 2008-2009 global recession did affect Turkey, economic growth quickly resumed in 2010. To illustrate, Turkey's GDP went from a 4.8 percent decrease in 2009 to a 9.2 percent increase the following year.[6] In fact, Turkey had the second highest growth rate in the

1. For a detailed analysis of Derviş' Program, *see* Chapter 3, Section III.B.3.
2. *See* HASAN SAYGIN & MURAT ÇIMEN, TURKISH ECONOMIC POLICIES AND EXTERNAL DEPENDENCY 22 (2013).
3. Anne O. Krueger, *Economic Policy Reform in Brazil and Turkey* 11 (Stanford Center for International Development Working Paper No. 445, 2011), *available at*: https://globalpoverty.stanford.edu/sites/default/files/publications/445wp.pdf.
4. *Id.*, at 13.
5. Temel Taşkın, *GDP Growth in Turkey: Inclusive or Not?*, 14 CENTRAL BANK REV. 31-64, 33 (2014).
6. *See* WTO Secretariat, *Trade Policy Review of Turkey*, WT/TPR/S/331, 10 (Feb. 9, 2016) [hereinafter Turkey TPR 2016].

world in 2011.[7] Such a robust recovery was impressive.[8] By 2019, the country's GDP had risen above $761 billion, with GDP per capita reaching $9,126.[9]

As far as trade is concerned, Turkish exporters could, finally, fully enjoy the benefits of lower foreign barriers and a devalued, yet stable currency. The new policy regime also led to a significant transformation in the Turkish manufacturing sector, which began transitioning from unskilled, labor-intensive mature industries to technology-intensive sectors.[10] As a result, exports jumped from $36 to $171 billion between 2002 and 2019, while imports increased from $51 to $202 billion, in the same period.[11] A parallel increase in the services trade (e.g., tourism, transportation, etc.) helped raise Turkey's overall trade in goods and services to around 60 percent of GDP.[12]

Nonetheless, Turkey still faces many trade challenges. Turkey's economy has run trade deficits since 1946 and had to diversify its exports, both by sector and by country of destination.[13] Turkey has also faced problems arising out of the application of the CU, particularly when the European Union signs new FTAs with major trading countries (e.g., South Korea, Mexico, and, more recently, the United Kingdom).[14] While Turkey remains a candidate to membership in the European Union, it cannot participate in trade negotiations along with the European Union and remains generally bound by the terms of any FTA the European Union signs.[15] With every new FTA, EU industrial exports enjoy immediate, greater market access, while Turkish industrial goods do not. Worse yet, Turkey has to accept transshipped merchandise cleared in EU countries, tariff free—a form of trade deflection that: (i) reduces tariff revenue; and (ii) further erodes Turkey's leverage in FTA negotiations.[16] Chapter 6 provides a detailed

7. *See Turkey's Economy, Istanbuls and Bears,* The Economist (Apr. 7, 2012), https://www.economist.com/finance-and-economics/2012/04/07/istanbuls-and-bears.
8. *See id.*
9. *See* The World Bank Data, GDP per Capita (current US$)–Turkey https://data.worldbank.org/indicator/NY.GDP.PCAP.CD?locations=TR (last visited Feb. 6. 2021).
10. *See* M. Sait Akman, Turkey in the World Trading System and the WTO: Activism under Global Challenges and the EU Process, 1:1 Afro Eurasian Studies 134, 144 (2012).
11. *See* Appendix I.
12. *See* Turkey TPR 2016, *supra* note 6 (using 2014 data).
13. *See* Akman, *supra* note 10, at 145-148.
14. *See id.*, at 152-153.
15. *See* Sait Akman, Dynamics of the European Union's Trade Strategy: Drawing Conclusions for Relations with Turkey, 19, Paper presented in UACES Exchanging Ideas on Europe 2012 "Old Borders—New Frontiers," Passau, Germany (Sept. 3-5, 2012) (requested permission). For a slightly different version of the work above, *see* Sait Akman, Dynamics of the European Union's Trade Strategy and Its Imperatives on Turkish Trade Policy: Prospects for a Functioning Customs Union, *in Turkey's Accession to the European Union: Political and Economic Challenges*, 127-160 (Belgin Akçay & Bahri Yilmaz eds., 2013).
16. *See* Onur Bülbül & Aslı Orhan, *Beyond Turkey-EU Customs Union: Predictions for Key Regulatory Issues in a Potential Turkey-U.S. FTA Following TTIP*, 9 Global Trade and Customs J. 444, 448 (2014); Trading Freedom for Stability, Turkey Strengthens EU Ties, Stratfor (Jun. 29, 2017), https://worldview.stratfor.com/article/trading-freedom-stability-turkey-strengthens-eu-ties; World Bank, *Evaluation of the EU-TURKEY Customs Union*, Report No. 85830-TR (Mar. 28, 2014), at 24, http://www.worldbank.org/content/dam/Worldbank/document/eca/turkey/tr-eu-customs-union-eng.pdf [hereinafter the World Bank Report]. For a more detailed discussion on trade deflection *see* Chad P. Brown and Meredith A. Crowley, Trade Deflection and Trade Depression, 72:1 J. Int'l Econ. 176, 176-187 (2007).

discussion of these issues and how TURK-SWITCH—a combined exit from the CU with a transition to several FTAs—should be implemented, so that a trade-sovereign Turkey has a fair chance to address its challenges.

## II. TRADE POLICY OBJECTIVES AND TOOLS IN THE NEW MILLENNIUM

Following the 2001 crisis, Turkey's economy underwent significant transformation. The JDP government reduced inflation, conducted privatizations, and decreased budget deficits.[17] Greater macroeconomic stability contributed to GDP rising from $183 to $761 billion between 2002 and 2019.[18] The government also vowed to make Turkey one of the top 10 economies by the Republic's Centennial (2023).[19] Because trade in goods and services plays an important role in its economy, President Erdoğan has maintained the trade architecture from the 1990s (e.g., multilateralism, the CU, financial liberalization, etc.), while innovating only at the margins (i.e., by diversifying exports and export destinations; increasing imports of intermediate goods and exports of finished goods, etc.). Thus, Turkey has set different trade policy objectives and deployed various trade policy tools. The following subsections analyze Turkey's trade policy objectives and the tools Turkey has used to pursue them since 2002.

### A. Policy Objectives

Since liberalizing its economy, Turkey's first and foremost objective has been to reduce its current account deficit.[20] As explained in Chapter 2,[21] current account deficits reflect a net outflow of money that results from "a country's international transactions with the rest of the world."[22] Current account *deficits* reflect a country's monetary policy, fiscal policy, budget deficits, low-level, private-sector savings (and borrowing), and, of course, trade deficits.[23] Although Turkey has shown improved monetary, fiscal, and budget discipline since the JDP rose to power, historically, it has run *trade* deficits, and its domestic savings have been low, meaning net interest payments flow abroad.[24]

17. *See* Saygin & Çimen, *supra note* 2, at 22-25.
18. *See* Appendix I.
19. *See Turkey: A Landmark Decade Vision 2023*, 3, Foreign Affairs (September-October 2013), http://files.foreignaffairs.com/legacy/attachments/Turkey%20pdf.pdf.
20. *See* 2 Temmuz 2013 Tarihli ve 1041 Nolu Onuncu Kalkinma Planinin (2014-2018) Onaylandigina Iliskin Karar [Decision No. 1041 Approving the Tenth Development Plan (2014-2018)], Türkiye Cumhuriyeti Resmi Gazete [the Official Gazette of the Republic of Turkey], July 6, 2013 No. 28699, 7 and 27, also *available at*: http://www.sbb.gov.tr/wp-content/uploads/2018/10/Onuncu_Kalkinma_Plani.pdf (last visited Oct. 25, 2018) [hereinafter the Tenth Development Plan].
21. *See supra* note 7 (Chapter 2).
22. *See* OECD, Current Account Balance, *available at*: https://data.oecd.org/trade/current-account-balance.htm (last visited Oct. 25, 2018).
23. *See* Saygin & Çimen, *supra* note 2, at 38-41; *The Economist Explains, What is a current-account deficit?*, The Economist (Apr. 7, 2017), https://www.economist.com/the-economist-explains/2017/04/06/what-is-a-current-account-deficit.
24. *See* the Tenth Development Plan, *supra* note 20, at 20 & 56.

Trade deficits and low private savings have been the chief determinants of Turkey's current account deficits.

When a country runs current account deficits, it must find external sources of financing, such as borrowing, greater FDI and short-term capital inflows. Turkey has experienced current account deficits since 2002 and has managed to find external sources to finance them.[25] However, using short-term, mostly speculative, foreign capital could risk the country's "macroeconomic stability" in the long run.[26] A rise in domestic savings and reduction in the trade deficit would help Turkey reduce its current account deficit and dependency on external capital inflows.[27]

Reducing the trade deficit has always been a difficult challenge, however. In fact, Turkey's trade deficit in goods has gone uninterrupted since 1946.[28] The export-import ratio has fluctuated between 0.521 and 0.846 in the last two decades.[29] This ratio was 0.846 in 2019.[30] Yet, as trade has expanded since 2002, Turkey's trade deficit has increased and, thus, the current account deficit. To reduce current account *and* trade deficits, Turkey has set two major trade policy goals: (1) reducing import dependency; and (2) expanding exports, while diversifying its export destination portfolio.

### 1. *Reducing Import Dependency*

A closer look at the composition of Turkey's imports reveals that its deficit originates mainly from importation of energy and intermediate goods. Turkey's energy imports, whose prices are largely set in global markets (i.e., Turkey is a price-taker), have amounted to about 25 percent of total imports.[31] Nearly half (i.e., 48 percent) of Turkey's total imports have been intermediate goods, which range from scrap metal to engines and drivetrains.[32] Together, Turkey's energy and intermediate-good imports constitute 73 percent of total imports, thus creating a *structural* obstacle to significant reductions in its trade deficit, for these classes of goods are essential to domestic production, consumption and exports.[33] Under such constraints, the remaining 27 percent of imports appear as the better candidates for punctual import management. Surely, strong yet legal enforcement of trade remedies could help reduce this amount. Because one must prove injury to domestic industry prior to imposing trade remedies and offsetting tariffs, aggressive import management has a very narrow focus, and, as such, is likely to have only a marginal impact on overall import levels. This makes export expansion the more promising alternative to help Turkey reduce its trade deficit,

25. World Bank Data, Turkey, Current Account Balance (% of GDP), *available at*: http://data.worldbank.org/indicator/BN.CAB.XOKA.GD.ZS?end=2016&locations=TR&start=1974&view=chart (last visited Oct. 25, 2018).
26. *See* the Tenth Development Plan, *supra* note 20, at 59.
27. *See id.*, at 20.
28. *See* Appendix I.
29. *See id.*
30. *See id.*
31. *See* the Tenth Development Plan, *supra* note 20, at 14.
32. *See* Turkey TPR 2016, *supra* note 6, at 139.
33. *See id.*

a goal that can only be accomplished through restructuring Turkey's trade arrangement with the European Union and a firm commitment to further trade liberalization.

## 2. *Expanding Exports and Diversifying Export Destinations*

Facing macroeconomic constraints, legal limitations (WTO and CU commitments), and structural impediments to reducing imports (reliance on energy and intermediate-good imports), Turkey must expand exports and diversify trade partners. Turkish exports have been mostly comprised of low- and medium-technology products, such as textiles and clothing, chemicals, iron and steel, household appliances, and automobiles.[34] By increasing its exporting sector's competitiveness, while also producing and exporting high value-added, technology-intensive products, Turkey should stand a chance to improve its trade balance.[35]

As far as export destinations are concerned, Turkey's main export markets have been the previous "EU-28" country area, with which it has a CU.[36] This overall beneficial trade relationship, however, also has some associated costs: when the European Union faces crisis or recession, Turkey's economy shrinks. To wit, Turkey's exports to the EU-28 declined from $60 to $47 billion (21.7 percent) during the Great Recession of 2008-2009, and, again from $62 to $59 billion (5.1 percent) during the milder Eurozone Crisis of 2011.[37] Moreover, Turkey's other important export destinations—neighboring countries, such as Syria, Iraq, Iran, and Russia—have had a share of internal conflicts and/or economic turmoil that created trade instability. So, Turkey's goal is to diversify its export destinations by increasing trade with other significant markets, such as the United States, the United Kingdom, Japan, and Southeast Asia, as well as countries in the Gulf Corporation Council ("GCC") area and Middle Asia (e.g., Azerbaijan, Kazakhstan, Pakistan, India, etc.).[38]

Diversification of exports, both by product and country of destination, would help Turkey at least come closer to the over-optimistic export goal set for the Republic's

34. *See id.*, at 23.
35. The authors realize that any increase in exports in higher value-added products would necessarily implicate greater importation of intermediate goods, which would increase imports. However, we also understand that the relationship between the increase in finished exports and increase in intermediate goods imports is not one-to-one.
36. *See* Turkey TPR 2016, *supra* note 6, at 24. Note that the cited source refers to the EU-28 area because it predates the United Kingdom's departure from the European Union, which occurred on January 31, 2020. *See* https://www.cnbc.com/2020/01/31/brexit-day-uk-formally-leaves-the-european-union.html. As this book went to print, the departure of the United Kingdom had not yet significantly affected the volume or destination of Turkey's exports to its remaining CU partners and the United Kingdom.
37. *See* Turkish Statistical Institute, Foreign Trade Statistics, Total Import and Export, *available at*: http://www.turkstat.gov.tr/UstMenu.do?metod=temelist (follow "main statistics" and then "foreign trade" hyperlink; then click "exports by country group and year.") [hereinafter TSI Exports by Country Group and Year].
38. *See* Turkish Exporters Assembly, *Economy and Foreign Trade Report 2016*, 144 (2016), http://www.tim.org.tr/files/downloads/Reports/2016_Economy_Foreign%20Trade_Report.pdf [hereinafter Tim Report 2016].

Centennial: $500 billion, by the end of 2023.[39] Execution of these objectives could also push Turkey toward capturing 1.5 percent of world trade in goods by 2023.[40] Although as of 2020, Turkey remains far from achieving these goals, it has great potential so long as the right combination of economic policies and trade diplomacy is deployed. To further familiarize the reader with Turkey's economic policymaking, the following section analyzes the trade policy tools that Turkey has deployed as it has attempted, so far with little success, to reach these objectives.

## B. Policy Tools

In its quest to achieve its ambitious trade policy objectives, Turkey has applied various trade policy tools since 2002. These goals focus on export promotion and import management, which we discuss in sequence, below.

### *1. Export-Promotion Tools*

Turkey has entrusted its export promotion and support programs to both governmental and nongovernmental organizations ("NGOs") and agencies. The private sector has also played an active role in the promotion of export activities.[41] The two major organizations promoting exports in Turkey are: the Turkish Exporters Assembly ("TIM") and the Foreign Economic Relations Board of Turkey ("DEIK").[42] An umbrella organization for Turkish exporting firms, TIM is responsible for coordinating private-sector and state-agency action.[43] TIM executes lobbying activities on behalf of exporters and conveys exporter problems to the highest governmental authorities.[44] DEIK, on the other hand, is the governmental organization that conducts foreign trade with the goal of promoting private-sector interests.[45] It also focuses on policy research and makes recommendations for government support to export sectors and domestic service industries deemed "strategic."[46] These two organizations are heavily engaged in promoting export activities, including lobbying, coordinating trade fairs, and facilitating private-sector integration into world markets.[47]

Other governmental organizations that have a role in trade are: the Ministry of Economy and the Turk EximBank, both of which support export activities. Among the tools they might deploy are: (i) inward-processing regimes for importing raw materials and intermediate goods with tariff-rebate commitments, contingent on exports;

39. *Id.*, at 136.
40. *Id.*
41. *See* Turkey TPR 2016, *supra* note 6, at 86.
42. *See id.*
43. *See* TIM, ABOUT US, *available at*: http://www.tim.org.tr/en/about-tim-about-us.html (last visited Oct. 25, 2018).
44. *See* Turkey TPR 2016, *supra* note 6, at 86.
45. DEIK HAKKINDA [ABOUT DEIK], *available at*: http://www.deik.org.tr/deik-deik-hakkinda# (last visited Oct. 25, 2018).
46. ABOUT DEIK, *available at*: http://www.taik.org.tr/about-deik.php (last visited on Oct. 25, 2018).
47. *See* Turkey TPR 2016, *supra* note 6, at 86.

(ii) low-level and quick export credits via Turk EximBank; (iii) financial support for branding activities under the Turquality program; (iv) export subsidies for agricultural products; (v) FTZs; and (vi) financial support for small and mid-sized enterprises ("SMEs").[48]

Turkey introduced the Inward-Processing Regime in 2006.[49] Under this Regime, exporters, who use imported inputs (i.e., raw materials and intermediate products) in their production, are entitled to duty-free or reduced-duty, input imports, so long as they re-export the finished goods.[50] This duty-drawback regime has been largely used by key sectors, such as agriculture, textile, clothing and leather goods.[51] Moreover, any Turkish company that engages in trade in goods or services may benefit from the services of Turk Eximbank.[52] Companies in textile, clothing, leather, machinery and electronic appliances, iron and steel, food and agriculture, and mining sectors have relied on export credits grants from Turk EximBank.[53] The total financial support of Eximbank was $31 billion in 2014, which amounted to 19.7 percent of total exports of Turkey in the same year.[54]

The other significant export-promotion tool is the Turquality branding program, operated by the Ministry of Economy, TIM, and Istanbul Textile and Apparel Exporters.[55] The program is designed to enhance and support Turkish brands (e.g., Turkish Airlines, Beko, DeFacto, Koton, Mavi, Vakko, etc.) throughout the world.[56] It aims at creating internationally accepted, well-known and high-quality Turkish brands.[57] Under the Turquality program, the Turkish Government funds 50 percent of the companies' expenses on patents, office rental space, office set-up costs, showroom rents, franchise fees, consulting fees, publicity, advertisement, and marketing costs.[58] Until 2013, 150 different brands and 50 companies have qualified for and received Turquality assistance.[59]

As the world's seventh-largest agricultural producer,[60] Turkey has provided subsidies for exporters of processed agricultural products.[61] These export subsidies have been granted according to the agricultural sector's potential for export growth.[62]

48. *See id.*, at 80-91 & 131.
49. *See id.*, at 80.
50. *Id.*
51. *See id.*, at 81.
52. Turkey TPR 2016, *supra* note 6, at 88.
53. *See* Annual Reports, Annual Report 2017, TURK EXIMBANK, 23 (2018), https://www.eximbank.gov.tr/en/investor-relations/annual-reports (last visited Mar. 4, 2019).
54. *See* Turkey TPR 2016, *supra* note 6, at 88.
55. *Id.*, at 96.
56. *See* TURQUALITY® PROJESININ TARIHÇESI [THE HISTORY OF THE TURQUALITY PROJECT], *available at*: http://www.turquality.com/hakkimizda/tarihce (last visited Oct. 25, 2018).
57. *See id.*
58. *See* Turkey TPR 2016, *supra* note 6, at 96; *see also* TURQUALITY® DESTEKLERI [THE FINANCIAL SUPPORTS OF TURQUALITY], *available at*: http://www.turquality.com/destekler/turquality-destekleri (last visited Oct. 25, 2018).
59. *See* Turkey TPR 2016, *supra* note 6, at 96.
60. Turkey is also net exporter of certain agricultural products (e.g., hazelnut, citrus fruits, grapes and tomatoes, etc.).
61. *See* Turkey TPR 2016, *supra* note 6, at 121-123.
62. *Id.*, at 131.

For example, exporters of certain processed agricultural products (e.g., frozen fruits and vegetables, olive oil, processed poultry products, etc.) received export subsidies rates, ranging between 2 and 14 percent, a.v., in 2016.[63] The government maintains that such subsidization has been granted in compliance with Turkey's WTO commitments.[64] Thanks to this program, Turkey's agricultural exports have increased from $9 to $18 billion between 2007 and 2014, with potential for further expansion.[65]

As discussed in Chapter 3, Turkey enacted FTZs to accelerate export-oriented investment and production in 1985. Since then, Turkey has established 18 FTZs, most of which are in coastal cities.[66] Companies operating in FTZs are entitled to exemptions from customs duties, corporate tax, value-added taxes, stamp duties, and income taxes on employee wages.[67] These companies are also not restricted from transferring their profits abroad.[68]

In 2016, 2,025 companies (530 of which were foreign) operated in FTZs.[69] Textile and leather, automotive, aircraft parts, medical devices, R&D and software, yacht manufacturing, and ship-building industries were the main users of FTZs.[70] The total trade volume of FTZs amounted to $22.4 billion, while their exports to third countries reached $7.9 billion in 2014.[71] Free-trade zones also employed more than 61,000 people in the same year.[72] In addition to FTZs, Turkey has applied a broad incentive program to attract more FDI and, thus, increased its domestic production and exports, while helping finance its trade and current account deficits.[73] Under the Investment Incentive Program ("IIP"), Turkey provided exemptions on value-added taxes and customs duties; deductions on corporate taxes; and support for companies' social security premia.[74] These incentives are allocated according to the amount, sector, and location of investment.[75] Investments on large scale (between $12 and $240 million)

63. *See* 26 Aralik 2016 Tarihli ve 2016/6 Nolu Tarimsal Urunlerde Ihracat Iadesi Yardimlarina Iliskin Para-Kredi ve Koordinasyon Kurulu Karari [Decision by Money-Credit and Coordination Council on Rebates for Exported Agricultural Products], Türkiye Cumhuriyeti Resmi Gazete [the Official Gazette of the Republic of Turkey], December 28, 2016, No. 29932, also *available at*: http://www.resmigazete.gov.tr/eskiler/2016/12/20161228-7.htm (last visited Oct. 25, 2018).
64. *See* Turkey TPR 2016, *supra* note 6, at 131.
65. 2015 Yili Ocak Dönemi Diş Ticaret Verileri [Foreign Trade Data for the 2015 January Period], *available at*: http://www.tarim.gov.tr/ABDGM/Belgeler/ET%C4%B0/Tar%C4%B1msal%20D%C4%B1%C5%9F%20Ticaret/D%C4%B1%C5%9F%20Ticaret%20OCAK-2015%20v1.pdf (last visited Oct. 25, 2018).
66. *See* Ali Bayraktar & K. Sevgin Güngör, *Countering Illicit Trade in Turkey's Free Zones*, 5-6 (Public Governance and Territorial Development Directorate Public Governance Committee, High Level Risk Forum GOV/PGC/HLRF/TFCIT/RD (2017)1), *available at*: http://www.oecd.org/officialdocuments/publicdisplaydocumentpdf/?cote=GOV/PGC/HLRF/TFCIT/RD(2017)1&docLanguage=En (last visited Oct. 25, 2018).
67. Investment Zones, *available at*: http://www.invest.gov.tr/en-US/investmentguide/investorsguide/Pages/SpecialInvestmentZones.aspx (last visited Oct. 25, 2018).
68. *See* Turkey TPR 2016, *supra* note 6, at 44.
69. *See* Bayraktar & Güngör, *supra* note 66, at 2.
70. *Id.*, at 7.
71. *See* Turkey TPR 2016, *supra* note 6, at 44.
72. *Id.*
73. *Id.*, at 40.
74. *Id.*, at 40-41.
75. *Id.*

and/or strategic sectors—i.e., sectors that produce intermediate and finished goods, with which Turkey has around 50-percent import dependency (excluding oil and natural gas), and high-value-added/high-tech sectors—have been the main IIP beneficiaries.[76] Any Turkish business (i.e., whether established by Turkish nationals or otherwise) and foreign company affiliates established in Turkey is able to benefit from IIP assistance.[77] In 2015, IIP-eligible businesses took advantage from the above-mentioned fiscal assistance and invested about ₺47 billion ($13.4 billion) themselves.[78]

Finally, the Turkish Government grants financial assistance to SMEs to promote domestic production and exports. SMEs are characterized as companies with less than 250 employees and whose balance sheet does not exceed ₺40 million.[79] About 99.8 percent of all businesses registered in Turkey as SMEs. They employ 75.8 percent of private-sector employees and produce 54.2 percent of Turkey's "value added at factor cost."[80] SMEs are also important for trade: they account for 37.8 percent of exports and 56.5 percent of imports.[81] The Small and Medium Enterprise Development Organization ("KOSGEB") administers government support for SMEs.[82] SMEs deemed to have promising business projects are eligible to receive KOSGEB's assistance in the form of direct grants, reimbursements, loans, or subsidized services, such as laboratory services.[83] These programs include rental fees, employee expenses, internal and external business visit expenses, machinery and equipment expenses, etc.[84] In 2019, KOSGEB provided ₺2.3 billion in support for SMEs.[85]

Clearly, a wide range of export-promotion tools has been in place since 2002. Next, we discuss Turkey's application of import management tools during the same period.

## *2. Import Management Tools*

In addition to export promotion, Turkey has applied various import management instruments to achieve its trade policy objectives. Among these import management tools are: (i) tariff management (i.e., within bound levels); (ii) imposition of special consumption taxes ("SCTs"); (iii) application of trade remedies (i.e., AD, CVD, and safeguards); and (iv) import licensing requirements.

76. *Id.*
77. *Id.*
78. *Id.*, at 42.
79. *See id.*, at 91.
80. *Id.*
81. *Id.*
82. *Id.*
83. *Id.*, at 92.
84. *See* KOSGEB Destekler [KOSGEB Supports], KOSGEB, https://www.kosgeb.gov.tr/site/tr/genel/destekler/3/destekler.
85. 2019 Yılı KOSGEB Faaliyet Raporu [KOSGEB 2019 Activity Report], 1 https://www.kosgeb.gov.tr/Content/Upload/Dosya/Mali%20Tablolar/Faaliyet%20Raporlar%C4%B1/KOSGEB_2019_Y%C4%B1l%C4%B1_Faaliyet_Raporu.pdf.

### a. *Tariffs: Turkey's Ceded Leverage*

As discussed in detail in Chapter 3, Turkey became a member of the WTO and signed the CU with the European Union in the mid-1990s. Since then, Turkey's has imposed tariffs rates pursuant to its commitments under the WTO and the CU. As a result of these commitments (e.g., especially the CU commitments), Turkey's trade regime has become one of the most liberal,[86] according to the MFN Tariff Trade Restrictiveness Index.[87] To wit, the "trade-weighted applied tariff rate on manufacturing goods was only 1.0 percent" in 2007.[88]

At the conclusion of the Uruguay Round, Turkey agreed to bind 50.4 percent of its tariffs (i.e., agricultural and otherwise).[89] Acquiescing to the general trend favoring greater transparency by the replacement of nontariff with tariff measures, Turkey bound *all* agricultural MFN tariff lines at 61 percent, on average.[90] It also agreed to bind about one-third (36.3 percent) of its industrial goods at an average 42.6 percent tariff.[91] Notably, despite strong, multilateral pressure to bind all trade to negotiated tariffs, Turkey managed to conclude the Uruguay Round with 63.7 percent of its industrial good tariff lines *unbound*. Whether through the significant number of tariff lines left unbound or its high tariff bindings, the WTO system gives Turkey much tariff discretion and, thus, leverage in trade negotiations.[92]

#### i. Turkey's Relinquished Tariff Discretion under the CU

Turkey's subsequent entry into the CU gave away much of its cleverly won tariff discretion. Pursuant to the CU, the European Union and Turkey eliminated *all* industrial good tariffs from their bilateral trade.[93] Moreover, Turkey adopted the EU preferential trade regime and applied CETs with the European Union on third-country industrial imports.[94] Because bound and applied EU MFN tariff rates are significantly lower (than Turkey's WTO tariff commitments), Turkey had to lower its tariffs on industrial imports from non-EU countries, as well.[95]

Thus, on industrial products, although Turkey's simple-average, bound (i.e., MFN, WTO/GATT) tariff rate sits at 42.6 percent, Turkey's *applied*-average tariff rate

86. Akman, *supra* note 10, at 151.
87. Tariff Trade Restrictiveness Index is described as "an index measuring the average level of tariff restrictions imposed on imports." *See Key Statistics and Trends in Trade Policy 2018*, United Nations Conference on Trade and Development (UNCTAD), UNCTAD/DITC/TAB/2019/1, viii (2019), https://unctad.org/en/PublicationsLibrary/ditctab2019d1_en.pdf.
88. Chad P. Brown, *Trade Policy Flexibilities and Turkey: Tariffs, Antidumping, Safeguards and WTO Dispute Settlement*, 5 (World Bank, Policy Research Working Paper No. 6322, 2013).
89. *See* Turkey TPR 2016, *supra* note 6, at 55.
90. *See* Appendix II, Table II.2.
91. *See* Appendix II, Table II.1.
92. *See* Appendix II, Tables II.1 & II.2.
93. With the exception of European Coal and Steel Community's products. *See* Subidey Togan & Bartlomiej Kaminski, The Foreign Trade Regime and Trade Liberalization in Turkey, *in Economic Liberalization and Turkey* 13, 17 (Subidey Togan ed., 2010).
94. Akman, *supra* note 10, at 139.
95. *See* Appendix II, Tables II.1 & II.2.

has plunged to below 6 percent since its entry in to the CU.[96,97] In fact, Turkey's trade-weighted average tariff rate was only 3.6 percent in 2018.[98] Obviously, *there is a huge gap*—around 36 percentage points—*between Turkey's average, bound and applied tariff rates, which demonstrates the sizable tariff leverage Turkey has waived by signing and remaining within the CU.*

While the CU Decision does allow Turkey to raise MFN tariff rates above CET limits, it does so subject to a finding of domestic industry injury.[99] Proving serious domestic industry injury (i.e., safeguards allegations) or ordinary domestic industry injury (i.e., AD and CVD allegations) is not, however, a matter of administrative discretion. As exceptional remedies authorized under CU and WTO rules, they require meticulous compliance with the legal requirements of the international trade system. Thus, the CU has exposed Turkey to a low-tariff regime that gives it only limited ability to obtain reciprocal tariff treatment from third countries. For instance, only after finding that its domestic textile industry had been seriously injured by a sudden influx of imports in 2011 was Turkey able to exceed, temporarily, the MFN (i.e., CU CET) tariffs from a range of 4-12 percent to 12-30 percent.[100] Also, as a result, Turkey rose its applied preferential tariffs from a range of 0-9.6 to 3-27 percent.[101] Such adjustments affected $4.8 billion in textile imports, in 2011.[102] Because under WTO rules, Turkey's simple *average* bound MFN tariff rate in textiles is 24.5 percent, the increase in these tariffs exceeded CETs (i.e., the CU level) but, overall, did not exceed Turkey's WTO bindings by much.[103] Obviously, Turkey's limited trade-remedy flexibility was never conceived to fully address the *effects* of third-country imports into Turkey (or zero-tariff transshipments via European Union) on Turkish domestic producers. Without tariff discretion, however, offsetting tariffs and safeguard tariffs are the only remedy to obtaining some—though not the full WTO-authorized—relief against fairly and unfairly traded imports for Turkish domestic industry.

After TURK-SWITCH, a restructuring of the EU-Turkey current trade arrangement that would restore Turkey's trade sovereignty, around two-thirds of industrial products would return to their unbound, WTO-negotiated status. The remaining one-third, whose applied rates have been held much below bound rates (by an average of about 36 percentage points), would provide Turkey more room to lawfully manage import tariffs.[104] That applied tariffs on one-third of EU industrial products could increase from 0 to 42.6 percent and that two-thirds of EU industrial products could see applied tariffs increase to uncertain levels, should help Turkey persuade EU negotiators to conclude an FTA that would reduce asymmetries Turkey has faced in its trade with

96. *See* Turkey TPR 2016, *supra* note 6, at 51.
97. World Trade Organization, World Tariff Profiles 2019, 178, *available at*: https://www.wto.org/english/res_e/booksp_e/tariff_profiles19_e.pdf [hereinafter World Tariff Profiles 2019].
98. *Id.*
99. *See* Brown, *supra* note 88, at 9 (citing Article 63 of Customs Union Decision–Decision No. 1/95; Degree on Safeguard Measures for Imports No. 2004/7305; etc.).
100. *See id.*, at 10-33.
101. *Id.*
102. *Id.*
103. *See* World Tariff Profiles 2019, *supra* note 97.
104. *See* Appendix II, Table II.1.

the European Union and EU FTA partners. Remarkably, under the WTO/GATT, the European Union has bound all its industrial imports at 4.1 percent.[105] Even in the event of EU recalcitrance or the unravelling of negotiations, Turkish industrial products would see only a minor increase in EU tariffs, so, unlike the EU-UK Brexit negotiations, where the United Kingdom basically returned to its pre-EU membership, low-WTO tariff schedule, the impact of a no-deal outcome in EU-Turkey negotiations would be distributed asymmetrically, in Turkey's favor.

Of course, as discussed in the introductory chapter, there is quite a bit more to agreement restructuring than tariffs. Surely, government agencies, political elites, and economic actors may have differing views on the national interest, and, as far as *trade* negotiations go, one must recognize that revisiting rules of origin (ROOs) can get quite involved, as entire supply chains might be disturbed. Yet, Turkey's continued waiver of trade sovereignty with dim EU-membership prospects might tip the balance in favor of TURK-SWITCH, a discussion we fully develop in Chapter 6.

Regardless of the trade policy path Turkey eventually chooses for itself, a middle-income country with developed-country-level tariffs on nonagricultural goods (5.5 percent average)[106] should be in a position to obtain similar concessions from other middle-income countries that have FTAs with the European Union. That goods from Mexico or South Africa get zero tariffs when transshipped through an EU Member into Turkey—regardless of any concession they offer to Turkey—amounts to a loss of substantial trade leverage.[107] Yet, this kind of asymmetry only partially captures the magnitude of Turkey's waived leverage: with every new trade deal Brussels makes, Turkey's trade leverage is further eroded as more countries enjoy similar benefits without having to make concessions to Turkey. *Only a trading system captured by financial and supply chain interests could engineer such an exorbitant waiver of trade sovereignty.*[108]

---

105. *See* Appendix II, Table II.1.
106. *See* Appendix II, Table II.2. For the sake of comparability, we shall use nonagricultural tariffs as a "rough" proxy for industrial tariffs whenever country-to-country, industrial-good-specific information for the *same* year is not available. We surmise the WTO stopped compiling *industrial* good tariffs by its members in 2003 because of the Doha Round's focus on Non-Agricultural Market Access ("NAMA"), a broader, more ambitious negotiation agenda. To our knowledge, the last WTO document containing yearly, country-to-country comparisons on *industrial* goods—and the main source of such information for this book—remains Marc Bacchetta and Bijit Bora, *Industrial Tariff Liberalization and the Doha Development Agenda*, 15 World Trade Organization, Development and Economic Research Division (2003) (using 2001 data), *available at*: https://www.wto.org/english/res_e/booksp_e/discussion_papers_e.pdf. Because of the failure of the Doha Round and other negotiations on nonagricultural—and thus industrial—tariff reductions, we believe Bacchetta and Bora's data on bound industrial good tariffs remains accurate. For convenience, the portion of their data pertaining to the European Union and Turkey is summarized in Appendix II, Table II.1.
107. *See* World Bank Report, *supra* note 16, at 24-25.
108. Note that, pursuant to the (EU) acquis communautaire, and, partly, to offset the revenue loss from CU implementation, the Turkish Parliament enacted Law No. 4760, creating a Special Consumption Tax ("ÖTV" or "SCT," its equivalent English acronym) in 2002. *See* Türkiye Büyük Millet Meclisi, Özel Tüketim Vergisi Kanunu Tasarisi ve Plan ve Bütçe Komisyonu Raporu (1/988) [Turkey's Grand National Assembly, Written Proposal of Special Consumption Tax and Report of Plan and Budget Commission], 883, http://www.gib.gov.tr/fileadmin/mevzuatek/gerekceler/KDV/tvk_4760_sayili_kanun.pdf [hereinafter Reasoning of SCT]. Since

Two and a half decades under the CU with no advancement on membership prospects should have prompted Turkey's policymakers to make a more forceful case for either membership or some version TURK-SWITCH. So far, however, they have merely urged updating the Turkey-EU Customs Union, ignoring, apparently, Turkey's sizable tariff leverage under the WTO system.[109] Yet, with EU leaders showing renewed unwillingness to grant Turkey EU membership, the country should consider a negotiated departure from the CU, particularly because the cost of leaving it could be viewed as not so substantial. Specifically, a post-CU Turkey could reconcile a strong trade relationship with the European Union with trade agreements with partners, such as Brazil, Mexico, the United Kingdom, the United States, Canada, and Japan. Turkey's current tariff schedule on industrial and agricultural products and its reserve of discretionary authority on tariffs might just prove to be right enticement for triggering new, realistic FTAs.[110]

### ii. Reserved Tariff Discretion on Agricultural Products

As mentioned earlier (Subsection B.2.a), Turkey bound agricultural products to an average MFN tariff of 61.0 percent.[111] While the simple average applied MFN tariff had fallen to 41.8 percent by 2018,[112] the *trade-weighted* average tariff was even lower, at 18.8 percent.[113] Because the CU does not cover agricultural products, Turkey has *significant* flexibility to impose higher tariff rates on agricultural imports. Turkey has also treated most neighboring countries, preferentially. For instance, Bosnia-Herzegovina's agricultural products enjoy almost duty-free access to the Turkish market. More importantly, because Turkey's MFN-bound tariff rates are quite high (61.0 percent), Turkey has wide discretion over agricultural imports. How Turkey should deploy potential future tariff concessions to achieve its export ambitions (i.e., growth and diversification) will be discussed in depth in Chapter 6.

---

then, Turkish taxpayers have been levied high internal consumption taxes on petroleum products (ranging from ₺2.15 to ₺2.29—per one-liter gasoline—almost 50 percent of the final consumer price); vehicles (up to 145 percent, a.v.); durable consumer goods (ranging between zero and 25), to name a few. SCT revenue amounted to 25.8 percent of total government tax revenue in 2014. *See* Turkey TPR 2016 *supra* note 6, at 60-64. Such revenue offset illustrates the monumental income transfer from the Turkish middle and lower classes to the export and banking sectors, the biggest winners from the CU.

109. *See Updating Customs Union with EU is Priority: Turkish Finance Minister*, HÜRRIYET DAILY NEWS (Feb. 28, 2019), http://www.hurriyetdailynews.com/updating-customs-union-with-eu-is-priority-turkish-finance-minister-141557.
110. It is important to note that Turkey's 73 percent of imports are mainly intermediate and energy products. In the case of a withdrawal from the CU, Turkey might apply higher tariff rates for these products, which may increase the cost of exportable production and also increase domestic inflation.
111. *See* Appendix II, Table II.2.
112. *See* World Tariff Profiles 2019, *supra* note 97.
113. *See id.*

### b. *Special Consumption Tax*

Low-level tariffs (mainly because of the CU) have reduced Turkey's control over import volumes as well as revenue. To cope with these effects and help Turkey recoup some of the lost revenue, the Parliament, invoking the EU *Acquis Communautaire*, enacted Law No. 4760, creating a Special Consumption Tax ("SCT") in 2002.[114] By 2014, SCT revenue alone amounted to 25.8 percent of total tax revenue.[115] SCT's alleged main objective is to provide social, environmental, and health benefits for Turks, by imposing additional consumption (rather than value-added) taxes on certain goods, such as petroleum products, alcoholic products, tobacco, durable consumer and luxury goods, etc.[116] Domestic and imported products belonging to these categories are subject to SCT.[117] Before 2018, still under the parliamentary system, the Council of Ministers had the authority to impose SCT on any type of product, at any desired rate. This power currently rests with the President. Thus, SCT remains an important revenue-raising tool that also shapes social, economic, health, and trade policies.[118]

SCT sets forth four main tax brackets or "Lists." List I covers petroleum products (e.g., gasoline, diesel, liquefied natural gas, etc.), whose rates are determined on a non-*ad valorem* basis.[119] Because Turkey is heavily dependent on energy imports, the specific SCT for these products is higher allegedly, at least, to encourage the purchase vehicles with lower fuel consumption. For instance, in August 2020, the average SCT on one liter of gasoline was ₺2.52 and total taxes on gasoline was 54 percent of the final price.[120] In the United States, the SCT alone (i.e., without including the value-added tax) would amount to $1.31 (i.e., ₺9.52) per gallon.[121] Indeed, Turks pay one of the highest gasoline taxes in the world.[122]

List II includes motor vehicles, aircrafts, and vessels, whose rates are determined on an a.v. basis, that ranged from zero to 220 percent in 2021.[123] Generally, vehicle SCT rates are determined according to the engine displacement (i.e., volume).[124] For instance, owners of automobiles that have less than 1,600 $cm^3$ of engine displacement

114. Reasoning of SCT, *supra* note 108, at 884.
115. *See* Turkey TPR 2016, *supra* note 6, at 60.
116. *See id.*; Reasoning of SCT, *supra* note 108, at 883-883.
117. *See* Turkey TPR 2016, *supra* note 6, at 60.
118. Yildirim Taylar, Vergi Teorisi Açisindan Özel Tüketim Vergileri ve Türk Özel Tüketim Vergisi Uygulamasi [Special Consumption Taxes and Application of Turkey's Special Consumption Tax from the Perspective of Tax Theory], Dokuz Eylül Üniversitesi Hukuk Fakültesi Dergisi, C12/Özel Sayi 435, 445 (2010).
119. *See* Turkey TPR 2016, *supra* note 6, at 60.
120. *See* Petrol ve LPG Piyasasi Fiyatlandirma Raporu, Enerji Piyasasi Düzenleme Kurumu, 6-8 (August 2020), https://www.epdk.gov.tr/Detay/DownloadDocument?id=34Kd0Y/F0UE=.
121. The dollar/lira rate was 7.2 in August 2020. *See* USDTRY:CUR, USD-TRY X-RATE, Bloomberg, https://www.bloomberg.com/quote/USDTRY:CUR.
122. *See Oil prices in Turkey reach record high*, Hürriyet Daily News (Oct. 01, 2012), http://www.hurriyetdailynews.com/oil-prices-in-turkey-reach-record-high-31348.
123. *See* (II) Sayili Liste [List Number II], Gelir Idaresi Başkanlıgı [Turkish Revenue Administration], https://www.gib.gov.tr/fileadmin/mevzuatek/otv_oranlari_tum/02022021_II_sayili_liste.pdf (the list was last updated on Feb. 2, 2021) (last visited Feb. 6, 2021).
124. *See* Turkey TPR 2016, *supra* note 6, at 61.

are assessed a range of 45-80 percent SCT at the point of first sale.[125] Owners of autos with engines between 1,600 and 2,000 $cm^3$ are assessed up to 150 percent; and those with autos exceeding 2,000 $cm^3$ are assessed up to 220 percent SCT.[126] By imposing taxes at such high rates, the government seeks to dissuade Turks from buying vehicles with more powerful and, thus, higher fuel-consuming engines. One would be naïve to ignore that invariably most of these vehicles are produced abroad.

List III comprises alcoholic beverages and tobacco products.[127] In 2021, the SCT rate on beer produced from malt was 63 percent, a.v., while the rate on cigarettes that contain tobacco was 65.25 percent, a.v..[128] List IV, the final category, includes durable consumer products (e.g., refrigerators and other home appliances), luxury goods (e.g., caviar and substitutes, digital cameras, perfumes, certain leathers and furs, etc.), and personal hygiene products (e.g., deodorants, etc.), all having SCT rates ranging from zero to 50 percent.[129]

Thus, SCT has been a de facto import management tool. Although under GATT, Article III National Treatment Principle Turkey cannot discriminate against imports, SCTs have targeted the sectors where Turkey has little or no domestic production, such as oil, natural gas, luxury goods, etc. As such, the government has deployed SCTs as an import management tool, ostensibly to help Turkey check its trade and account deficits.

### c. *Trade Remedies*

Because Turkey's tariff discretion is restricted (i.e., bound) under the CU, temporary trade barriers—namely, AD, CVD, and safeguard measures—can be a useful trade management tool. These remedies are subject to strict disciplines under the WTO system, but are limited to use only against unfairly traded (i.e., AD and CVD) and fairly traded but surging (i.e., safeguards) imports, though only to the extent that the government can demonstrate injury (in AD and CVD investigations) or serious injury (in safeguard investigations).[130]

Notably, Turkey was among the top ten users of AD measures, while it is the third highest user of safeguard measures at the WTO.[131] On the AD side, Turkey initiated 231

125. *See* (II) Sayili Liste, *supra* note 123.
126. *Id.*
127. *See* Turkey TPR 2016, *supra* note 6, at 60-63.
128. *See* (III) Sayili Liste [List Number III], GELIR IDARESI BAŞKANLIGI [TURKISH REVENUE ADMINISTRATION], https://www.gib.gov.tr/fileadmin/mevzuatek/otv_oranlari_tum/04012021_III_sayili_liste.pdf (the list was last updated on Jan. 4, 2021) (last visited Feb. 6, 2021).
129. *See* ÖTV (IV) Sayili Liste [List Number IV], GELIR IDARESI BAŞKANLIGI [TURKISH REVENUE ADMINISTRATION], https://www.gib.gov.tr/fileadmin/mevzuatek/otv_oranlari_tum/01072019_IV_sayili_liste.pdf (the list was last updated on Jan. 7, 2019) (last visited Feb. 6, 2021).
130. *See* Juscelino F. Colares, *The Limits of WTO Adjudication: Is Compliance the Problem?*, 14 J. OF INT'L ECON. L. 403, 407 (2011).
131. Turkey TPR 2016, *supra* note 6, at 68-69.

AD investigations between 1995 and 2020.[132] Pursuant to these investigations, Turkey has imposed 199 AD measures.[133] Imports of textile and textile articles, plastic and rubber, and iron and steel products were the most frequent targets of Turkey's AD measures.[134] During this period, Turkey's AD investigations and their resulting offsetting tariffs targeted, mostly, emerging economies, particularly, China, Indonesia, Taiwan, India, Malaysia, Thailand, and Vietnam.[135] As of December 2019, Turkey had 134 AD measures in force.[136] China has been the most targeted country.[137] By contrast, Turkey has rarely used CVDs. Since 1995, it has initiated only three CVD investigations[138] imposing only one CVD measure.[139]

As far as safeguard measures are concerned, Turkey did not have domestic legislation authorizing the application of safeguard measures until 2004.[140] So, safeguard application is only a recent development.[141] Since 2004, however, Turkey has initiated 27 safeguard investigations.[142] Among these, only 17 resulted in the imposition of safeguards.[143] Turkey has applied safeguards on the following products: footwear; matches; motorcycles; cotton yarn; polyethylene terephthalate; terephthalic acid; travel goods; handbags; certain electronic appliances; wallpapers; and similar wallcovering.[144] Although safeguards are not country-specific—unlike AD and CVD remedies—the main exporters affected by Turkey's safeguard measures have been: Pakistan; South Korea; Spain; Belgium; and China.[145]

Although AD and CVD remedies target imports only from producers in subject countries, fairly traded imports from *other* countries may benefit from application of

132. *See* World Trade Organization, Anti-dumping Initiations by Reporting Member 01/01/1995—30/06/2020, https://www.wto.org/english/tratop_e/adp_e/AD_InitiationsByRepMem.pdf (last visited Feb. 6, 2021).
133. *See* World Trade Organization, Anti-dumping Measures by Reporting Member 01/01/1995—30/06/2020, https://www.wto.org/english/tratop_e/adp_e/AD_MeasuresByRepMem.pdf (last visited Feb. 6, 2021).
134. *See* Turkey TPR 2016, *supra* note 6, at 68.
135. *See* WTO Documents, Committee on Anti-Dumping Practices, Semi-Annual Report Under Article 16.4 of the Agreement Turkey, *20-6434*, G/ADP/N/342/TUR (Sept. 23, 2020), https://docs.wto.org/dol2fe/Pages/SS/directdoc.aspx?filename = q:/G/ADP/N342TUR.pdf&Open = True (last visited Feb. 6, 2021).
136. World Trade Organization, World Tariff Profiles 2020, 202, *available at*: https://www.wto.org/english/res_e/booksp_e/tariff_profiles20_e.pdf.
137. *See* Turkey TPR 2016, *supra* note 6, at 200-204.
138. *See* World Trade Organization, Countervailing Initiations: By Reporting Member 01/01/1995—30/06/2020, https://www.wto.org/english/tratop_e/scm_e/CV_InitiationsByRepMem.pdf (last visited Feb. 6, 2021).
139. *See* World Trade Organization, Countervailing Measures: By Reporting Member 01/01/1995—30/06/2020, https://www.wto.org/english/tratop_e/scm_e/CV_MeasuresByRepMem.pdf (last visited Feb. 6, 2021).
140. *See* Turkey TPR 2016, *supra* note 6, at 27 & 69.
141. *See id.*, at 69.
142. *See* World Trade Organization, Safeguard Initiations by Reporting Member Period: 01/01/1995 to 30/06/2020, https://www.wto.org/english/tratop_e/safeg_e/safeg_e.htm#statistics (last visited Feb. 6, 2021).
143. *See* World Trade Organization, Safeguard Measures by Reporting Member Period: 01/01/1995 to 30/06/2020, https://www.wto.org/english/tratop_e/safeg_e/SG-MeasuresByRepMember.pdf (last visited Feb. 6, 2021).
144. Turkey TPR 2016, *supra* note 6, at 69.
145. *Id.*

these disciplines, resulting in some trade creation. This might be the case, particularly, because of Turkey's low tariffs. The same cannot be said about safeguard measures, however. Safeguards target both fairly and unfairly traded imports, regardless of country of origin. Yet, proving *serious* domestic industry injury by surging imports—the injury standard for safeguard actions—requires a much higher showing of harm than proving ordinary injury in AD and CVD cases. Thus, despite targeting fairly traded imports, the efficiency loss due to safeguards is mitigated by the adoption of a stricter injury requirement.

Because Turkey trade policy is under significant legal constraints under the CU, trade remedies remain useful tools for import management and punctual domestic industry protection. We now turn to Turkey's last primary trade management tool: import licensing or Turkey's disguised QR regime.

### *d. Import Licensing*

Turkey has applied import licensing on a significant variety of products (e.g., radioactivity-related items, petroleum and liquefied petroleum gas ("LPG"), civil aircraft-related items, fertilizers, certain sugar substitutes, various armaments and chemicals, etc.) arguably aiming to affect import levels.[146] Typically import-licensing schemes create an obligation on importers to disclose the source and quantity of proposed imports and to obtain licenses prior to the importation of such products.[147] This requirement encumbers the process of importation and may create delays or impede the entry of foreign products altogether. Yet, some import licensing may arise from legitimate regulatory purposes, such as compliance with international commitments (e.g., Convention on International Trade in Endangered Species of Wild Fauna and Flora ), enforcement of public health regulations, and attention to national security and public safety concerns.[148] Under licensing requirements, importers of controlled or dual-use products have been required to obtain licenses from specified authorities, such as the Turkish Atomic Energy Authority, the Ministry of Transportation, the Ministry of Food, Agriculture and Livestock, etc.[149]

Other less meritorious concerns may have given rise to the imposition of import licenses in Turkey, however. For instance, in 2011, importers of telecommunication products (e.g., telephone answering machines, radars, etc.) and household machines (e.g., refrigerators, clothes driers, sewing machines, vacuum cleaners, etc.) were required to obtain a license from the Ministry of Science, Industry and Technology.[150] To obtain import licenses for household machines, importers had to demonstrate that they would provide after-sale services (e.g., service technicians for maintenance and

146. Akman, *supra* note 10, at 151.
147. *See* World Trade Organization, Import Licensing: Technical Information, Technical Information on Import Licensing, https://www.wto.org/english/tratop_E/implic_e/implic_info_e.htm (last visited Mar. 4, 2019).
148. *See* Turkey TPR 2016, *supra* note 6, at 66-68.
149. *See id.*, at 67-68.
150. WTO Secretariat, *Trade Policy Review of Turkey*, WT/TPR/S/259/Rev.1, 42 (2012) [hereinafter Turkey TPR 2012].

repair, spare parts, etc.) to consumers.[151] Importers of telecommunication products also had to assure conformity with Turkey's national network.[152] In 2013, the government removed import-licensing requirements for all these products.[153] While one cannot fully ascertain whether the imposition of such import licensing was meritorious, one cannot rule out their potential protectionist motivation.

The energy sector has also had to comply with import-licensing requirements. Importers of electricity, natural gas, petroleum, and LPG have been required to obtain licenses from the Energy Market Regulatory Authority.[154] According to government officials, the main purpose of this requirement is "to prevent the unorthodox use of those items out of purpose and to ensure fuel quality."[155] Again, the vagueness of and paternalism underlying such rationale does not allow us to determine the economic soundness of imposing import licenses to this sector. They do raise our skepticism, though.

Turkey has also applied import licenses for various motor vehicles and trailers.[156] Importers of these products are required to obtain licenses from the Ministry of Science, Industry and Technology.[157] By requiring such licenses, the government seeks to ensure that those vehicles are suitable for Turkey's highways.[158] Of course, dual-use products, such as various armaments, ammonium nitrate, fireworks, knives, propellant powders, prepared explosives, etc. should and have been covered by import license requirements.[159]

Thus, the Turkish Government has used national security, public safety, consumer protection and international obligations as rationales for requiring import licenses.[160] Although the government alleges its intent has not been to restrict imports, import-licensing requirements can have such an effect.[161] In addition to these import management tools and the export-promotion tools discussed earlier, Turkey has deployed two additional mechanisms to achieve its trade goals: trade diplomacy and trade litigation, topics to which we now turn.

151. *Id.*
152. *Id.*, at 41-43.
153. *See* WTO Notification under Article 7.3 of the Agreement on Import Licensing Procedures for 2015 by Turkey, G/LIC/N/3/TUR/14 [hereinafter Import Licensing Notification, 2015]; WTO Notification under Article 7.3 of the Agreement on Import Licensing Procedures for 2016 by Turkey, G/LIC/N/3/TUR/15 [hereinafter Import Licensing Notification, 2016].
154. Turkey TPR 2016, *supra* note 6, at 67.
155. *Id.*
156. *See id.*, at 66.
157. *See id.*, at 67.
158. *Id.*
159. *Id.*
160. *See* Turkey TPR 2016, *supra* note 6, at 67-68; Import Licensing Notification, 2015, *supra* note 153; Import Licensing Notification, 2016, *supra* note 153.
161. *See* Import Licensing Notification, 2015, *supra* note 153; Import Licensing Notification 2016, *supra* note 153.

### 3. *Trade Diplomacy*

Since 1980, when Turkey changed its trade policy to outward-oriented industrialization, trade-related issues (e.g., new export markets, export diversification, energy supply, tourism, etc.) have helped shape government decision-making, including foreign policy. According to Kutlay, "the major driving force for ... Turkish foreign policy has [become] economy and trade."[162] Unsurprisingly, trade diplomacy has been an important policy tool for Turkey as it attempts to adapt to a changing world trade environment while accomplishing redefined trade policy goals. This section examines: (i) Turkey's ambivalent stance at the Doha Round; (ii) Turkey's negotiations of bilateral trade agreements; and (iii) Turkey's efforts to attract foreign investment and expand its service trade (e.g., tourism, aviation and energy transportation, etc.). Because of the failure of the Doha Round and Turkey's inability to freely negotiate new bilateral trade agreements under the CU, we demonstrate that, thus far, Turkey's efforts in attracting FDI and expanding its trade in services have been its most fruitful diplomatic efforts.

#### a. *Turkey's Ambivalence in the Doha Round*

A few years after the conclusion of the Uruguay-Round trade negotiations, which culminated with the creation of the WTO in 1994, WTO Members initiated a new round of multilateral negotiations, known as the "Doha Round" or "Doha Development Agenda" ("DDA").[163] The main objective of the Doha Round was to reform the international trading system by lowering trade barriers and revising the trade rules of the WTO.[164] WTO Members agreed the Doha Round would include negotiations on improving non-agricultural market access ("NAMA"), reducing agricultural subsidies, liberalizing trade in services, adopting uniform practices to facilitate trade, addressing intellectual property rights issues (e.g., geographical indications), and revising AD and subsidy disciplines.[165]

As of this writing, the consensus is that the Doha Round failed by not delivering on most of the trade issues it undertook.[166] For instance, two significant areas, namely,

162. Mustafa Kutlay, *Economy as the "Practical Hand" of "New Turkish Foreign Policy": A Political Economy Explanation*, 13 Insight Turkey 67, 76 (2011).
163. These negotiations were named after Doha, Qatar, which hosted the WTO's Fourth Ministerial Conference in 2001. *See* The Doha Round, World Trade Organization https://www.wto.org/english/tratop_e/dda_e/dda_e.htm (last visited Oct. 25, 2018).
164. *See id.*
165. *See* Bozkurt Aran, *The Doha Development Round of International Trade Negotiations*, Ministry of Foreign Affairs, http://www.mfa.gov.tr/data/Kutuphane/yayinlar/EkonomikSorunlarDergisi/sayi30/aran.pdf (last visited Oct. 25, 2018).
166. *See The Doha round ... and round ... and round*, The Economist (Jul. 31, 2008), http://www.economist.com/node/11848592; *The Doha Round Finally Dies a Merciful Death*, Financial Times (Dec. 21, 2015), https://www.ft.com/content/9cb1ab9e-a7e2-11e5-955c-1e1d6de94879; *Global Trade After the Failure of the Doha Round*, Editorial NY Times (Jan. 1, 2016), https://www.nytimes.com/2016/01/01/opinion/global-trade-after-the-failure-of-the-doha-round.html?mcubz=3.

removal of agricultural subsidies and NAMA, have remained deadlocked.[167] On one hand, developing countries (e.g., India, China, Brazil, etc.) have demanded the removal of agricultural subsidies (e.g., crop insurance, etc.) of developed countries (mainly the European Union and United States), while, on the other, developed countries have sought to increase NAMA rights by having developing countries reduce tariffs.[168] Both parties could not reach an agreement on these negotiations, and, thus, the Round has largely failed.[169] To date, the Round has one major achievement to its credit: the conclusion of the Trade Facilitation Agreement, which improved customs procedures and made trade more transparent, easier, and cheaper.[170]

As far as Turkey is concerned, the Doha Round could produce significant results in its favor, hence its active participation.[171] Turkey's main interest in the Round's Development Agenda has been "a fair, competitive, and predictable trading environment where trade[-] (including export[-]) distorting support measures are eliminated."[172] Having liberalized trade to developed country levels, Turkey views multilateral negotiations as a vehicle to improve its export performance.

Historically, Turkey adopted a developing country posture in multilateral negotiations. In the Doha Round, however, Turkey has followed a "sui generis" approach, acting as a "middle power" that sides with developed or developing countries depending on the matter under consideration.[173] Because of Turkey's CU with the European Union, Turkish diplomacy largely reflects the EU position, particularly in NAMA negotiations.[174] In agriculture, however, Turkey has worked with the developing countries to phase out "trade-distorting-" agricultural subsidies, while voicing its support for keeping "special safeguard mechanisms for developing countries."[175]

Bound to low, EU-set industrial-good CETs, Turkey—not unlike its developed peers in the European Union—has sought lower tariffs in NAMA negotiations. Indeed, tariffs on nonagricultural imports—a category that includes industrial goods as well as leather, petroleum, other mining goods, etc.[176]—were 5.0 and 5.8 percent in 2011 and

---

167. *See* William E. Keating, *The Doha Round and Globalization: A Failure of World Economic Development?*, 40 (Aug. 24, 2015) (B.A. Dissertation, City University of New York), *available at*: http://academicworks.cuny.edu/cgi/viewcontent.cgi?article=1008&context=hc_sas_etds (last visited Oct. 25, 2018).
168. *See id.*
169. *See id.*
170. *See* Doha Development Agenda, European Commission, http://ec.europa.eu/trade/policy/eu-and-wto/doha-development-agenda/ (last visited Oct. 25, 2018).
171. *See* Akman, *supra* note 10, at 153; Turkey TPR 2012, *supra* note 150, at 14.
172. *See* Akman, *supra* note 10, at 153.
173. *Id.*, at 135, 157 & 166.
174. *Id.*, at 154.
175. *Id.*
176. We use nonagricultural instead of industrial tariffs here, because the WTO stopped compiling Member *industrial* good tariffs in 2003. We surmise this might have been motivated by the Doha Round NAMA's negotiation agenda, which bundled industrial goods with other nonagricultural goods to simplify negotiations, thus excluding only the more politically sensitive agricultural goods category.

2018, respectively.[177] While third-country imports, including developing-country imports, have benefited from greater access and lower CETs in Turkey,[178] Turkish exports have not been granted reciprocal access. Knowing that Turkey is bound to CETs, most developing countries have little incentive to lower tariffs and carry on applying MFN tariffs to Turkish products.[179] Turkey has no leverage in this regard (a topic discussed in detail in Chapter 6). Therefore, Turkey's only alternative is to coordinate with developed nations to reduce developing countries' nonagricultural tariffs.[180]

In alignment with NAMA's purposes, Turkey has proposed that: (i) all WTO Members bind nonagricultural tariffs; and (ii) developing countries reduce their simple-average bound tariffs on such products.[181] Note that Turkey bound only about one-third of its industrial good tariffs at an average 42.6 percent at the WTO, so by offering to bind the remaining two-thirds of its industrial good tariffs and to reduce its average bound MFN tariff rates, Turkey is making a seemingly significant concession.[182] Of course, this is only an apparent concession: Turkey is already bound to apply EU CETs, which, fixed at 3.9 percent in 2018 (for nonagricultural products), are already built in the system and taken for granted, as explained earlier in this chapter.[183] To be clear, so long as Turkey stays in the CU, its proposal to bind all tariff lines and reduce WTO bound tariffs amounts to "no concession" to most third countries (i.e., countries outside the European Union and with which Turkey has no FTAs, such as, Brazil, China, India, Mexico, the United States, etc.). Yet, scoring reductions in bound MFN tariffs from such countries would provide easier access for Turkey's exports, such as automobiles, textiles and clothing, machinery, household appliances, chemicals, and iron and steel.[184] Understandably, enjoying lower EU-set CETs upfront, such countries have passed on Turkey's "offer."

Although agriculture constitutes only a small portion of world trade and, thus, would be a good candidate for liberalization, its domestic political significance in most WTO Members has inhibited liberalization efforts.[185] For Turkey, with a rural population hovering around 30 percent, such negotiations are no different.[186] Still, because the EU-Turkey CU does not cover agricultural products, Turkey has more discretion (than in NAMA negotiations) to further its agricultural interests in the Doha Round. When appearing as a "developing country," Turkey has coordinated with its peers (e.g., India, Brazil, China, Indonesia, etc.) in agriculture negotiations to resist significant tariff reductions for agricultural products.[187] With them, Turkey pressed developed nations to cut domestic support and eliminate trade-distorting subsidies.[188] Not

177. Turkey TPR 2016, *supra* note 6, at 51.
178. *See* Akman, *supra* note 10, at 155.
179. *Id.*
180. *Id.*
181. *See id.*
182. *See* Appendix II, Table II.1.
183. *See* World Tariff Profiles 2019, *supra* note 97, at 88 & 178.
184. *See* Turkey TPR 2016, *supra* note 6, at 139.
185. Akman, *supra* note 10, at 158.
186. *See id.*, at 154.
187. *See id.*, at 159.
188. *Id.*, at 158.

unlike developing countries, Turkey can ill afford to provide massive government support to the agricultural sector, because of budgetary constraints.[189] Turkey's advocacy for elimination of developed-country, agricultural subsidies is also linked to its aspiration for greater agricultural exports. Its support for greater export competitiveness motivated its coordination with the European Union on eliminating export subsidies for agricultural products. Turkey's embrace of agricultural competitiveness is not complete; however, it agreed with developing countries' demand to keep a 10-percent *de minimis* requirement before subsidies are deemed WTO inconsistent. Agriculture remains, after all, a politically sensitive sector.[190]

That the Doha Round failed to solve current trade issues has contributed, partially, to Turkey's lack of success in achieving its trade objectives. Whether Turkey would be able to achieve more favorable outcomes through WTO litigation or, once freed from CU constraints, whether Turkey would have better chances of extracting trade concessions from other countries in successive bilateral negotiations are questions we attempt to answer in Chapters 5 and 6, respectively.

### *b. Turkey's Bilateral Trade Agreements*

As discussed in Chapter 3, Turkey's trade policy has been tethered to EU trade policy under the CU. To analyze Turkey's usage of bilateral trade agreements, one must examine both Turkey's commitments arising out of the application of the CU and the EU bilateral trade agenda, which Turkey must follow to comply with GATT, Article XXIV. Briefly stated, Turkey's most significant commitments can be described, thusly: (i) Article 13 of the CU Decision provides that Turkey shall apply EU-determined CETs against third-country products;[191] (ii) Article 14 requires Turkey not to impose tariffs, under any circumstance, that are lower than the mandated CETs;[192] and (iii) Article 16 prescribes that "Turkey shall align itself progressively with the preferential customs regime of the [EU] … ."[193] These three provisions have profoundly restricted Turkey's ability to offer tariff concessions in any negotiation.

Since the failure of the Doha Round, numerous countries have sought alternative ways to further their trade interests. Multilateralism has lost its luster, and bilateralism is on the rise. Thus, a commentator has stated that bilateral trade agreements have become "the rule rather than the exception"[194] in world trade. The EU trade agenda has also shifted to bilateralism.[195] The European Union has signed trade agreements with

189. *Id.*, at 159.
190. Such a rule would "provide the opportunity to give domestic support not exceeding 10 percent of the production value." *Id.*
191. *See* Decision No. 1/95 of the EC–Turkey Association Council of 22 December 1995 on implementing the final phase of the Customs Union, 96/142/EC, Art. 14, 1996 O.J. (L 035) [hereinafter CU Decision].
192. *Id.*, Art. 14.
193. *Id.*, Art. 16.
194. Canan Balkir, Europeanization of Trade Policy: An Asymmetric Track, *in The Europeanization of Turkish Public Policies: A Scorecard* 17 (Aylin Guney & Ali Tekin eds., 2016).
195. *See* Akman, *supra* note 15, at 13-14.

around 70 different countries, including Canada, Mexico, South Korea, and Japan.[196] Moreover, the European Union has been in trade negotiations with other major economies, such as the United States, MERCOSUR (e.g., Argentina, Brazil, Uruguay, etc.), and ASEAN countries (e.g., Vietnam, Singapore, Indonesia, Malaysia, etc.).[197]

Legally bound to follow the EU preferential trade regime and apply CETs, Turkey has no voice and cannot participate in the EU trade decision-making process.[198] Put simply, Turkey's "external trade relations" on industrial goods have been determined in Brussels.[199] The European Union has not granted Turkey a seat in EU bilateral trade negotiations on grounds that Turkey is not a member of the European Union.[200] The "Turkey clause," which encourages EU FTA-negotiating partners to start separate FTA negotiations with Turkey, "has no binding effect on [these] countr[ies]."[201] Such a framework has constrained Turkey's *bargaining* in direct FTA negotiations with these countries. Bound by the GATT and CU Decision, Turkey must apply substantially the same duties to countries outside the CU, regardless of what they offer in return. In an attempt to comply with these requirements and keep pace with the European Union, Turkey has signed 22 FTAs[202] and is currently engaged in negotiations with more than a dozen countries or trading blocks. These do not include four FTAs pending ratification by Parliament.[203] Moreover, Turkey has made official attempts to start FTA negotiations with 9 more countries, including the United States, Canada, and India.[204]

Turkey's challenges in these negotiations are immense, if not insurmountable. The "Turkey clause" has no binding effect on third countries, but because EU FTA partners gain automatic concessions from Turkey upon signing with the European Union, they are naturally reluctant "to make reciprocal concessions."[205] Thus, the asymmetric trade relation between Turkey and the European Union works in favor of EU FTA partners, further eroding Turkey's tariff leverage.[206] Because of this asymmetry, Turkey loses inbound tariff revenue—as EU FTA-partner products can enter duty free or at reduced tariff rates—while being unable to obtain pro-export concessions

196. Dominic Webb, *List of EU Trade Agreements*, 1 (Briefing Paper Number 7792, House of Commons Library, Feb. 28, 2019), http://researchbriefings.files.parliament.uk/documents/CBP-7792/CBP-7792.pdf.
197. Overview of FTA and other Trade Negotiations, EUROPEAN COMMISSION, http://trade.ec.europa.eu/doclib/docs/2006/december/tradoc_118238.pdf (last updated December 2018) (last visited Feb. 28, 2019).
198. Balkir, *supra* note 194, at 18.
199. Haluk Kabaalioglu, Turkey-EU Customs Union: Problems and Prospects, 12:2 DOKUZ EYLÜL ÜNIVERSITESI SOSYAL BILIMLER ENSTITÜSÜ DERGISI 47, 49 (2010).
200. *See* Akman, *supra* note 15, at 19.
201. Kabaalioglu, *supra* note 199, at 50.
202. *See Serbest Ticaret Anlaşmaları* [Free Trade Agreements], TICARET BAKANLIGI [REPUBLIC OF TURKEY DEPARTMENT OF COMMERCE], https://www.ticaret.gov.tr/dis-iliskiler/serbest-ticaret-anlasmalari (last visited Feb. 6, 2021).
203. *See* Onay Süreci Devam Eden STA'lar [FTAs Pending for Ratification], TICARET BAKANLIGI [REPUBLIC OF TURKEY DEPARTMENT OF COMMERCE], https://www.ticaret.gov.tr/dis-iliskiler/serbest-ticaret-anlasmalari/onay-sureci-devam-eden-stalar (last visited Feb. 6, 2021).
204. *See* Müzakere Süreci Devam Eden STA'lar [Ongoing FTA Negotiations], TICARET BAKANLIGI [REPUBLIC OF TURKEY DEPARTMENT OF COMMERCE], https://www.ticaret.gov.tr/dis-iliskiler/serbest-ticaret-anlasmalari/muzakere-sureci-devam-eden-stalar.
205. Balkir, *supra* note 194, at 18.
206. *Id.*

from such partners.[207] Turkey's domestic industry is also harmed by third-country products entering into Turkey duty free, or at reduced rates.[208] The Turkish export sector also faces strong competition in the EU market (most of EU FTA partners are developing countries, such as Mexico, India, Indonesia, Malaysia, etc., which export similar products to the European Union) and elsewhere (particularly in the markets of the countries that signed FTA with the European Union).[209] With so much leverage *ex ante*, EU FTA partners' main motivations to negotiate with Turkey are to reduce uncertainty (by encouraging goodwill) and maintain supply-chain stability.

The mismatch between Turkish and EU trade policies and priorities creates another significant hindrance for Turkey in FTA negotiations.[210] For instance, both European Union and Turkey want to have market access for their exporting sectors, yet their target countries, sectors, and aims are quite different. EU exports target big consuming markets (e.g., the United States, China, Japan, India, Russia), while Turkey exports target the smaller economies in its neighborhood.[211] The European Union also prioritizes market access for technology-intensive products, while Turkey seeks access for its medium-low- and medium-high-technology sectors, such as motor vehicles, electrical machinery, chemicals, etc.[212] As far as the trade in services is concerned, Turkey prioritizes tourism, transportation, and construction, while the European Union wants more access for its telecommunications, financial, and banking sectors.[213] Thus, EU and Turkey trade objectives are far from identical. Subjugation of the latter to the first, however, imposes significant costs to Turkey.

CU Decision Article 14 imposes yet another significant hurdle for Turkey concerning FTA initiation: "[u]nder no circumstances may the Customs Union Joint Committee authorize Turkey to apply a customs tariff which [sic] is lower than the Common Customs Tariff for any product."[214] This proscription hinders Turkey from independently negotiating and concluding FTAs with other countries *until* the European Union has a first crack at negotiating an FTA with them.[215] To date, Turkey has obtained only one waiver: to negotiate an FTA with North Macedonia (previously named "Macedonia") (1999).[216]

As mentioned above, unlike industrial products, Turkey retains significant WTO-flexibility in agricultural goods, for the CU does not cover such products. In fact, Turkey has used its wider tariff discretion in agriculture to obtain trade concessions on industrial goods from other countries, including Iran.[217] Furthermore, in pursuit of its geopolitical interests, Turkey has granted agricultural imports from majority-Muslim

207. *Id.*
208. *Id.*
209. *See id.*
210. Akman, *supra* note 15, at 17.
211. *Id.*
212. *Id.*, at 21-22.
213. *Id.*, at 28.
214. CU Decision, *supra* note 191, Art. 14.
215. Balkir, *supra* note 194, at 18.
216. *Id.*
217. *See* Turkey TPR 2016, *supra* note 6, at 36 (attributing Turkey's obtaining Iranian market access for 125 industrial products to its agricultural tariff leverage).

Bosnia-Herzegovina nearly duty-free access.[218] That Turkey has exercised its remaining tariff discretion on agricultural goods to pursue regional goals provides a glimpse of how a CU-free Turkey could become a dynamic trade-liberalizing player.

Thus, because of commitments arising out of the CU, Turkey's ability to negotiate FTAs and further its trade policy objectives, particularly on industrial products, is significantly limited. Turkey is not able to participate in the EU decision-making process and has no voice in the EU FTA negotiations, but is legally bound by them. The erosion of Turkey's trade discretion is only likely to increase as the European Union continues on its FTA-negotiating path.[219] The following section analyzes Turkey's efforts to attract foreign investment and expand its service sector (e.g., tourism, aviation, transportation, and energy).

### c. *Diplomatic Efforts to Attract Foreign Investment and Expand the Service Sector*

Stagnant multilateralism and restrained trade sovereignty, combined, made it impossible for Turkey's trade diplomacy to make significant progress toward achieving the country's trade goals. However, Turkey still has some cards to play: it can attract more foreign investment and expand its trade in services. Notably, Turkey successfully enlarged its diplomatic network in the last decade.[220] In 2016, it included 235 diplomatic missions, which gives Turkey the world's sixth largest diplomatic network, only surpassed by the five permanent members of the United Nations Security Council (i.e., United States, France, China, Russia, and the United Kingdom).[221]

#### i. Attracting Foreign Investment

Along with the global trade and financial liberalization of the 1980-1990 period, developed and developing countries also pursued greater FDI, hoping to increase employment, tax revenue, and growth.[222] Domestic regulation and macroeconomic and political stability play a significant role in attracting FDI.[223] In the pre-2002 period, Turkey could not attract significant FDI, because of regulatory uncertainty and instability. After the 2001 economic crisis, however, single-party, Erdoğan governments succeeded in restabilizing the economy, which restored Turkey's credibility as

---

218. *Id.*, at 55-56 (Table 3.4).
219. *See* Turkey TPR 2016, *supra* note 6, at 31-34.
220. *See* Nazli Yuzbasioglu & Sultan Cogalan, *Turkey boasts no. 6 diplomatic network in the world*, ANADOLU AGENCY (Dec. 26, 2016), *available at:* http://aa.com.tr/en/todays-headlines/turkey-boasts-no-6-diplomatic-network-in-the-world/714459.
221. *Id.*
222. Magnus Blomström & Ari Kokko, *The Economics of Foreign Direct Investment Incentives*, 2 (NBER Working Paper Series, Working Paper No. 9489, National Bureau of Economic Research, 2003), http://www.nber.org/papers/w9489.pdf.
223. *See* Burcak Polat & Cem Payaslıoglu, *Determinants of Foreign Direct Investment to Turkey: A Sectoral Approach*, 17:2 TOPICS IN MIDDLE EASTERN AND AFRICAN ECONOMIES 1, 3-9 (2014).

an investment host state.[224] In 2003, Turkey also enacted Foreign Direct Investment Law, No. 4875, whose main objective is "to encourage foreign investments [and] protect the rights of foreign investors ... ."[225] To attract more investment, Turkey also applied a broad IIP (e.g., exemptions on value-added taxes and customs duties, deductions on corporate taxes, etc.).[226]

Turkey also deployed diplomatic efforts in pursuit of greater FDI inflows. When visiting other countries, President Erdoğan usually brings a cadre of diplomats and more than 100 Turkish businesspeople, who seek to create or expand opportunities with their hosts. Partially due to these efforts, Turkey has concluded Bilateral Investment Treaties with 105 countries, including China, Japan, the Russian Federation, and the United States.[227] Moreover, the official launch of Turkey's EU accession negotiations in 2005 provided a great opportunity for Turkey to attract FDI.[228] These initiatives have turned Turkey into an FDI destination.[229] Inbound investment totaled around $217 billion between 2003 and 2019—around $13 billion per year.[230] However, the global financial crisis of 2008-2009, deterioration of the EU-Turkey relationship, greater regional instability, trade friction with the United States, and, more recently, COVID-19 all contributed to a decline in FDI inflows.[231]

As to the origin of FDI, European countries (e.g., Austria, Germany, Luxembourg, Spain, the United Kingdom, and the Netherlands) have been the major sources of investment in Turkey.[232] Between 2003 and 2019, more than 62 percent of Turkey's FDI came from EU-28 countries.[233] In the same period, Asian countries constituted less than

224. *See* Krueger, *supra* note 3, at 11-13.
225. *See* 5 Haziran 2003 Tarihli ve 4875 Sayili Dogrudan Yabanci Yatirimlar Kanunu [May 5, 2003, Law No. 4875, Foreign Direct Investment Law], Türkiye Cumhuriyeti Resmi Gazete [the Official Gazette of the Republic of Turkey], June 17, 2003 No. 25141, Art. 1 (English version *available at*: http://www.invest.gov.tr/en-US/infocenter/publications/Documents/FDI%20Law%20in%20Turkey.pdf) (last visited Oct. 25, 2018).
226. *See* Turkey TPR 2016, *supra* note 6, at 40; *see also* Section II.B.1.
227. *See* Bilateral Investment Treaties, Republic of Turkey, Ministry of Trade, https://www.trade.gov.tr/legislation/bilateral-investment-treaties (last visited Feb. 8, 2021).
228. Sebnem Kalemli-Ozcan, Miguel Eduardo & Sánchez-Martín Gilles Thirion, *A Difficult Relationship: Declining (but Productive) FDI Inflows in Turkey* 23 (Policy Research Working Paper No. 7918, the World Macroeconomics and Fiscal Management Global Practice Group December 2016).
229. *See* Turkey TPR 2016, *supra* note 6, at 24.
230. *See* FDI in Turkey, Presidency of the Republic of Turkey, Investment Office, INVEST, https://www.invest.gov.tr/en/whyturkey/pages/fdi-in-turkey.aspx (last visited Feb. 8, 2021). [hereinafter FDI in Turkey].
231. *See* Foreign direct investment, net inflows (% of GDP), Turkey, OECD, *available at*: https://data.worldbank.org/indicator/BX.KLT.DINV.WD.GD.ZS?locations=TR; Gökhan Önder & Zeynep Karal, Determinants of Foreign Direct Investments Outflow from a Developing Country: The Case of Turkey, 11:2 BUSINESS, MANAGEMENT AND EDUCATION 241, 241-243 (2013); The Office of the United States Trade Representative, Countries & Regions, Europe & Middle East, Europe, Turkey, https://ustr.gov/countries-regions/europe-middle-east/europe/turkey#:~:text=U.S.%20foreign%20direct%20investment%20(FDI,wholesale%20trade%2C%20and%20depository%20institutions (last visited Feb. 7, 2021); UNCTAD Prosperity for all, Investment flows to developing Asian countries to fall 30% to 45% due to COVID-19, says UN report, Press Release, UNCTAD/PRESS/PR/2020/018, https://unctad.org/press-material/investment-flows-developing-asian-countries-fall-30-45-due-covid-19-says-un-report (last visited Feb. 7, 2021).
232. *See* FDI in Turkey, *supra* note 230.
233. *See id.*

19 percent of Turkey's FDI inflows, while investment coming from the United States was only 7.6 percent of Turkey's total FDI inflows.[234] The latter figure shows too low a rate of US investment—an interesting area for subsequent inquiry—and indicates a major source of FDI growth for the future.

A look at different economic sectors shows that finance (e.g., commercial banking, investment banking, and insurance) led in inbound investment, receiving 33.1 percent of FDI between 2003 and 2019.[235] The manufacturing sector (e.g., computers and electronic devices, food, beverages, tobacco and chemicals, etc.) came second, with 24.4 percent.[236] Utilities (e.g., electric power generation and distribution, gas and water supply), the third-largest sector, captured 11.3 percent of FDI in the same period.[237] Because of its unique geographical location, further trade and FDI expansion would most benefit Turkey's utilities, not only finance or manufacturing, as might be the case in other countries.

### ii. Expanding Trade in Services

With a mild, Mediterranean climate, a rich history, and long coastline, Turkey is one of the world's leading tourist destinations. The sixth tourist destination in the world with over 51 million visitors and $34.5 billion revenue in 2019, Turkey has sought to attract more tourists[238] by entering into agreements with countries and lifting visa requirements. As of 2019, Turkey grants visa-free or visa-on-arrival access to citizens from more than 100 countries, including Brazil, Mexico, Iran, Japan, South Korea, and Russia, but not to US citizens, due to lack of reciprocity.[239]

In transportation, Turkey has sought to leverage its geographical location and become an aviation hub. Turkey has built the world biggest airport in Istanbul, a $28 billion investment,[240] which started operations in 2018.[241] Turkish Airlines, the national flag carrier, 49 percent owned by the state-controlled, Turkish Wealth Fund, should help Turkey become both a major aviation hub and tourism destination.[242] To

234. *See id.*
235. *See id.*; Polat & Payaslıoglu, *supra* note 223, at 12.
236. *See* FDI in Turkey, *supra* note 230.
237. *See id.*; *see also* Polat & Payaslıoglu, *supra* note 223, at 12.
238. *See* Tuba Sahin, *Turkey's tourism revenues hit $34.5B high in 2019*, ANADOLU AGENCY (Jan. 31, 2020), https://www.aa.com.tr/en/economy/-turkeys-tourism-revenues-hit-345b-high-in-2019/1719889; *Turkey named world's 6th most favorite tourism destination in 2019*, DAILY SABAH (Feb. 11, 2020), https://www.dailysabah.com/business/2020/02/11/turkey-named-worlds-6th-most-favorite-tourism-destination-in-2019.
239. *See* Visa Information for Foreigners, MINISTRY OF FOREIGN AFFAIRS, http://www.mfa.gov.tr/visa-information-for-foreigners.en.mfa.
240. Francesca Street, *Istanbul's New Airport Aims to Be One of World's Largest*, CNN TRAVEL (Oct. 31, 2018), https://www.cnn.com/travel/article/istanbul-new-airport-turkey/index.html.
241. *Id.*
242. *See* Portfolio, TURKEY WEALTH FUND, http://turkiyevarlikfonu.com.tr/EN/Portfoy/5 (last visited Feb. 28, 2019).

illustrate, Turkish Airlines flies to 306 different destinations in 124 countries, which makes it the airline "that flies to the [greatest number of] countries in the world."[243]

China's "one road, one belt" project has also played an important role in Turkey's transportation plans.[244] The ambitious Chinese project, expected to include 65 countries and cover $21 trillion in global trade,[245] will supposedly create a railroad between Beijing and London, whose route, starting from Northern China, will cross Central Asia, Turkey, and Europe.[246] The planned maritime "silk" route will allegedly connect the South China Sea, Indian Ocean, Red Sea, Mediterranean Sea and the remainder of the European coast. Turkey's strategy as a middle passageway is to become a major hub in the belt. In furtherance of this plan, Turkey has conducted significant infrastructure projects, such as the Marmaray (railroad) and Eurasia (road) tunnels under the Bosporus, two more Bridges on the Bosporus and the new airport in Istanbul.[247] Turkey also seeks to create a Kars-Edirne high-speed railroad, connecting Turkey's east and west.[248] To complete its middle corridor plan, Turkey has also collaborated with the Azerbaijani and Georgian Governments to build a railroad connecting Baku, Tbilisi, and Kars, through which any Asian cargo could reach Europe within 15 days.[249] On October 30, 2017, the Baku-Tbilisi-Kars railroad started operations. It can transport "1 million people and 6.5 million tons cargo" per year.[250] Turkey seems well positioned to take advantage of the "one road, one belt" initiative to become one of the important centers of global trade.

As far as energy is concerned, Turkey, located in the vicinity of 70 percent of the world's oil and natural gas reserves (i.e., Russia, Central Asian Countries and Middle East)[251] is both heavily dependent on energy imports and a "'natural bridge' between

243. Turkish Airlines and Oman Air extend their existing codeshare agreement Press Release Turkish Airlines (Mar. 4, 2019), https://www.turkishairlines.com/en-us/news-press-release/?p = 1.

244. *See* Tao Zan, "Turkey Dream" and the China-Turkish Cooperation under "One Belt and One Road" Initiative, 10:3 J. OF MIDDLE EASTERN AND ISLAMIC STUDIES (IN ASIA) 50, 57-63 (2016).

245. Metin Can, *Modern Silk Road a New Phase in Turkish-Chinese Ties*, DAILY SABAH (Mar. 17, 2017) https://www.dailysabah.com/economy/2017/03/17/modern-silk-road-a-new-phase-in-turkish-chinese-ties.

246. *See* Umut Ergunsu, *Belt and Road will make Turkey-China cooperation a success*, CHINA DAILY (Jul. 1, 2017), http://www.chinadaily.com.cn/opinion/2017-06/01/content_29580844.htm; Anna Bruce-Lockhart, *China's $900 billion New Silk Road. What you need to know*, WORLD ECONOMIC FORUM (Jun. 26, 2017), https://www.weforum.org/agenda/2017/06/china-new-silk-road-explainer/.

247. Erdogan: Modern Ipek Yolu Vatandaşlarımızın Hayat Standardını Artıracak, BBC NEWS / TURKCE (May 14, 2017), http://www.bbc.com/turkce/haberler-dunya-39913491.

248. *Id.*

249. Huaxia, *Turkey builds massive high-speed railway to mark centennial anniversary*, NEW CHINA (May 14, 2017), http://news.xinhuanet.com/english/2017-05/14/c_136282781.htm.

250. *Turkey, Azerbaijan and Georgia launch "Silk Road" rail link*, TRT WORLD (Oct. 30, 2017), http://www.trtworld.com/turkey/turkey-azerbaijan-and-georgia-launch-silk-road-rail-link-11789.

251. Muhammed Oral & Ünal Özdemir, *Küresel Enerji Jeopolitiginde Türkiye: Fırsatlar ve Riskler* [*Global Energy Geopolitics and Turkey: Opportunities and Risks*], 6 JOURNAL OF HISTORY CULTURE AND ART RESEARCH 948, 953 (2017).

energy producers and consumers."[252] The European Union, Turkey's Western neighbor, imports more than €1 billion in energy per day.[253] Collection of transit fees and taxes should help Turkey modernize its physical infrastructure. Becoming an energy shipment hub in Eurasia would further Turkey's interests in two "interrelated" ways.[254] First, Turkey, a net importer of oil (i.e., 93 percent) and natural gas (i.e., 99 percent),[255] would benefit from diversifying its supply of energy.[256] Second, by becoming a major hub, Turkey would help Europe become less dependent on one single supplier, namely Russia.[257] Oil and natural gas transshipments from the Middle East and Central Asia through Turkey would be a win-win solution for Turkey and the European Union.

Four pipelines supply Turkey's domestic demand: (1) the Russia-Turkey Natural Gas Pipeline (West Line); (2) the Russia-Turkey Blue Stream Gas Pipeline; (3) the Iran-Turkey Eastern Anatolian Natural Gas Pipeline; and (4) the Azerbaijan-Turkey Baku-Tbilisi-Erzurum Natural Gas Pipeline.[258] Turkey imports gas from these countries to meet domestic demand while also exporting the remaining of the imported gas to Greece through the Turkey-Greece Natural Gas Interconnection.[259] Two through-pipelines—i.e., pipelines that do not supply Turkey's domestic network—complete Turkey's energy transportation architecture: (1) the Baku-Tbilisi-Ceyhan ("BTC") Pipeline; and (2) the Iraq-Turkey Pipeline ("ITP").[260] The BTC pipeline has brought Asian (particularly Azeri) crude oil from Shah Deniz Phase (Baku) through Tbilisi (Georgia) to Ceyhan Marine Terminal (Turkey) since 2006.[261] The ITP has brought crude oil from Iraq to Ceyhan (Turkey) since 1977. In 2010, Turkey and Iraq extended the oil transit contract for 15 more years.[262] Furthermore, the Iraq-Kurdistan Regional Government also connected a new pipeline to the ITP, transferring Kirkuk crude oil to Ceyhan Marine Terminal in Turkey.[263] Thus, crude oil coming from Azerbaijan and Iraq is shipped to world markets via Turkey.[264]

252. Diyar Guldogan & Handan Kazanci, *Turkey a "bridge" between energy producers, consumers*, ANADOLU AGENCY (Jul. 10, 2017), http://aa.com.tr/en/corporate-news/turkey-a-bridge-between-energy-producers-consumers/858082 (quoting President Erdogan).
253. Energy, Energy Security, EUROPEAN COMMISSION, https://ec.europa.eu/energy/en/topics/imports-and-secure-supplies (last visited Feb. 28, 2019).
254. Madeleine K. Albright & Stephen J. Hadley, *U.S.-Turkey Relations a New Partnership* 33 (Project Director Independent Task Force Report No. 69, 2012).
255. Oral & Özdemir, *supra* note 251, at 954.
256. *Id.*
257. *Id.*
258. Natural Gas Pipelines and Projects, MINISTRY OF ENERGY, http://www.enerji.gov.tr/en-US/Pages/Natural-Gas-Pipelines-and-Projects (last visited Feb. 28, 2019).
259. *Id.*
260. These pipelines are operated by BOTAS.
261. Natural Gas Pipelines and Projects, *supra* note 258.
262. *See* Energy Policies of International Energy Agency (IEA) Countries 2016 Review, Turkey, 81, https://www.iea.org/publications/freepublications/publication/EnergyPoliciesofIEACountriesTurkey.pdf (2016) [hereinafter IEA Turkey Report].
263. *Id.*
264. *Id.*, at 82.

In addition to these pipelines, Turkey has new pipeline projects. One of them is the Trans-Anatolian Natural Gas Pipeline ("TANAP") connection with the Trans-Adriatic Pipeline ("TAP"), whose combined aim is to bring Azeri natural gas to European markets via Turkey.[265] TANAP, the first stage of the connection, started operating in 2018 and transfers natural gas from Shah Deniz Phase II (Azerbaijan), through Georgia, to Turkey.[266] Turkey has also built a 1,850 km pipeline from the border of Georgia to the border of Greece to transfer natural gas to European Markets.[267] TAP, the second stage of the connection, begins at the Turkey-Greece border and convey Caspian natural gas (i.e., coming from Azerbaijan to Turkey, via TANAP) to European markets, crossing Greece, Albania, the Adriatic Sea, then, finally reaching Southern Italy.[268] Turkey is also encouraging Kazakhstan, Turkmenistan and Azerbaijan to collaborate on a second major pipeline.[269] This project would convey natural gas from Kazakhstan and Turkmenistan to Azerbaijan under the Caspian Sea. As a result, Kazak and Turkmen natural gas might also be transferred to Europe by using the TANAP-TAP connection, by way of Turkey.[270]

Furthermore, the TurkStream Gas Pipeline Project, a Russia-Turkey initiative,[271] would deliver Russian natural gas to Turkey's northwestern coast under the Black Sea and, then, all the way to European markets.[272] Turkey's initial objective is, obviously, to secure its natural gas supply, which could be jeopardized as a result of the Russia-Ukraine dispute over Crimea.[273] TurkStream would also help Russia bypass Ukraine and reach both Turkish and European markets.[274] Finally, Turkey has been involved in developing its own natural gas in the Black Sea and Eastern Mediterranean Sea.[275] Regardless of Turkey's success in finding gas in the Mediterranean Sea, Turkey is likely to also coordinate with Israel in building an undersea gas pipeline for shipment of Mediterranean-extracted, Israeli natural gas (Tamar and Leviathan gas fields) to

265. *See Turkey opens natural gas pipeline from Azerbaijan*, REUTERS (Jun. 12, 2018), https://www.reuters.com/article/energy-turkey-tanap-idAFL8N1TE5BE; Arye Gut, *Trans-Anatolian gas pipeline (TANAP) will bring Azerbaijan gas resources to Europe*, THE JERUSALEM POST (Jun. 21, 2018), https://www.jpost.com/Blogs/News-from-Arye-Gut/Trans-Anatolian-gas-pipeline-TANAP-will-bring-Azerbaijan-gas-resources-to-Europe-560036.
266. Natural Gas Pipelines and Projects, *supra* note 258.
267. Trans-Anatolian Natural Gas Pipeline Project, Why TANAP, http://www.tanap.com/tanap-project/why-tanap/ (last visited Feb. 28, 2019).
268. *See* Trans-Adriatic Pipeline, TAP at a Glance, https://www.tap-ag.com/the-pipeline (last visited Jan. 10, 2021).
269. *See* IEA Turkey Report, *supra* note 262, at 112.
270. *See id.*
271. *See* Natural Gas Pipelines and Projects, *supra* note 258.
272. *Id.*
273. *Id.* Note that Turkey imports 55 percent of its energy from Russia. Cüneyt Kazokoglu, *Rusya, Türk Akımı için neden bastırdı?*, BBC NEWS / TURKCE (Oct. 11, 2016), http://www.bbc.com/turkce/haberler-turkiye-37619204.
274. Kazokoglu, *supra* note 273.
275. *See* Reuters Staff, *Turkey lifts Black Sea gas field estimate after new find: Erdogan*, REUTERS (Oct. 17, 2020), https://www.reuters.com/article/us-turkey-energy-blacksea-idUSKBN2720LC; Can Sezer, *Turkish ship to drill for oil and gas in Mediterranean: minister*, REUTERS (Oct. 30, 2018), https://www.reuters.com/article/us-turkey-cyprus/turkish-ship-to-drill-for-oil-and-gas-in-mediterranean-minister-idUSKCN1N41LC.

Turkey.[276] Israel's Energy Minister, Yuval Steinitz observed that Israeli natural gas could also be delivered to the Balkans and Europe by using Turkey's pipeline system.[277] According to him, building a "natural gas pipeline from Israel to Turkey is a *high priority* for [Israel]."[278]

Thus, Turkey's project of becoming an energy shipment hub is now a reality, one that is under fast, sustained expansion. When fully developed, Turkey's regional and global role on energy distribution will grow. Greater pipeline investment in Turkey is already creating more jobs and raising revenue in the form of taxes and transit fees.[279] Notably, these projects have enabled Turkey to secure its domestic pipelines and improve its relations with neighbors, such as Azerbaijan, Russia, Iraq, the European Union, and, eventually, Israel—thus creating favorable conditions for further diplomatic success. Yet, Turkey still needs to work on increasing storage capacity, enacting an investor-friendly regulatory framework and decreasing regional instability.[280]

### *d. Making Sense of Turkey's Trade Toolkit*

Turkey's use of diplomacy has been constrained because of its commitments arising out of the CU and the failure of multilateral trade negotiations. Despite these constraints, Turkish diplomacy has attempted to leverage the country's natural resources and geostrategic location, by attracting FDI and expanding trade in the form of tourism, transportation, and energy. This multilateral, multisector approach is promising given Turkey's unique geographical location. Another tool that Turkey has deployed to further its economic interest is engagement with the WTO dispute settlement system, the subject of a more comprehensive and deeper analysis in Chapter 5. In conclusion, since 2002, Turkey has used varied trade policy tools (e.g., export promotion, import management, diplomacy and trade litigation) to improve chances of achieving its trade policy objectives, namely reducing trade and current account deficits, reducing import dependency on intermediate goods, and expanding exports and diversifying export destinations. The following section briefly analyzes some specific trade challenges Turkey has faced since 2002.

## III. TURKEY'S TRADE CHALLENGES (2002-PRESENT)

Turkey has faced four major political-economic challenges in the last two decades: (1) global macroeconomic instability (e.g., the Global Recession, Eurozone Crisis, etc.); (2) asymmetric relations with the European Union; (3) regional instability; and (4)

276. Money Talks: Israel's gas plan in Turkey-TRT World, YouTube (Jan. 23, 2017), https://www.youtube.com/watch?v=eYxQNgL3nlo.
277. *Id.*
278. *Id.*
279. *See* Harun Bal & Ali E. Alper, Baku-Tiflis-Ceyhan Petrol Boru Hatti ve Turkiye Ekonomisine Etkileri [The Effects of Baku-Tiblisi-Ceyhan Pipeline on Turkey's Economy], 19:3 Ç.Ü. Sosyal Bilimler Enstitüsü Dergisi 354, 351 (2010).
280. IEA Turkey Report, *supra* note 262, at 118.

domestic economic and political turmoil. The subsections below explain how these challenges have affected Turkey's ability to further its trade objectives.

## A. Global Macroeconomic Instability

Adverse global economic developments, such as the 2008-2011 Global Recession, are mostly exogenous to Turkey. Because Turkey runs an open economy with a high current account deficit, global economic developments can directly affect FDI inflows, growth, trade policy, and trade performance.[281] For instance, the Global Recession, starting in 2008, caused an "unprecedented decline in foreign demand,"[282] which decreased Turkey's exports from $132 to $102 billion between 2008 and 2009.[283] Imports also decreased from $201 to $140 billion in the same period.[284] As a result of the significant decline in foreign trade, Turkey's GDP fell 5 percent, while the unemployment rate rose from 11 to 14 percent in 2009.[285]

The 2009 Eurozone crisis, a sovereign debt crisis, followed by euro-US dollar depreciation also affected Turkey's trade with the European Union.[286] To illustrate, Turkey's exports to the EU-28 declined from $62 to $59 billion (5.1 percent) between 2011 and 2012.[287] However, Turkey's total export volume *increased* from $134 to $152 billion (13 percent), in the same period.[288] Although the Eurozone crisis harmed the Turkish economy, Turkey was able to find alternative markets (e.g., Middle East) for its exports, because it has an open economy that allows it to mitigate eventual bilateral trade setbacks.[289]

## B. Growing Asymmetries with the European Union

Turkey's second trade policy challenge is the uncertainty resulting from its asymmetric relation with the European Union.[290] As noted before, Westernization has been a priority for Turkey, which has sought to become a member of the *growing* EU (that is, until Brexit) since 1959.[291] Turkey officially applied for EU membership in 1987, which the European Union rejected. This led to negotiations, which concluded with Turkey settling for a CU in 1996. Turkey viewed the CU as an important step for future membership, so it accepted quite asymmetric conditions, such as having to follow EU trade policy without participating in the EU trade decision-making process.[292]

281. *See* Turkey TPR 2016, *supra* note 6, at 10.
282. Turkey TPR 2012, *supra* note 150, at 1.
283. *See* Appendix I.
284. *Id.*
285. *See* Appendix I; Turkey TPR 2012, *supra* note 150, at 2.
286. *See* Turkey TPR 2016, *supra* note 6, at 21.
287. *See* TSI Exports by Country Group and Year, *supra* note 37.
288. *Id.*
289. *Id.*
290. *See* Chapter 4, Section II.B.2.c.
291. Referring the European institutions.
292. *See* Chapter 3, Section III.B.2.b.

Following CU establishment and protracted negotiations to address resistance from some EU Members, Turkey received its "candidate status" in 1999. Six years later, Turkey persuaded the European Union to begin accession negotiations.[293] Despite an early, positive atmosphere, these negotiations—spread over 35 different chapters, including free movement of workers, external relations, transport policy, judiciary and fundamental rights[294]—stalled in the mid-2000s.[295] In fact, since 2006, the EU Council has blocked eight chapters, related to concerns over Turkey's restrictions on Cyprus.[296] A few years later, Southern Cyprus[297] also "unilaterally" blocked six more chapters, including free movement of people and energy; and security and defense policy.[298] As of July 2019, 16 out of 35 chapters remained open for negotiations, while only one chapter was "provisionally" concluded (i.e., Chapter 25: Science and Research).[299] As a result, while the European Union has embarked on an enlargement campaign that has seen 13 new countries join the Union,[300] Turkey remains excluded.[301]

In 2015, concerned with the possibility of losing control over the flow of Middle Eastern and South-Central Asian refugees, and seeking to ensure Turkey would continue accepting Syrian refugees, EU officials embarked on an effort to improve their relationship with Turkey.[302] The host of more than three million refugees from Syria, Iraq, and other Asian countries, Turkey seized this opportunity to restart its frozen relations with the European Union.[303] Soon, both Parties reached an agreement: Turkey agreed to stop refugee flows in the Aegean Sea and host those who had reached the Greek islands,[304] while the European Union promised to take the same amount of refugees, but only after selecting among the most educated, and who had also passed strict background verification.[305] The European Union also agreed to: (i) give Turkey € 6 billion to defray a portion of Turkey's refugee-hosting expenses;[306] (ii) expand

293. Selim Yenel, *Resetting the Turkey-EU Relationship,* 16:1 TURKISH POL'Y Q. 29, 30-31 (2017).
294. Current Situation, DIRECTORATE FOR EU AFFAIRS, ORGANIZATION, DIRECTORATE FOR ACCESSION POLICY, *available at*: https://www.ab.gov.tr/65_en.html (last visited Oct. 25, 2018).
295. Yenel, *supra* note 293, at 31.
296. Current Situation, *supra* note 294.
297. Cyprus, the biggest island in the Mediterranean Sea, has been divided into two portions: the Northern Cyprus and Southern Cyprus. The European Union controversially recognizes Southern Cyprus as Cyprus and accepted it as an EU Member.
298. Current Situation, *supra* note 294.
299. *Id.*
300. Ten countries (2004), Romania and Bulgaria (2007) and Croatia (2013). *See European Neighbourhood Policy and Enlargement Negotiations, From 6 to 28 members*, EUROPEAN COMMISSION (last updated Jun. 03, 2017), https://ec.europa.eu/neighbourhood-enlargement/policy/from-6-to-28-members_en.
301. Yenel, *supra* note 293, at 31.
302. *See* Tuncay Sahin, *How does the EU-Turkey refugee deal work?*, TRT WORLD (Oct. 24, 2017), https://www.trtworld.com/turkey/how-does-the-eu-turkey-refugee-deal-work--11588.
303. Yenel, *supra* note 293, at 33.
304. *See* Sahin, *supra* note 302.
305. Patrick Kingsley, *Refugee crisis: What does the EU's deal with Turkey mean?*, THE GUARDIAN (Mar. 18, 2016 14.14 EDT), https://www.theguardian.com/world/2016/mar/18/eu-deal-turkey-migrants-refugees-q-and-a.
306. *Id.*

visa-free travel to Turks; (iii) speed up Turkey's accession negotiations; and (iv) upgrade the CU.[307]

According to EU authorities, the flow of unverified refugees to Europe dropped dramatically.[308] Thanks to Turkey's coordinated efforts in the Aegean Sea, thousands of refugees were rescued.[309] To date, the European Union has yet to expand visa-free travel to Turkish citizens and provide the final half of the promised €6 billion reimbursement for Turkey's refugee-related expenses. Worse yet, the European Union has refused to update the CU, and Turkey's accession process remains blocked. Again, EU officials seem to realize that the accession carrot is all it needs to waive to obtain further concessions from Turkey. Arguably, this negotiating behavior is likely to continue so long as Turkey's negotiators sign agreements that bestow, upfront, benefits to the European Union in exchange for undated or opaque promises.

In fact, since the failed coup attempt in July 2016, EU-Turkey relations have deteriorated. To Turkish officials, the European Union's delayed reaction in denouncing those who attempted the coup against Erdoğan's democratically elected government was most concerning.[310] The 2017 Constitutional Referendum also increased tensions between the European Union and Turkey. Because Turkey has millions of registered electors in the European Union, most Turkish political parties sought to campaign in EU-member countries. The Netherlands, Austria, and Germany did not allow rallies for "yes" (i.e., pro-constitutional reform) campaigners.[311] Yet, "no" campaigners (i.e., Erdoğan opposition) were welcomed by those countries.[312] Finally, tensions escalated after Dutch authorities refused granting landing permission to the plane carrying Turkey's Minister of Foreign Affairs. The Minister had planned meetings with Turkish expatriates in Dutch soil. In response, President Erdoğan used highly inflammatory language to condemn what he perceived as discriminatory, partisan action.[313] Since then, conduct and statements by both sides have further deteriorated EU-Turkey relations. Matters got appreciably worse when the EU Parliament voted to

307. Lesley Dudden & Kadir Ustun, *EU-Turkey Refugee Agreement: Too Big to Fail* 9 (Analysis No. 34, SETA-Foundation for Political, Economic and Social Research, 2017), http://setadc.org/wp-content/uploads/2017/06/Report_34_EUTurkey_Refugee_Agreement-1-1.pdf.

308. *Id.*

309. News Release-Fewer migrants at EU borders in 2016, FRONTEX (EUROPEAN BORDER AND COAST GUARD AGENCY) (Jan. 6, 2017), http://frontex.europa.eu/news/fewer-migrants-at-eu-borders-in-2016-HWnC1J.

310. Yenel, *supra* note 293, at 33.

311. *See Turkey Rallies Row: Germany and Netherlands Harden Stance*, BBC NEWS (Mar. 12, 2017), https://www.bbc.com/news/world-europe-39251216; *Former Main Opposition CHP Chair Cancels Meeting in Germany*, HÜRRIYET DAILY NEWS (Mar. 5, 2017), http://www.hurriyetdailynews.com/former-main-opposition-chp-chair-cancels-meeting-in-germany-110453.

312. *See Germany allows "No" meeting for CHP politician 2 days after bans on Turkish ministers*, DAILY SABAH (Mar. 4, 2017), https://www.dailysabah.com/eu-affairs/2017/03/04/germany-allows-no-meeting-for-chp-politician-2-days-after-bans-on-turkish-ministers. Note that some opposition leaders decided not to attend their political meetings held in these countries to protest this double standard..

313. Lizzie Dearden & Harriet Agerholm, *Erdogan calls Dutch government "Nazis" after Turkish foreign minister's plane prevented from landing in Netherlands*, INDEPENDENT (Mar. 11, 2017), http://www.independent.co.uk/news/world/europe/netherlands-withdraw-permission-turkish-foreign-minister-mevlet-cavusoglu-plane-landing-rotterdam-a7624246.html.

suspend accession talks with Turkey in July 2017.[314] In June 2018, the European Union also suspended earlier negotiations to alleviate asymmetries within the CU itself, such as giving Turkey a seat in future EU-initiated FTA negotiations, an issue that had been a part of the previously proposed CU-modernizing package.[315]

In sum, Turkey's EU accession process remains deadlocked. Facing EU rejection and CU-based constraints, Turkey has sought a CU update, which has not materialized and whose prospects are dim. Given the remaining impasse and Turkey's need to address its trade challenges, we propose a significant, forward-looking alternative in Chapter 6.

## C. Regional Instability

Perennial regional instability has been a third trade policy challenge for Turkey. Since 2002, Turkey has adopted a so-called zero-problem-with-neighbors policy, aiming to expand trade relations with Russia, Armenia, Iran, and other neighboring countries. For instance, former President Abdullah Gul's visit to Armenia in 2008 was a historical step toward restarting diplomatic and economic relations.[316] However, since the Arab Spring (starting in 2010), regional instability has increased. Popular movements overthrew the governments of Tunisia, Libya, and Egypt.[317] As of January 2021, armed conflict is still ongoing in Libya, Yemen, Syria, and Iraq. Hundreds of thousands were also killed while millions were forced to abandon their lands.[318] Failed states or weakened governments are common in the region. Terrorist organizations, such as DEASH, also known as ISIS, Hezbollah, and the PKK also grew in the absence of state power, increasing instability in the region.[319] According to UN estimates, regional

314. *See* European Parliament/Legislative Observatory, 2016/2308(INI)—06/07/2017, *Text adopted by Parliament, single reading, available at*: http://www.europarl.europa.eu/oeil/popups/summary.do?id = 1497554&t = e&l = en. The EU Parliament acted in the same manner in 2019 as well, *see* Viktor Almqvist, *Parliament Wants to Suspend EU Accession Negotiations with Turkey*, Press Releases, EUROPEAN PARLIAMENT NEWS (Mar. 13, 2019), http://www.europarl.europa.eu/news/en/press-room/20190307IPR30746/parliament-wants-to-suspend-eu-accession-negotiations-with-turkey.

315. *See* Council of the European Union, *Enlargement and Stabilisation and Association Process—Council Conclusions*, Doc. No. 10555/18, para. 35 (Jun. 26, 2018), http://www.Consilium.europa.eu/media/35863/st10555-en18.pdf (stating that "Turkey has been moving farther away from the European Union" and that "no further chapters can be considered for opening or closing and no further work toward the moderni[z]ation of the EU-Turkey Customs Union is foreseen").

316. *See Gul in landmark visit to Armenia*, BBC NEWS (Sept. 6, 2008), http://news.bbc.co.uk/2/hi/europe/7602066.stm; Paul de Bendern & Hasmik Mkrtchyan, *Soccer diplomacy brings Turkey's Gul to Armenia*, REUTERS (Sept. 6, 2008), http://www.reuters.com/article/us-armenia-turkey/soccer-diplomacy-brings-turkeys-gul-to-armenia-idUSL634500720080907.

317. *The Arab Spring: A Year of Revolution*, NPR (Dec. 17, 2011), http://www.npr.org/2011/12/17/143897126/the-arab-spring-a-year-of-revolution; Primoz Manfreda, *Arab Spring Impact on the Middle East How Did the Uprisings of 2011 Change the Region?* (Jun. 26, 2018), https://www.thoughtco.com/arab-spring-impact-on-middle-east-2353038.

318. Syria Events of 2016, HUMAN RIGHTS WATCH, https://www.hrw.org/world-report/2017/country-chapters/syria (last visited Feb. 27, 2019).

319. DAESH is an acronym of al-Dawla al-Islamiya fi al-Iraq wa al-Sham, while ISIS is the Islamic State in Iraq and Syria. *See* Becky Pemberton & Patrick Knox, *What does ISIS stand for, what*

turmoil cost about $600 billion or 6 percent of regional growth, in the 2011-2015 period.[320]

These developments affected Turkey in several ways. Since 2011, Turkey has had to open its borders to Syrian and Iraqi war refugees. As of this writing, Turkey is a safe haven for more than 4 million displaced people[321] (3.6 million of them being from Syria), which makes Turkey the biggest refugee host in the world.[322] Notably, according to Turkish officials, Turkey has spent about $30 billion to manage the refugee crisis between 2011 and 2017.[323]

During this period Turkey has also lost a big portion of its former trade. For instance, in 2011, Turkey suspended its FTA with Syria because of the Assad regime violence against civilians.[324] As a result, Turkey's exports to Syria decreased from $1.8 billion to $0.4 billion between 2010 and 2012.[325] Moreover, Turkey faced terrorist attacks by Al Qaida, DEASH (known in the West as "ISIS," or the Islamic State of Iraq and Syria) and Kurdistan Worker's Party ("PKK") affiliates, who filled the power vacuum in the region and are still able to cross the 911-kilometer Turkish-Syrian border. These terrorist attacks caused thousands of deaths and injuries. Main targets were tourist attractions (e.g., Sultanahmet district (2016), a famous nightclub (2017), a stadium (2016), etc.), wedding ceremonies, political gatherings, and, most notably,

---

*does Daesh mean and what is the right name for the terrorist organisation?*, THE SUN (Feb. 14 2019), https://www.thesun.co.uk/news/2595042/isis-islamic-state-daesh-terrorist-group/.

320. *See ESCWA: "Arab Spring" cost Middle East economies $614bn*, ALJAZEERA (Nov. 11, 2016), http://www.aljazeera.com/news/2016/11/escwa-arab-spring-cost-middle-east-economies-600bn-161111034453699.html; *Arab Spring "cost region $600bn" in lost growth, UN says*, BBC NEWS (Nov. 11, 2016), http://www.bbc.com/news/world-middle-east-37945757.

321. *See Turkey Hosts Largest Number of Refugees Worldwide*, UNITED NATIONS POPULATION FUND (Oct. 5, 2019), https://www.unfpa.org/sites/default/files/resource-pdf/19-255-MHPSS-Case-TURKEY-2019-10-04-1711.pdf; Sevil Erkus, *Migrants Day: Turkey hosts largest number of refugees in the world*, HÜRRIYET DAILY NEWS (Dec. 18, 2018), http://www.hurriyetdailynews.com/migrants-day-turkey-hosts-largest-number-of-refugees-in-the-world-139803; Selcan Hacaoglu, *A Flood of Refugees Tests Turkey's Tolerance*, BLOOMBERG BUSINESSWEEK (Dec. 12, 2018), https://www.bloomberg.com/news/features/2018-12-12/an-endless-flood-of-syrian-refugees-tests-turkey-s-tolerance.

322. *See Syria Refugee Crisis Explained*, UNHCR (Feb. 5, 2021), https://www.unrefugees.org/news/syria-refugee-crisis explained/#: ~ :text = Turkey%20alone%20hosts%20the%20largest,percent%20living%20in%20refugee%20camps; Which countries host the most refugees?; UNITED NATIONS HIGH COMMISSIONER FOR REFUGEES (Feb. 27, 2017), http://www.unhcr.org/en-us/news/videos/2017/2/58b3f4714/which-countries-host-the-most-refugeesquest.html.

323. *Turkey spends $30 billion on Syrian refugees: FM*, HÜRRIYET DAILY NEWS (Nov. 06, 2017), http://www.hurriyetdailynews.com/turkey-to-continue-responding-to-humanitarian-crises-121982.

324. Can Sezer, *Turkey shrugs off Syria free trade suspension*, REUTERS (Dec. 5, 2011), http://in.reuters.com/article/turkey-syria-trade/turkey-shrugs-off-syria-free-trade-suspension-idINDEE7B40FW20111205.

325. *See* Türkiye ile Ticaret, Genel Durum [Trade with Turkey, General Situation], TURKIYE CUMHURIYETI TICARET BAKANLIGI [REPUBLIC OF TURKEY, MINISTRY OF TRADE] (Aug. 31 2018), https://ticaret.gov.tr/yurtdisi-teskilati/orta-dogu-ve-korfez/suriye/ulke-profili/turkiye-ile-ticaret.

Ataturk Airport in Istanbul (2016).[326] Such attacks have reduced Turkey's attractiveness to foreign tourists and may have affected FDI inflows.[327] Not uncoupled from and much like trade, regional instability has required the use of scarce resources and much diplomacy.

## D. Domestic Economic and Political Turmoil

Maintaining domestic economic stability has been another significant challenge. Under single-party, JDP rule since 2002,[328] Turkey has faced domestic political crises, which have threatened macroeconomic performance and trade. The most recent and serious one occurred on July 15, 2016: militants belonging to the Fetullah Gülen Terrorist Organization attempted a military coup that involved kidnapping and/or assassinating President Erdoğan. Turks took the streets, stopped the tanks, took back occupied public spaces, and courageously disrupted the coup plot.[329] The majority of Turks, regardless of political orientation, acted decisively in defense of Turkish democracy. Most coup plotters were captured and arrested, while some escaped to Greece.[330]

The foiled military coup attempt has directly affected the Turkish economy, damaging its creditworthiness. Only five days after the failed coup attempt, Standard & Poor's "downgraded" Turkey's credit score from BB + to BB, with other rating agencies (e.g., Moody's, Fitch, etc.) moving in the same direction.[331] Foreign capital inflows fell by 50 percent, while capital outflows *doubled* in 2016, resulting in a forced lira depreciation against the dollar and euro.[332] In the week following the coup attempt, the Istanbul Stock Exchange Index dropped 18 percent.[333]

The disruption resulting from the July 2016 coup attempt affected trade, which fell by more than 10 percent that month.[334] Tourism also dropped 30 percent, and Turkey lost around $8 billion in tourism revenue during the year.[335] Turkey's GDP contracted by 1.3 percent in the third quarter, the first GDP contraction since 2009.[336] However, growth quickly resumed in late 2016 and reached near five percent per

326. *See* Hugh Morris, *Is Turkey safe for tourists and can I cancel my holiday?*, The Telegraph (Feb. 3, 2017), http://www.telegraph.co.uk/travel/advice/is-turkey-safe-for-tourists/.
327. Such as the Government of the United Kingdom warning their citizens not to visit Turkey since it had high-security risks. *See id.*
328. Except for a five-month period in 2015. *See Turkey in review 2015*, Hürriyet Daily News (Jan. 1, 2016), http://www.hurriyetdailynews.com/turkey-in-review-2015-93313.
329. Ali Osman Mert, *15 July Coup Attempt and The Parallel State Structure, Turkish Presidency Department of Corporate Communications*, 18 (2016), https://www.tccb.gov.tr/assets/dosya/15Temmuz/15temmuz_en2.pdf.
330. Constantinos Georgizas, *Turkey Angered as Greece Blocks Extradition of Soldiers over Coup Attempt*, Independent (Jan. 26, 2017), http://www.independent.co.uk/news/world/europe/greece-turkey-coup-attempt-soldiers-extradition-recep-tayyip-erdogan-a7548256.html.
331. Levent Aydın, *Economic Implications of Fethullahist Terrorist Organization and Parallel State Constitution on Turkish Economy*, 9:3 Research in Applied Economics 31, 35-36 (2017).
332. *Id.*
333. *Id.*, at 40.
334. *Id.*, at 36.
335. *Id.*, at 34.
336. *Id.*, at 33.

quarter the following year.[337] Thus, domestic political turmoil, terrorism-related, or otherwise has been an unfortunate drag on Turkey's economy and trade. Billions of dollars were allocated to fight the PKK and DEASH.

As a middle-income country with high current account and trade deficits, Turkey has sought to put its own house in order. To maintain and further stability, Turkey must strengthen its secular institutions to keep any group (religious or otherwise) from capturing its politics and undermining its democracy. Turkey must also strive to root out terrorism and decrease regional instability. Yet, the political and economic benefits from success in these three areas will not materialize fully unless the government adopts pro-growth changes to regulatory, fiscal, and trade policies. We now discuss the Turkey's *trade* performance since 2002—a prelude to further analysis of what might have to change in this domain for Turkey to succeed in the next decade.

## IV. TURKEY'S 2002-2019 TRADE PERFORMANCE

Following the economic crisis of 2001, successive governments stabilized the economy by decreasing inflation to single digits, applying major privatization programs, stabilizing the lira,[338] and reforming the tax and fiscal systems.[339] This positive economic environment helped Turkish exporters benefit from lower foreign barriers under the CU and WTO regimes. The following subsections provide an analysis of Turkey's export, import, and macroeconomic performance in the 2002-2019 period.

### A. Export Performance

Turkey's exports increased over fourfold between 2002 and 2019. However, export volumes fluctuated much in this period. Thus, Turkey's export performance went through four different periods: (1) the 2002-2008 export boom; (2) the 2008-2010 Global Recession; (3) the 2011-2014 recovery period; and (4) the 2015-2020 period, where international and domestic instability returned and affected Turkey's export performance.[340] From 2002 to 2008, Turkey experienced a "dramatic export boom," with exports increasing from $36 to $132 billion or growing "by 265 percent."[341] Macroeconomic stability, lira depreciation, and lower trade barriers, resulting from CU

337. *See* Turkish Statistical Institute, Press Release, Quarterly Gross Domestic Product, Quarter IV: October-December, 2017, Press Release No. 27825, TURKISH STATISTICAL INSTITUTE (Mar. 29, 2018), *available at*: http://www.turkstat.gov.tr/PreHaberBultenleri.do?id=27825 [hereinafter TSI-Press Release].
338. Tolga Cebeci & Ana M. Fernandes, *Micro Dynamics of Turkey's Export Boom in the 2000s*, 3 (Policy Research Working Paper No. 6452, the World Bank Development Research Group, Trade and Integration Team, 2013).
339. Krueger, *supra* note 3, at 3 & 11.
340. Although the writers offer three categories in their paper, we include one more because of the current fluctuation in the 2015-2018 period. *See* Cebeci & Fernandes, *supra* note 338.
341. *See id.*, at 2.

and WTO membership, led to greater FDI and modernization that contributed to making Turkish products more competitive in world trade markets.[342]

The 2008-2010 Global Recession caused an "unprecedented decline in foreign demand,"[343] which adversely affected Turkey's industrial production, GDP, and employment.[344] Decreasing global demand and a gradual lira appreciation in mid-2009 reduced Turkish exporters' ability to compete in foreign markets.[345] Export volume decreased from $132 billion in 2008 to $102 billion in 2009.[346] Exports slightly increased in 2010 ($113 billion), but failed to return to the export-boom level of 2008.[347]

The adverse effects of the Global Recession withered in the 2011-2014 period, however. Exports recovered and finally exceeded their pre-recession level in 2011 ($134 billion).[348] Turkish exports to EU markets would decline in 2012 and 2013, as both the dollar and lira appreciated against the euro, because of the Eurozone Crisis.[349] Turkish businesses succeeded in finding alternative markets (e.g., Middle East and Northern Africa) to make up that decline and even increased exports.[350] In fact, exports grew to their highest level in 2014, totaling $157 billion.[351]

The more recent period (i.e., 2015-2020) has been marked by lira depreciation and some export volatility. Although the dollar appreciated from 2014 to 2016 (i.e., from ₺2.17 to ₺3.51),[352] exports fell from $157 billion to $142 billion in the same period, a 9 percent decline.[353] After 2016, however, Turkey, payed a price for the return of instability—to wit, the military coup attempt, terrorism, the Syrian Civil War and diplomatic friction with the United States—and, thus, saw the lira devaluate, sharply. The dollar appreciated to ₺7.07 by February 2021.[354] Turkish exporters benefitted from lira depreciation, again. Exports increased from $142 billion in 2016 to $167 and $171

342. *Id.*, at 3.
343. Turkey TPR 2012, *supra* note 150, at 1.
344. Dani Rodrik, the Turkish Economy after the Global Financial Crisis, 1:1 EKONOMI-TEK 41, 47 (2012).
345. *Id.*; CRAIG K. ELWELL, CONG. RESEARCH SERV., RL34582, THE DEPRECIATING DOLLAR: ECONOMIC EFFECTS AND POLICY RESPONSE 1 (2012); Eren Erdogan, Osman Nuri Aeas Mustafa Ozturk, *Does Overvalued Turkish Lira Affect Turkey's Foreign Trade Competitiveness?* 4:2 INT'L J. OF SOCIAL SCIENCES AND HUMANITY STUD. (2012).
346. *See* Appendix I.
347. *Id.*
348. *Id.*
349. *See* Turkey TPR 2016, *supra* note 6, at 21.
350. *See* TSI Exports by Country Group and Year, *supra* note 37.
351. *See* Appendix I.
352. *Indicative Exchange Rates Announced at 15:30 on 01/02/2014 by the Central Bank of Turkey Bülten No: 2014/1*, CENTRAL BANK OF TURKEY, https://www.tcmb.gov.tr/wps/wcm/connect/TR/TCMB+TR/Main+Menu/Istatistikler/Doviz+Kurlari/Gosterge+Niteligindeki+Merkez+Bankasi+Kurlarii/; *Indicative Exchange Rates Announced at 15:30 on 12/30/2016 by the Central Bank of Turkey Bülten No: 2016/249*, CENTRAL BANK OF TURKEY, https://www.tcmb.gov.tr/wps/wcm/connect/TR/TCMB+TR/Main+Menu/Istatistikler/Doviz+Kurlari/Gosterge+Niteligindeki+Merkez+Bankasi+Kurlarii/.
353. *See* Appendix I.
354. *See Indicative Exchange Rates Announced at 15:30 on 02/05/2021 by the Central Bank of Turkey Bülten No: 2021/25*, CENTRAL BANK OF TURKEY, *available at*: https://www.tcmb.gov.tr/kurlar/kurlar_tr.html (last visited Feb. 6, 2021).

billion in 2018 and 2019, respectively.[355] Turkey's 2019 export performance broke all records.[356]

As far as countries of destination, the EU-28 remained the main buyers of Turkish exports in this period. Approximately 57 percent of Turkey's exports went to the European Union between 2002 and 2007.[357] However, the EU-28 share of Turkey's exports declined after 2008, reaching the lowest level in 2012 (39 percent).[358] Because regional instability in MENA countries also depressed Turkish exports around that time, the EU-28 share of Turkish exports began increasing after 2012 and hit 45 percent in 2019.[359] Other important destinations for Turkish exports were the Turkic countries (mostly unchanged), United States (i.e., between 3 and 5.7 percent), and Russia (mostly unchanged).[360]

### B. Import Performance

Turkey's manufacturing sector is heavily dependent on the importation of capital and intermediate goods, including oil and natural gas. For instance, energy imports constitute about 25 percent of Turkey's overall imports, but vary according to global energy prices.[361] According to the Turkish Statistical Institute, intermediate goods, oil and natural gas, together, are responsible for 73 percent of total imports.[362] Because Turkey is heavily dependent on imports, there is a strong correlation between import and export volumes.[363]

This explains why, while experiencing an export boom between 2002 and 2008, Turkey saw a dramatic increase in imports. In fact, imports increased from $51 to $201 billion between 2002 and 2008.[364] As a result of the Global Recession, imports decreased by 30 percent, by value, from $201 in 2008 to $140 billion in 2009.[365] Starting in 2010, imports experienced a recovery, reaching a record $251 billion in 2013.[366] Yet, imports began decreasing in 2014, falling to $242, $207, and $198 billion in 2014, 2015,

355. *See* Appendix I.
356. *See id.*
357. *See* Turkish Statistical Institute, Statistics by Theme, Foreign Trade Statistics, *available at*: http://www.turkstat.gov.tr/PreTablo.do?alt_id=1046 (follow "Foreign Trade by Country Groups" hyperlink; then click "Exports by Country Groups") (calculation was made by the authors).
358. *Id.*
359. *Id.* The data for the United Kingdom was included.
360. *Id.*
361. *See* the Tenth Development Plan, *supra* note 20, at 14.
362. *See* Turkish Statistical Institute, Statistics by Theme, Foreign Trade Statistics, *available at*: http://www.turkstat.gov.tr/PreTablo.do?alt_id=1046 (follow "Foreign Trade by Classifica tion of Broad Economic Categories (BEC)" hyperlink; then click "Imports by Classification of Broad Economic Categories (BEC)") (calculation was made by the authors).
363. *See* Appendix I.
364. *See id.*
365. *See id.*
366. *See id.*

and 2016, respectively.[367] The most probable reason for this decline was lira depreciation, with the dollar increasing dramatically from ₺2.1 in 2014 to ₺5.3 in 2019.[368] Obviously, lira depreciation made imports more expensive, although this effect was somewhat offset by the decrease in global energy prices,[369] whose decline started in mid-2014.[370] Since Turkey is fully dependent on energy imports, the decline in oil prices decreased Turkey's energy costs.[371] To illustrate, Turkey's *monthly* energy imports totaled $4.5 billion in June 2014, decreasing to $3.3 billion in June 2015.[372] Starting in 2016, increasing global oil prices hurt Turkey's import costs, and thus, its trade deficit. Turkey's imports jumped from $198 to $223 billion between 2016 and, then increased to $202 billion in 2019.[373]

## C. Trade and Current Account Deficits in the 2002-2019 Period

Reflecting both export and import fluctuations, Turkey's trade volume (in goods) jumped from $87 to $374 billion in the 2002-2019.[374] With the contribution of trade in services, Turkey's GDP increased from $238 to $761 billion between 2002 and 2019.[375] However, Turkey still faces trade and current account deficits. In regard to the trade deficit, the increase in exports did not match the increase in imports. As a result, Turkey's trade deficits rose from $15 to $31 billion in the period.[376] Thus, the structural, trade-deficit problem remains unsolved since 1946.[377]

Having chronic trade deficits in goods, Turkey is under constant pressure to achieve trade surpluses in services. Turkey's service trade surplus, which includes tourism, transportation, construction, insurance, and pension services, increased from $7.8 to $30.1 billion between 2002 and 2019.[378] However, because of sizeable trade deficits in goods and lack of significant growth in the trade in services, Turkey ran

367. *See id.*
368. *Indicative Exchange Rates Announced at 15:30 on 01/02/2015 by the Central Bank of Turkey, Bülten No: 2015/1*, Central Bank of Turkey, http://www.tcmb.gov.tr/kurlar/201501/02012015.xml; *Indicative Exchange Rates Announced at 15:30 on 03/04/2019 by the Central Bank of Turkey, Bülten No: 2019/44*, Central Bank of Turkey, https://www.tcmb.gov.tr/wps/wcm/connect/TR/TCMB+TR/Main+Menu/Istatistikler/Doviz+Kurlari/Gosterge+Niteligindeki+Merkez+Bankasi+Kurlarii.
369. *See* Central Bank Report 2017, Central Bank of Turkey, 8 (2017), http://www.tcmb.gov.tr/wps/wcm/connect/TR/TCMB+TR/Main+Menu/Yayinlar/Raporlar/Yillik+Rapor/.
370. Crude oil prices declined from $119 to $62 per barrel, in 2014-2015 period. Oil prices decreased further to less than $40 in the 2015-2016 period. *See* Crude Oil Brent, Latest Price & Chart for Crude Oil Brent, *available at*: http://www.nasdaq.com/markets/crude-oil-brent.aspx?timeframe=5y (last visited Oct. 25, 2018).
371. *See* Central Bank Report 2017, *supra* note 369.
372. *Id.*
373. *See* Appendix I.
374. *See id.*
375. *See id.*
376. *See* Appendix I.
377. *See id.*
378. *See Balance of Payments Statistics, November 2020*, Republic of Turkey, Central Bank Report, 13, Table 5. https://www.tcmb.gov.tr/wps/wcm/connect/2c897137-850e-4d15-9a2a-c0d4735d9986/bop.pdf?MOD=AJPERES&CACHEID=ROOTWORKSPACE-2c897137-850e-4d15-9a2a-c0d4735d9986-nrMfFRO.

nearly uninterrupted current account deficits in the 2002-2020 period.[379] A current account deficit of $626 million, in 2002, ballooned to $74.4 billion, its highest level, in 2011, but eventually disappeared, becoming a $6.8 billion surplus in 2019.[380] Unofficial estimates for 2020 show a return to a sizable current account deficit ($34.5 billion), however.[381]

Since 2002, Turkey has managed to find external sources to finance current account deficits.[382] Inbound FDI totaled $217 billion between 2003 and 2019.[383] Because FDI inflows were not enough to offset usual current account deficits, Turkey has relied on short-term investment flows. The financial crises of the late 1990s and early 2000s should caution Turkish officials against reliance on short-term, speculative foreign capital, which exposes the country's to destabilizing runs on the lira.[384] Cognizant of the close connection between trade performance and macroeconomic stability in Turkey, we now attempt to gauge the *effectiveness* of the trade policy tools Turkey deployed in the 2002-2019 period.

## V. MATCHING TRADE POLICY OBJECTIVES AND TOOLS

Turkey has deployed numerous policy tools to help it advance its trade objectives, namely: (i) decrease trade and current account deficits; (ii) reduce import dependency; and (iii) expand exports and diversify export destinations. Most of these tools (e.g., export promotion, import management and trade diplomacy) were discussed in this chapter. At a first glance, although Turkey managed to increase exports, it continues to run growing trade and current account deficits and has largely failed to reduce its dependency on imports and diversify export destinations. Hence, one may conclude that the trade policy tools resorted to, thus far, have not, *adequately*, helped Turkey attain its major trade objective: reducing its trade deficit.

Judgment on the effectiveness of each of these tools requires some nuanced thinking. For instance, a particular policy tool may have succeeded (e.g., export promotion), while others may have been either partially successful (e.g., trade agreements, like the CU, which opened EU markets, but hindered Turkey's liberalization efforts) or complete failures (e.g., diplomatic efforts in the Doha Round). Ascertaining whether or the extent to which a particular trade policy tool has been effective, however, is far from a trivial task. It involves, among other things, analyzing multiple

379. *See id.*
380. *See id.*
381. *See* Gokhan Ergocun, *Turkey: Current account balance sees $273M gap*, ANADOLU AGENCY (Dec. 11, 2020), https://www.aa.com.tr/en/economy/turkey-current-account-balance-sees-273m-gap/2073379#:~:text=The%20survey%20showed%20the%20end,item%2C%20increasing%20by%20%24514%20million (stating the December deficit while reporting surveys forecasting the "2020 current account balance ... to show a deficit of $34.5 billion").
382. *See* Current Account Balance (% of GDP), Turkey, WORLD BANK, http://data.worldbank.org/indicator/BN.CAB.XOKA.GD.ZS?end=2016&locations=TR&start=1974&view=chart (last visited Feb. 28, 2019).
383. *See* FDI in Turkey, *supra* note 230.
384. *See* the Tenth Development Plan, *supra* note 20, at 59.

variables and determining the extent to which the particular policy instrument selected matches the goals it should help achieve.

After providing a thorough review of Turkey's economic history, the rationale for the EU-Turkey CU, and the current challenges Turkey faces on the economic and trade fronts while operating under the constraints of the CU, we concluded Part II of this book with a discussion of Turkey's major policy tools (e.g., export promotion, import management, and trade diplomacy) and with an assessment of their effectiveness in addressing these challenges. While helpful, these tools fall far short of what the country needs to address its current challenges: more, diversified, and liberalized trade. In Part III, we fully flesh out the steps Turkey must take to best position itself to benefit from further trade liberalization. For that to occur, however, Turkey must pursue a full restructuring of its trade relationship with the European Union and recover its trade sovereignty. Next, Chapter 5 introduces Part III, the policy-prospective portion of the book. We begin with a frank assessment of the last major policy tool Turkey has—short of CU restructuring—that might affect the nature and composition of its trade: trade litigation. Could WTO litigation, with its bilateral focus and prospective-only remedial nature, do much for Turkey?

# PART III Restructuring the EU-Turkey Trade Framework: TURK-SWITCH

CHAPTER 5

# Turkey's Needs and Why WTO Litigation Cannot Meet Them*

## I. OVERVIEW

As discussed in Part II of this book, Turkey faces challenges common to sizeable middle-income countries, like Brazil, Mexico, and Russia—where social and economic conditions lag behind more advanced economies. Yet, unlike these countries, Turkey experiences high perennial trade and current account deficits.[1] When a country runs current account deficits, it needs deficit-offsetting external sources of financing, such as borrowing, greater FDI, and short-term capital inflows.[2] Turkey has experienced current account deficits for decades, but has managed (mostly) to find external sources to finance them.[3] However, reducing the trade deficit—the main item in Turkey's current account deficit—has always proved a difficult challenge. In fact, Turkey's trade deficit in goods has gone uninterrupted since 1946.[4] The export-import ratio has fluctuated between 0.521 and 0.846 in the last two decades.[5] This ratio was 0.772 in 2020.[6] Yet, as trade has expanded since Turkey's last major crisis (2001), its trade deficit has increased and, thus, its current account deficit.

* An earlier version of this chapter, titled *Turkey as a WTO Litigant: A Case of Waived Leverage and Mismatched Policy Ends and Means*, appeared in 51.4 GEORGETOWN JOURNAL OF INTERNATIONAL LAW 854 (2020).

1. *See* IMF, Turkey: 2017 Article IV Consultation—Press Release; Staff Report; and Statement by the Executive Director for Turkey, IMF Staff Country Report 17/23, 1 (February 2017).
2. *See* Atish Ghosh & Uma Ramakrishnan, *Current Account Deficits: Is There a Problem?*, IMF FIN. & DEV. (Dec. 18, 2018), https://www.imf.org/external/pubs/ft/fandd/basics/current.htm.
3. *See* Current Account Balance (% of GDP)—TURKEY, WBG, http://data.worldbank.org/indicator/BN.CAB.XOKA.GD.ZS?end=2016&locations=TR&start=1974&view=chart (last visited Aug. 12, 2019).
4. *See* Appendix I.
5. *See id.*
6. *See id.*

To reduce both trade and current account deficits, Turkey has set two major trade policy goals: (1) reducing import dependency; and (2) expanding exports while diversifying its portfolio of export destinations.[7] Despite conspicuous state involvement in managing imports (e.g., imposition of import-licensing requirements, application of antidumping remedies, etc.)[8] and in promoting exports (e.g., granting small export credits via EximBank, bestowal of agricultural export subsidies, etc.),[9] Turkey has only rarely been the target in WTO dispute settlement proceedings.[10]

This chapter offers a thorough analysis of Turkey's involvement in the entire range of WTO litigation—as Complainant, Respondent, or interested Third Party—and explains why WTO adjudication was neither designed for nor could be effective in helping Turkey address its perennial trade challenges (and, thus, its current account deficits). Some major clues lie in Turkey's restricted trade autonomy under the CU, and the delayed membership or non-membership of its non-EU neighbors—factors that would significantly curtail the benefits of litigation as a trade policy tool for any WTO Member. Section II briefly examines the operation of the WTO dispute settlement system. Section III lays out our methodology for empirically analyzing Turkey's litigation performance and summarizes our findings. Section IV examines the extent to which WTO litigation has helped Turkey address its trade policy objectives. Because we conclude that this has not been the case, we analyze, in Section V, the extent to which such de minimis impact stems from: (i) limitations related to litigation itself (e.g., its remedial nature, bilateral reach, etc.); and/or from (ii) Turkey's diminished ability to sue its non-EU neighbors (most of which remain non-WTO Members) and the European Union (Turkey's senior partner in the CU). Because trade litigation—not unlike the combination of trade policy tools Turkey has used so far—cannot be relied upon to address Turkey's macroeconomic and trade-specific challenges, this chapter concludes with a call for Turkey to look for solutions in further trade liberalization, thus setting the stage for the needed restructuring of the EU-Turkey trade framework whose legal and transactional implementation we explain in Chapter 6.

## II. THE WTO DISPUTE SETTLEMENT SYSTEM

Among the WTO's major achievements is the establishment of a rules-based trade order with an accompanying dispute settlement system, the DSB, a mechanism designed to further "multilateral trade cooperation," and, when necessary, provide a

7. *See* Onuncu Kalkinma Planinin (2014-2018) Onaylandigina Iliskin Karar, 66-68, 75-76, 99-101, 174-175 R.G.: 02.07.2013 Sayi: 1041, *translated in* SBB.GOV.TR, http://www.sbb.gov.tr/wp-content/uploads/2018/11/The_Tenth_Development_Plan_2014-2018.pdf (last visited Sept. 9, 2020); *see also* Onbirinci Kalkinma Planinin (2019-2023) Onaylandigina Iliskin Karar 29, 30, 32, 37-40 R.G.: 18.07.2019 Sayi: 1225.
8. *See* WTO Secretariat, *Trade Policy Review of Turkey*, WT/TPR/S/331 11, 66-70 (Feb. 9, 2016) [hereinafter Turkey TPR 2016].
9. *See id.*, at 87-89, 126-140.
10. *See* MEMBER INFORMATION: TURKEY AND THE WTO, WTO, https://www.wto.org/english/thewto_e/countries_e/turkey_e.htm (last visited Jan. 30, 2021).

forum for litigation.[11] Members are expected to comply with the WTO agreements.[12] If a Member acts inconsistently with its WTO commitments, another Member whose "benefit ... is being nullified or impaired" by such inconsistency can use the DSB to seek redress.[13] The DSB is specifically regulated under the Dispute Settlement Understanding ("DSU"),[14] a compendium of rules that, among other things, authorizes the DSB to "administer [all] rules and procedures" applicable to all Members.[15] DSU Article 2 provides that the DSB has "the authority to establish panels, adopt panel or Appellate Body ("AB") reports, maintain surveillance of implementation of rulings and recommendations, and authorize suspension of concessions ... " in cases of noncompliance.[16] Therefore, despite the fact that only WTO Members, collectively, can adopt binding interpretations,[17] the DSB exercises de facto supreme authority over decisions that govern Member conduct regarding and following litigation.[18]

Dispute settlement under the DSB may involve four major phases.[19] First, an "aggrieved Member" may request consultations.[20] The Member to whom such a request is directed shall respond within ten days and shall enter into such consultations *in good faith*.[21] Should such a Member fail to respond "within 10 days," fail to enter consultations within 30 days, or should both parties "fail to settle the dispute within 60 days," the Member who requested the holding of consultations may request the DSB to form a panel.[22] Second, pursuant to a Complainant's request, the DSB establishes a panel.[23] Members with a "substantial interest" in a given dispute may request to participate as Third Parties, and the DSB invariably accommodates such requests.[24] Panels are expected to rule on the dispute and submit final reports within six months, yet the time for deliberations may be extended, as necessary.[25] Once submitted, the panel report shall be adopted by the DSB within 60 days, unless the losing Member

11. Some commentators have referred to the GATT as the "constitution" of the WTO. *See* JACK L. GOLDSMITH & ERIC A. POSNER, THE LIMITS OF INTERNATIONAL LAW 135-158 (2005).
12. *See* Dani Rodrik, Commentary, *Rethinking the World Economy*, STANFORD.EDU 3, 7 (March 2001), http://web.stanford.edu/class/polisci243c/readings/v0002088.pdf (last visited Feb. 5, 2021).
13. General Agreement on Tariffs and Trade 1994, Art. XXIII, Apr. 15, 1994, Marrakesh Agreement Establishing the World Trade Organization, Annex 1A, 1867 U.N.T.S. 187 [hereinafter *GATT 1994*].
14. *See* Understanding on Rules and Procedures Governing the Settlement of Disputes, Apr. 15, 1994, Marrakesh Agreement Establishing the World Trade Organization, Annex 2, 1869 U.N.T.S. 401 [hereinafter *DSU*].
15. *Id.*, Art. 2.
16. *Id.*, Art. 2.1.
17. *See* Marrakesh Agreement Establishing the World Trade Organization Art. II, Apr. 15, 1994, 1867 U.N.T.S. 154.
18. *See* Raj Bhala, *The Myth About Stare Decisis and International Trade Law (Part One of a Trilogy)*, 14 AM. U. INT'L L. REV. 845, 936-956 (1999).
19. *See* JOHN H. JACKSON, WILLIAM J. DAVEY & ALAN O. SYKES, JR., LEGAL PROBLEMS OF INTERNATIONAL ECONOMIC RELATIONS CASES, MATERIALS AND TEXT 286 (6th ed. 2013).
20. *GATT 1994*, *supra* note 13, Art. XXII.
21. *See DSU*, *supra* note 14, Art. 4.3.
22. *See id.*, Arts. 4.3-4.7. Note that the time period might differ in case of urgency (e.g., perishable goods). *See DSU*, *supra* note 14, Arts. 4.8 and 4.9.
23. *See id.*, Art. 6.1. Panel members are elected by their qualities among international trade scholars, former senior trade policy officers, etc. *See DSU*, *supra* note 14, Art. 8.1.
24. *Id.*, Art. 10.2.
25. *Id.*, Arts. 12.8 and 12.9.

(Respondent or Complainant) decides to appeal the report, or all Members, by consensus, agree not to adopt it.[26] Third, should there be an appeal, the AB,[27] whose decision is final, "may uphold, modify or reverse the legal findings and conclusions of the panel."[28] As with unappealed panel reports, AB reports "shall be unconditionally accepted by the parties" and shall be adopted by the DSB, unless all Members decide, by consensus, not to adopt them.[29] Fourth, and finally, any eventual losing Respondent is required to implement final panel or AB recommendations.

Ordinarily, the losing Respondent must comply with the recommendations of the panel or AB report within a reasonable time.[30] In cases where immediate withdrawal of Respondent's inconsistent measure is impracticable, that Member is expected to provide compensation to the successful Complainant.[31] Should such Member fail to comply with the recommendations in a timely fashion or provide compensation, the Complainant may request consultations to reach a mutually agreed compensation.[32] If the parties fail to agree on a mutually acceptable compensation or disagree on whether the violating Respondent has complied, the Complainant may request authorization to suspend concessions against the noncompliant, recalcitrant Respondent.[33] As of January 2021, WTO Members had resorted to the DSB 600 times.[34] Turkey was involved in 121 disputes.[35] The following section provides a review of Turkey's litigation performance under the DSB.

## III. TURKEY'S LITIGATION PERFORMANCE AT THE WTO

Before summarizing Turkey's litigation performance, we provide, first, a note on our data and methodology. The nonempirically inclined reader may skip to subsection B.

26. *Id.*, Art. 16.4.
27. The Appellate Body is a standing body composed of seven members nominated for potential, once-renewable four-year terms. *See id.*, Arts. 17.1 and 17.2.
28. *Id.*, Art. 17.13.
29. *Id.*, Art. 17.14. That the Appellate Body ceased operations in December 2019 does not mean dispute settlement work has stopped at the WTO. Panels can still be formed and function, as before. Though important, this development might be seized as an opportunity for regional dispute settlement systems to take on a greater role in trade adjudication going forward.
30. *See id.*, Art. 21.3.
31. *See id.*, Art. 3.7.
32. *See id.*, Art. 22.1.
33. *See id.*, Art. 22.2.
34. *See* Chronological List of Disputes Cases, WTO, https://www.wto.org/english/tratop_e/dispu_e/dispu_status_e.htm (last visited Jan. 30, 2021). The data is current as of January 2021, and the most current case at the WTO DSB could be found at *European Union and certain member states — Certain measures concerning palm oil and oil palm crop-based biofuels*, WTO Doc. WT/DS600 (Jan. 15, 2021), https://www.wto.org/english/tratop_e/dispu_e/cases_e/ds600_e.htm.
35. *See* Member Information: Turkey and the WTO, WTO, https://www.wto.org/english/thewto_e/countries_e/turkey_e.htm (last visited Jan. 30, 2021). The data is current as of January 2021.

## A. Data and Methods

WTO website data show that, since DSB began operations in 1995, Turkey has been involved in six cases as Complainant, 12 cases as Respondent, and 102 cases as Third Party, totaling 120 cases or 20 percent of all disputes.[36] However, WTO data fails to account for one case: *United States—Measures Concerning the Importation, Marketing and Sale of Tuna and Tuna Products*.[37] Turkey participated in the *US–Tuna* panel proceedings but decided to withdraw its Third-Party appearance at the appellate stage.[38] As a result, Turkey appeared as Third-Party litigant 103 times, thus being involved in a total of 121 disputes.

Although nominally involved in 121 cases, some of these are double counted. Pursuant to DSB Article 9.1, "more than one Member [may] request[] the establishment of a panel ... [on] the same matter," and the DSB may form a single panel for more than one request.[39] To illustrate, in 1996, Hong Kong, China, India, and Thailand separately requested consultations with Turkey on the same subject matter, namely Turkey's restrictions on imports of textiles and clothing.[40] However, Hong Kong, China, and Thailand decided to participate as Third Parties in the dispute initiated by India.[41] Although the WTO database reports Hong Kong's, China's, and Thailand's filings as still "in consultations," the claims raised in the India-prosecuted case—a dispute in which these three countries appeared as Third Parties—are substantially the same and were adjudicated in that case, making their original filings, effectively, data aberrations. In another example, the European Union, Japan, South Korea, China, Switzerland, Norway, New Zealand, and Brazil requested the establishment of a panel regarding U.S. safeguard measures on imports of certain steel products in 2002.[42]

36. *See id.*
37. Appellate Body Report, United States–Measures Concerning the Importation, Marketing and Sale of Tuna and Tuna Products, WTO Doc. WT/DS381/AB/R (adopted May 16, 2012) [hereinafter *US–Tuna*].
38. *See id.*, ¶ 7.
39. *See DSU, supra* note 14, Art. 9.1. For a detailed discussion on combining disputes into a single panel, *see* Eun Sup Lee, World Trade Regulation: International Trade Under the WTO Mechanism 320-321 (2012).
40. *See, e.g.*, Turkey–Restrictions on Imports of Textile and Clothing Products, WTO Doc. WT/DS29 (Feb. 12, 1996) (Complainant: Hong Kong and China); Turkey–Restrictions on Imports of Textile and Clothing Products, WTO Doc. WT/DS34 (Jul. 19, 2001) (Complainant: India); Turkey–Restrictions on Imports of Textile and Clothing Products, WTO Doc. WT/DS47 (Jun. 20, 1996) (Complainant: Thailand).
41. *See* Turkey–Restrictions on Imports of Textile and Clothing Products, WTO Doc. WT/DS34 (Jul. 19, 2001) (Complainant: India).
42. *See, e.g.*, United States–Definitive Safeguard Measures on Imports of Certain Steel Products, WTO Doc. WT/DS248 (Dec. 16, 2003) (Complainant: European Union); United States–Definitive Safeguard Measures on Imports of Certain Steel Products, WTO Doc. WT/DS249 (Dec. 16, 2003) (Complainant: Japan); United States–Definitive Safeguard Measures on Imports of Certain Steel Products, WTO Doc. WT/DS251 (Dec. 16, 2003) (Complainant: South Korea); United States–Definitive Safeguard Measures on Imports of Certain Steel Products, WTO Doc. WT/DS252 (Dec. 16, 2003) (Complainant: China); United States–Definitive Safeguard Measures on Imports of Certain Steel Products, WTO Doc. WT/DS253 (Dec. 16, 2003) (Complainant: Switzerland); United States–Definitive Safeguard Measures on Imports of Certain Steel Products, WTO Doc. WT/DS254 (Dec. 16, 2003) (Complainant: Norway); United States–Definitive Safeguard Measures on Imports of Certain Steel Products, WTO Doc. WT/DS258 (Dec. 16, 2003) (Complainant:

Turkey also reserved its third-party rights in all (eight) disputes involving these safeguard measures. Because the DSB established a single panel to hear the dispute by the eight Complainants (plus Turkey and others, as Third Parties) against the United States, Turkey's eight filings amounted to an appearance in one case, rather than eight.[43]

There are also 12 prior instances where more than one Member requested the establishment of a panel, and the DSB established a single panel for all requests.[44] The DSB will likely consolidate a recent set of disputes the European Union, Japan, Taiwan,

---

New Zealand); United States–Definitive Safeguard Measures on Imports of Certain Steel Products, WTO Doc. WT/DS259 (Dec. 16, 2003) (Complainant: Brazil).

43. *See* Appellate Body Report, *United States–Definitive Safeguard Measures on Imports of Certain Steel Products*, WTO Docs. WT/DS248/AB/R, WT/DS249/AB/R, WT/DS251/AB/R, WT/DS252/AB/R, WT/DS253/AB/R, WT/DS254/AB/R, WT/DS258/AB/R, and WT/DS259/AB/R (adopted Dec. 10, 2003).

44. *See, e.g.*, European Communities–Protection of Trademarks and Geographical Indications for Agricultural Products and Foodstuffs, WTO Docs. WT/DS174 and WT/DS290 (Apr. 11, 2006) (Complainants: United States and Australia); European Communities and Its Member States–Tariff Treatment of Certain Information Technology Products, WTO Doc. WT/DS375, WT/DS376, and WT/DS377 (Jul. 11, 2011) (Complainants: United States, Japan, and Taiwan); China–Measures Related to the Exportation of Various Raw Materials, WTO Docs. WT/DS394, WT/DS395, and WT/DS398 (Jan. 23, 2013) (Complainants: United States, European Union, and Mexico); Dominican Republic–Safeguard Measures on Imports of Polypropylene Bags and Tubular Fabric, WTO Docs. WT/DS415, WT/DS416, WT/DS417, and WT/DS418 (May 9, 2012) (Complainants: Costa Rica, Guatemala, Honduras, and El Salvador); China–Measures Related to the Exportation of Rare Earths, Tungsten and Molybdenum, WTO Docs. WT/DS431, WT/DS432, and WT/DS433 (May 26, 2015) (Complainant: United States, European Union, and Japan); Australia–Certain Measures Concerning Trademarks and Other Plain Packaging Requirements Applicable to Tobacco Products and Packaging, WTO Doc. WT/DS434 (Jun. 30, 2016) (Complainants: Ukraine); Australia–Certain Measures Concerning Trademarks and Other Plain Packaging Requirements Applicable to Tobacco Products and Packaging, WTO Docs. WT/DS435, and WT/DS441 (Jul. 2, 2020) (Complainants: Honduras, Dominican Republic); Australia–Certain Measures Concerning Trademarks and Other Plain Packaging Requirements Applicable to Tobacco Products and Packaging, WTO Docs. WT/DS458 and WT/DS467 (Aug. 30, 2018) (Complainants: Cuba, and Indonesia); Argentina–Measures Affecting the Importation of Goods, WTO Docs. WT/DS438, WT/DS444, and WT/DS445 (Jan. 20, 2016) (Complainants: European Union, United States, and Japan); China–Measures Imposing Anti-Dumping Duties on High-Performance Stainless Steel Seamless Tubes from Japan, WTO Docs. WT/DS/454 and WT/DS460 (Feb. 23, 2016) (Complainants: Japan and European Union); Brazil–Certain Measures Concerning Taxation and Charges, WTO Docs. WT/DS/472 and WT/DS/497 (Jan. 17, 2020) (Complainants: European Union and Japan); United States–Certain Measures on Steel and Aluminium Products, WTO Docs. WT/DS/544, WT/DS548, WT/DS/552, WT/DS/554, and WT/DS/556 (Sept. 10, 2019) (Complainants: China, European Union, Norway, Russia, and Switzerland); United States–Certain Measures on Steel and Aluminium Products, WTO Docs. WT/DS/550 and WT/DS/551 (Jul. 11, 2019) (Complainants: Canada, Mexico); Canada–Additional Duties on Certain Products from the United States, WTO Doc. WT/DS/557 (Jul. 11, 2019) (Complainant: United States); China–Additional Duties on Certain Products from the United States, WTO Doc. WT/DS/558 (Sept. 11, 2019) (Complainant: United States); European Union–Additional Duties on Certain Products from the United States, WTO Doc. WT/DS/559 (Sept. 11, 2019) (Complainant: United States); Mexico–Additional Duties on Certain Products from the United States, WTO Doc. WT/DS/560 (Jul. 11, 2019) (Complainant: United States); Russian Federation–Additional Duties on Certain Products from the United States, WTO Doc. WT/DS/566 (Sept. 11, 2019) (Complainant: United States).

and the United States filed, separately, against India.[45] Thus, to provide a more accurate count of disputes, we will consider all disputes decided by a single panel as one even where, nominally, they appear as "separate" cases. After eliminating such instances of double counting, one can conclude that Turkey has been involved in six cases as Complainant, ten cases as Respondent, and 64 cases as Third Party.[46]

In the following subsections, we assess Turkey's litigation performance by focusing on the following variables: Case Type, Product Type, Opposing Country, and Win-Loss rate. As explained in a previous general WTO litigation study, these variables allow us to analyze whether differences in the invoked trade agreements (e.g., trade-remedy versus non-trade-remedy claims), types of products affected (e.g., commodities versus non-commodities), or Members challenged (e.g., high-income versus middle-income countries) have affected Turkey's litigation performance, which we measure by the Win-Loss rate variable.[47] To determine Win-Loss rates under this methodology, a dispute counts as a win for Complainant (and loss for Respondent) whenever Complainant wins on any claim.[48] Thus, when litigation effectively changes the status quo *ex ante*—triggering Respondent's obligation to bring its violating measure(s) into compliance[49]—Complainant scores a win (and Respondent, a loss), even if Complainant fails in other claims.

## B. Turkey's Performance as Complainant

A six-time Complainant, Turkey has brought disputes against Egypt (2000), South Africa (2003), Morocco (2016), the United States (2017 and 2018), and the European Union (2020).[50] Because two disputes are still nominally in consultations, one is currently in the panel stage, and two were pending before the AB on December 2019 (when AB operations came to a halt), to date, Turkey has fully prosecuted only one dispute: *Egypt–Definitive Anti-Dumping Measures on Steel Rebar from Turkey* (2003), which it won.[51]

45. *See* India–Tariff Treatment on Certain Goods in the Information and Communications Technology Sector, WTO Doc. WT/DS/582 (Aug. 31, 2020) (Complainant: European Union); India–Tariff Treatment on Certain Goods, WTO Doc. WT/DS/584 (Oct. 7, 2020) (Complainant: Japan); India–Additional Duties on Certain Products from the United States, WTO Doc. WT/DS/585 (Jan. 7, 2020) (Complainant: United States); India–Tariff Treatment on Certain Goods in the Information and Communications Technology Sector, WTO Doc. WT/DS/588 (Aug. 31, 2020) (Complainant: Taiwan).
46. As the same phenomenon (i.e., having one panel hear challenges by or against different Members to a set of measures that share common legal and/or factual issues) may have also occurred in disputes in which Turkey did not participate, we refrain from providing total participation rates for Turkey, because refining the denominator would require eliminating potential double counting for other countries, a task that falls outside the scope of this book.
47. *See* Juscelino F. Colares, *The Limits of WTO Adjudication: Is Compliance the Problem?*, 14 J. INT'L ECON. L. 403, 413-422 (2011).
48. *See* Juscelino F. Colares, *A Theory of WTO Adjudication: From Empirical Analysis to Biased Rule Development*, 42 VAND. J. TRANSNAT'L L. 383, 401 (2009).
49. *See DSU*, *supra* note 14, Art. 21.1.
50. *See* Appendix III, Table III.1.
51. In this case, Turkey alleged that Egypt had violated the Anti-Dumping Agreement, Arts. 2, 3, and 6; and the GATT, Art. X. Although the Panel rejected most of Turkey's claims since Turkey failed

Although such a low number of observations do not warrant statistical analysis, Turkey's role as a Complainant appears to reveal two interesting "patterns." As far as Case Type is concerned, Turkey has filed only trade-remedy claims. These claims appear in three antidumping ("AD") disputes, one countervailing duty ("CVD") dispute, and two safeguard disputes.[52] As to Product Type, iron and steel products (i.e., steel rebar, hot-rolled steel, and steel pipe and tube products) were the object of five disputes, while one dispute concerned blankets.[53] Notably, Turkey seems focused on challenging other Members' trade remedy determinations, presumably in an attempt to increase, or at least maintain, market access for its commodity and low-tech exports.

Clearly, Turkey has not been a frequent Complainant before the DSB. Remarkably, Turkey did not use the DSB offensively for a thirteen-year period (2003-2016).[54] Moreover, despite the fact that membership in the CU does not bar filing WTO disputes against its senior partner, Turkey took 25 years to file its first direct complaint against the European Union (2020).[55] Arguably, one would expect the junior partner in a customs union to be naturally disinclined from adopting an aggressive litigation strategy independent from its partner, much less against it. Thus, Turkey's infrequent offensive appearances are no surprise. Perhaps, the more interesting question is its newfound interest in bringing cases (four) since 2016.[56]

### C. Turkey's Performance as Respondent

Since the establishment of the DSB, Brazil (2000), Ecuador (2001), Hungary (2002) India (1996 and 2012), the United States (1996, 2005 and 2018), Thailand (2018), and the European Union (2019) have requested consultations with Turkey, pursuant to GATT Article XXII.[57] Because three disputes remain in consultations,[58] two were settled during consultations,[59] and three are still active (i.e., at the panel stage), Turkey has been a Respondent, effectively, in only two disputes before the DSB: *Turkey–Restrictions on Imports of Textile and Clothing Products*; and *Turkey–Measures Affecting*

to establish its claims under the Anti-Dumping Agreement, Arts. 2 and 3, the panel found that Egypt was in violation of the Anti-Dumping Agreement, Arts. 3 and 6. *See* Panel Report, *Egypt–Definitive Anti-Dumping Measures on Steel Rebar from Turkey*, WTO Doc. WT/DS211/R (adopted Aug. 8, 2002).

52. *See* Appendix III, Table III.1.
53. *See id.*
54. *See* Appendix III, Table III.1.
55. *See* Meltem Saribeyoglu, Dunya Ticaret Orgutu, Gümrük Birligi ve Turkiye [World Trade Organization, Customs Union and Turkey] 276-277 (2010).
56. Turkey initiated four of its six disputes after 2016. *See* Appendix III, Table III.1.
57. *See* Appendix III, Table III.2. As explained earlier, Hong Kong and China (i.e., Turkey–Restrictions on Imports of Textile and Clothing Products, WTO Doc. WT/DS29 (Feb. 12, 1996)) and Thailand (i.e., Turkey–Restrictions on Imports of Textile and Clothing Products, WTO Doc. WT/DS47 (Jun. 20, 1996)) requested consultations with Turkey, yet those countries decided to participate as Third Parties in the dispute raised by India: *Turkey–Textiles*. We counted these disputes as one despite the fact that they remain in consultations. *See* Appendix III, Table III.3.
58. *See id.*
59. *See id.*

*the Importation of Rice.*[60] In both cases, the panel and/or AB found that Turkey's measures were inconsistent with the WTO agreements (i.e., Turkey lost both cases).[61] Later, Turkey would notify the DSB that it had reached mutually acceptable implementations of report recommendations with India and the United States.[62] Thus, Turkey has a perfect record of compliance.

As far as Case Type is concerned, Complainants bringing cases against Turkey raised non-trade-remedy claims (e.g., GATT Articles I, II, III, and XI claims) in seven out of ten disputes.[63] Turkey was the target of trade-remedy claims (e.g., one AD and two safeguard challenges) in only three disputes.[64] Again, although the number of cases here is too small, cautioning one against making extrapolations, a seven-to-three, non-trade-remedy-to-trade-remedy ratio is intriguing. When one considers that Turkey has been among the most frequent users of trade remedies,[65] one would expect Turkey to be sued more frequently for alleged misapplication of trade remedies than otherwise. That Turkey's frequent application of trade remedies seems mostly *consistent* with its WTO commitments (or at least infrequently challenged) might be an indicator of its fair, rules-based behavior.

In regard to Product Type and Opposing Country, we cannot discern any "patterns." Complainants challenged orders imposing restrictions on textiles and clothing and related products (e.g., cotton yarn) in two disputes.[66] They also targeted orders affecting agricultural products (banana and rice) twice.[67] The remaining challenges focused on orders involving foreign movie pictures, iron pipe fittings, pet

60. *See id.*
61. In *Turkey–Textiles,* India alleged that Turkey had restricted textiles and clothing imports in violation of the GATT, Arts. XI, XIII and XXIV and the Agreement on Textiles and Clothing, Art. 2.4. The panel found that Turkey's measures were inconsistent with the GATT, Arts. XI and XIII and the Agreement on Textiles and Clothing, Art. 2.4. On appeal, while conceding having taken measures restricting the importation of textiles and clothing, Turkey argued that such measures had been enacted pursuant to the EU–Turkey CU, thus qualifying under the GATT, Art. XXIV exception. The panel rejected Turkey's resort to Article XXIV because Turkey had less restrictive, alternative options (e.g., rules of origin) that would meet its CU commitments. As such, Turkey could not claim that "the formation of a customs union ... would be prevented if it were not allowed to adopt [the challenged] quantitative restrictions." *See* Appellate Body Report, *Turkey–Restrictions on Imports of Textile and Clothing Products,* ¶¶ 46, 61, 63, WTO Doc. WT/DS34/AB/R (adopted Oct. 22, 1999). In *Turkey–Rice,* the United States alleged that Turkey's measures on the importation of rice had violated the GATT, Arts. III:4, X:1, X:2, and XI:1; the Agreement on Agriculture, Art. 4.2; the Agreement on Import Licensing Procedures, Arts. 1, 3, and 5; and TRIMs, Art. 2.1. The panel found that Turkey's measures were inconsistent with the Agreement on Agriculture, Art. 4.2 and the GATT, Art. III:4. Furthermore, the panel did not address most of the claims raised by the United States on the grounds of judicial economy. *See Turkey–Measures Affecting the Importation of Rice,* Panel Report, WTO Doc. WT/DS334/R (adopted Oct. 22, 2007).
62. *See* Appendix III, Table III.2.
63. *See id.*
64. *See id.*
65. *See* Turkey TPR 2016, *supra* note 8, at 68-70.
66. *See* Appendix III, Table III.2.
67. *See id.*

food, air conditioners and, more recently, pharmaceuticals.[68] Among Members challenging Turkey's measures were the United States (three times), India (twice),[69] and a few single-filers: Brazil, Ecuador, the European Union (the author of the most recent request for consultations),[70] Hungary, and Thailand.[71]

Thus, Turkey has been involved in ten disputes as Respondent. Six of these disputes were filed before 2005.[72] Since then, Turkey has been involved in four disputes, one of which remains in consultations, while the others are currently under panel consideration.[73] This record suggests Turkey's trade policies and actions have been largely WTO-compliant.

## D. Turkey's Performance as Third-Party Litigant

Because Turkey has appeared seldom as main Complainant or Respondent, its frequent participation as Third-Party litigant (64 disputes)[74] is both intriguing and deserving of closer scrutiny. Table 5.1 shows the current status of these disputes. Because two were settled or terminated by the Parties,[75] and 20 are still active, a total of 42 disputes have been finalized by a panel or the AB, and adopted by the DSB.[76] Together with the main Complainants in these cases, Turkey has won 37 times,[77] losing in only five instances.[78] Turkey's success rate in these finalized "Third-Party" cases is quite high: 88.09 percent. Such a high success rate is unremarkable, however. Prior empirical research has showed high Complainant success rates in *all* WTO substantive litigation (i.e., regardless of Case Type, Product Type, or Respondent Type).[79] According to Colares (2009), Complainants have won about 90 percent of substantive disputes that see final

68. *See id.*
69. *See id.*
70. As indicated earlier, the European Union filed, recently, a request for consultations with Turkey on Turkey's localization and technology transfer requirements for certain pharmaceutical products. *See* European Union, Permanent Mission of the World Trade Organization, the Ambassador 1-2 (Apr. 2, 2019), http://trade.ec.europa.eu/doclib/docs/2019/april/tradoc_ 157 821.pdf (last visited Aug. 12, 2019) [hereinafter EU Request for Consultations].
71. *See* Appendix III, Table III.2.
72. *See id.*
73. *See id.*
74. *See* Appendix III, Table III.3 (listing Turkey's Third-Party appearances). As we have explained in Section III.A, to account for the commonality of issues of law and fact and to avoid double counting of Third-Party disputes decided by a single panel, we count any grouping of overlapping disputes as one.
75. The cases that were settled or terminated are: United States–Measures Affecting Imports of Women's and Girls' Wool Coats, WTO Doc. WT/DS32 (Apr. 30, 1996) and European Union–Measures on Atlanto-Scandian Herring, WTO Doc. WT/DS469 (Aug. 25, 2014).
76. *See* Appendix III, Table III.3.
77. *See id.*
78. *See id.*
79. *See* Colares, *supra* note 48, at 402-412. *See also* ROBERT E. HUDEC, ENFORCING INTERNATIONAL TRADE LAW: THE EVOLUTION OF THE MODERN GATT LEGAL SYSTEM 253 (1993) (reporting similar Complainant success rates during the pre-WTO, GATT panel period).

adjudication before the DSB.[80] In a broader perspective, Turkey's Third-Party success merely replicates the major systemic trends found in WTO litigation.

*Table 5.1 Turkey as Third Party: Case Status*

| *Case Status* | *N* | *Win Rate (%)* |
|---|---|---|
| DSB-Adopted Report | 42 | 88.09 |
| Settled | 2 | N/A |
| Active | 20 | N/A |
| Total | 64 | N/A |

Table 5.2 shows that, as Third Party, Turkey took a keen interest in closely monitoring litigation against high-income countries. Such countries were the Respondents nearly two-thirds of the time (65.62 percent). In 24 of such disputes, Turkey appeared against the United States,[81] and, in 12, against the European Union.[82] As far as middle-income countries are concerned, China was Respondent in six of these disputes, and Russia in three.[83] Hoping to gain greater market access for its exports, Turkey has concentrated its Third-Party appearances on challenges against high income (e.g., the United States, European Union, Australia, and South Korea) and large middle income (e.g., Brazil, China, India, Mexico, and Russia) countries, presumably because they have larger and more dynamic markets. Together, both groups, appearing as Respondents, account for 92.18 percent of Turkey's participation as Third-Party litigant.[84]

80. *See* Colares, *supra* note 47, at 402-413. For a discussion of erstwhile Complainant success rates in *compliance* litigation, *see* Colares, *supra* note 47, at 419-426.
81. *See* Appendix III, Table III.3.
82. *See id.* Note that Turkey is participating as Third-Party litigant in *European Union–Additional Duties on Certain Products from the United States,* WTO Doc. WT/DS/559 (Sept. 11, 2019), a case in which the United States challenges EU's unauthorized retaliation against US-imposed Section 232, national security tariffs on steel and aluminum. Although included in our database, this case does not appear in our Third-Party statistics because Turkey was also sued by the United States regarding the same subject matter in a parallel case, namely *Turkey–Additional Duties on Certain Products from the United States*, WT/DS/561 (Sept. 11, 2019), and it is likely that the DSB will establish a single panel for these and other similar, parallel disputes. Furthermore, because Turkey and the European Union share similar positions in this controversy, Turkey's Third-Party appearance in this case should not be coded as adversarial to the European Union. *See* Appendix III, Tables III.2 and III.3.
83. *See* Appendix III, Table III.3.
84. *See id.*

*Table 5.2 Turkey as Third Party: Respondent Type*

| *Respondent Type*[85] | *N (%)* |
|---|---|
| High Income | 42 (65.62) |
| Middle Income | 22 (34.38) |
| Total | 64 (100) |

As with Table 5.2, Table 5.3 contains enough observations to allow some extrapolation. At the outset, one specific trend can be detected: in nearly 61 percent of cases in which Turkey has participated as Third Party, the Complainants were targeting Respondent's use of *trade remedies*.[86] Among these cases, only seven were related to safeguards,[87] while 32 involved AD or CVD challenges.[88] Arguably, Turkey has remained vigilant of other Members' "misuse" of trade remedies in a proactive attempt to protect its export interests, even when Turkish products are not directly implicated. By monitoring challenges to Member-imposed trade remedies, Turkey maintains a watchful eye on potential abuse of such disciplines in its direct trade relations. This suggests that Turkey might be following a subtle play-for-precedent strategy in its choice of Third-Party litigation.[89]

*Table 5.3 Turkey as Third Party: Case Type*

| *Case Type* | *N (%)* |
|---|---|
| Trade Remedies | 39 (60.93) |
| Non-trade Remedies | 25 (39.07) |
| Total | 64 (100) |

Table 5.4 summarizes the interface between Turkey's appearance as Third-Party litigant and the types of product involved in such disputes. Along with other Third-Party litigants, Turkey joined disputes where the main Complainant(s) challenged orders affecting *commodities* and mature-industry products over 87 percent of the time. Among such products, the main targets were: iron and steel products (11 disputes); automobiles and auto parts (nine disputes); agricultural foodstuffs (12 disputes); and textile and clothing products (six disputes).[90] Notably, Turkey is an exporter of all such products, which, again, demonstrates its concern with ensuring market access even when its products are not directly targeted.

85. *See* World Bank Country and Lending Groups—Lower-Middle-Income Economies-Upper-Middle-Income Economies-High-Income Economies, *available at*: https://datahelpdesk.worldbank.org/knowledgebase/articles/906519-world-bank-country-and-lending-groups (last visited Jan. 30, 2021).
86. *See* Appendix III, Table III.3.
87. *See id.*
88. *See id.*
89. For a similar argument, *see* Colares, *supra* note 47, at 418.
90. *See* Appendix III, Table III.3.

*Table 5.4 Turkey as Third Party: Product Type*

| *Product Type* | *N (%)* |
|---|---|
| Commodities | 56 (87.50) |
| Non-commodities | 8 (12.50) |
| Total | 64 (100) |

Turkey's Third-Party filings also illustrate its close commercial relationship (and frictions) with the European Union. In all of Turkey's Third-Party appearances (64 disputes), the European Union was a participant.[91] The latter appeared either as the main Complainant (15 times), fellow Third-Party litigant (37 times),[92] or the Respondent (12 times).[93] The 52 clearly non-adversarial appearances indicate that, as the junior partner in the CU, Turkey has largely incorporated and followed the senior partner's litigation positions at the DSB. Yet, the 12 quasi-adversarial appearances (i.e., disputes where Turkey appeared as a Third Party while the EU was the Respondent) suggest a nontrivial level of divergence. Of these 12, nine were challenges to EU use of trade remedies (i.e., seven AD, one CVD, and one safeguard challenge).[94] Besides revealing a measure of independence, Turkey's participation as Third Party in these nine trade-remedy disputes "against" the European Union might be viewed as an attempt by Turkey to change EU trade-remedy regulations, which it cannot pursue as the CU's junior party. Remarkably, eight of these nine cases were brought in the last decade.[95] This suggests Turkey has a growing interest in revisiting aspects of its trade relationship with the European Union, short of leaving the CU. Next, we examine the nexus between Turkey's trade policy goals and its litigation performance.

## IV. THE RELATIONSHIP BETWEEN TURKEY'S TRADE OBJECTIVES AND LITIGATION PERFORMANCE

As set out in Section I, Turkey's first and foremost trade policy objective has been to reduce its current account deficit, which largely stems from the country's high trade deficit in goods. To reduce this deficit, uninterrupted since 1946, Turkey has deployed two strategies: (1) reducing import dependency on intermediate goods; and (2) expanding exports, while diversifying export destinations. In pursuit of these two goals, Turkey has applied various trade policy tools (*see* Chapter 4), which could have impacted its litigation performance at the WTO.

91. *See id.*
92. *See id.*
93. Specifically, these "Turkey vs. European Union," indirect clashes occurred in: EC–Trademarks and Geographical Indications; EC–Provisional Steel Safeguards; EC–IT Products; EC–Fasteners (China); EU–Footwear (China); EU–Fatty Alcohols (Indonesia); EU–Herring; European Union–Anti-Dumping Measures on Biodiesel from Argentina; EU–Cost Adjustment Methodologies (Russia); EU–Biodiesel (Indonesia); and EU–Price Comparison Methodologies. *See id.*
94. *See id.*
95. *See id.*

## A. Red Flags on the Intermediate Goods Front

Because Turkey is bound to apply EU-set, *low-level* tariffs (CETs), reducing import dependency on intermediate goods has required Turkey to aggressively implement measures that protect domestically produced, intermediate goods. To assist the intermediate goods industry, Turkey has also granted a wide range of subsidies and incentives.[96] Arguably, one would expect that such trade management would nullify or impair the benefits of Turkey's WTO counterparts, thus triggering the filing of disputes before the DSB. Turkey's infrequent appearance as a Respondent seems to indicate, however, that its trade policies have been either mostly consistent with its WTO commitments or not so conspicuous as to trigger other Members' trade sensitivities.

Although officials have adopted measures favoring Turkey's manufacturing sector, the country seldom has been challenged before the DSB. For instance, as of January 2021, Turkey has been the target of consultations requests only ten times. Compared to Argentina (22 cases); Brazil (17 cases); Chile (13 cases); China (45 cases); India (32 cases); Indonesia (15 cases); and Mexico (15 cases)[97]—all middle-income countries[98]—Turkey has been targeted less often, despite being a frequent user of subsidies and trade remedies. Although it lost the only two disputes that made it to the final panel stage, one cannot say, based on two instances, that Turkey has done much worse than any other Respondent. Rather, the more important lesson here might be that Turkey has calibrated its trade policy to further its intermediate-good industry with measures that, though deviating from market principles at times, have not drawn much attention of its trade partners.

## B. Benign Export Measures

Expanding exports and diversifying export destinations is the other major trade strategy that would help Turkey decrease its trade and current account deficits.[99] Indeed, Turkey intends to reach $500 billion worth of exports by 2023.[100] This overly ambitious objective has been pursued in two ways. First, Turkey has deployed various export-promotion tools.[101] Not unlike the measures designed to reduce Turkey's dependence on intermediate goods, export promotion has not led to much trade friction—Turkey's measures have only been the target of requests for consultations ten times, definitely less than comparable middle-income countries.

Second, to help promote its exports, Turkey has been a seemingly strategic and definitely frequent user of indirect trade litigation (64 appearances as Third-Party litigant). As Third-Party adjudicator, Turkey has taken advantage of trade-remedy law

96. *See* Turkey TPR 2016, *supra* note 8, at 29, 41.
97. *See* Dispute Settlement: The Disputes, Disputes by Member, WTO [hereinafter *WTO Disputes by Member*], https://www.wto.org/english/tratop_e/dispu_e/dispu_by_country_e.htm (last visited Jan. 30, 2021).
98. *See* World Bank Country Income, *supra* note 85.
99. *See supra* Section II.
100. *See* Turkey TPR 2016, *supra* note 8, at 17.
101. *See id.*, at 87-96.

litigation (seven safeguard and 32 AD/CVD challenges) to protect existing (safeguard disputes) or open potential markets (AD/CVD disputes) for its significant export sectors (iron and steel, automobiles, textiles and clothing, agriculture, etc.). Notably, because safeguards are not country-specific measures, Turkey benefits directly from defeating them—while also saving resources—by entering Third-Party appearances. Yet, Turkey's Third-Party appearance in country-specific, AD/CVD disputes can be viewed as part of a "play-for-precedent" strategy that involves suing with an interest in undermining other Members' trade-remedy practices that could eventually jeopardize Turkish exporters.[102]

That said, Turkey has been a rather infrequent (direct) Complainant. It has brought only six cases: three targeting countries not among Turkey's top-ten exporting partners (e.g., Egypt, South Africa, and Morocco), two targeting the United States, and one targeting the European Union.[103] Although, technically, the CU does not restrict Parties from suing each other in other fora, Turkey abstained from suing the European Union for more than two-and-half decades at the DSB. Remarkably, despite agriculture's exclusion from the CU, Turkey has yet to challenge the EU Common Agricultural Policy's (CAP) massive agricultural subsidies. In fact, as of January 2021, Turkey has been a Complainant less frequently than: Argentina (21 cases); Brazil (33 cases); Chile (ten cases); China (21 cases); Guatemala (ten cases); Honduras (eight cases); India (24 cases); Indonesia (12 cases); Mexico (25 cases); Panama (seven cases); Russia (eight cases); Taiwan (seven cases); Thailand (14 cases); and Ukraine (nine cases).[104] At a time when Complainants typically win 90 percent of their challenges, Turkey's infrequent use of direct litigation is intriguing. Setting aside its close ties with the European Union and the litigation-inhibiting effect that being in a CU might have, Turkey's lack of interest in direct litigation is perhaps best explained by a certain reluctance to restrain its trade management options in case it succeeds in challenging those of other Members.

Regardless, Turkey's performance as a WTO litigator has not (and, as we demonstrate in the next Section, could not have) secured its trade policy objectives. As previously discussed, Turkey's dependence on intermediate-good imports has remained too high—intermediate-good imports amounted to 75.3, 77.1, and 74.2 percent of Turkey's total imports in 2018, 2019, and 2020, respectively.[105] This dependence makes it hard for Turkey to reduce trade deficits via greater exports. Further, although Turkey's exports increased to $171 billion in 2019, the highest level in Turkey's history,[106] its main export destinations remained the same (i.e., the Europe—including

102. For a different application of such strategy, *see* Colares, *supra* note 47, at 418.
103. *See* Appendix III, Table III.1 (indicating the Respondents in Turkey's six direct filings); Turkish Statistical Institute, Statistics By Theme, Foreign Trade Statistics, Exports by Country and Year, http://www.turkstat.gov.tr/PreIstatistikTablo.do?istab_id=2889 (last visited Jan. 30, 2021).
104. *See* WTO Disputes by Member, *supra* note 97.
105. *See* Turkish Statistical Institute, Foreign Trade Statistics, Foreign Trade by Classification of Broad Economic Categories (BEC), New Imports by Classification of Broad Economic Categories (BEC), https://data.tuik.gov.tr/Kategori/GetKategori?p=dis-ticaret-104&dil=1 (last visited Feb. 4, 2021). We made the percentage calculations above based on data from this source.
106. *See* Appendix I.

the United Kingdom and other non-EU countries—capturing 55.9 percent of Turkey's total exports; and the Near/Middle East and Northern African countries, receiving 22.6 percent of Turkey's total exports).[107] Together, these two factors largely account for Turkey's uninterrupted trade deficit (1946-present), which reached $31 billion in 2019.[108] Having such structural constraints in its trade profile, even the most successful trade litigation strategy would be of limited efficacy for Turkey. As such, trade litigation holds little promise for advancing Turkey's export growth goals.

In the following section, we examine the extent to which the inefficacy of trade litigation for Turkey, at least, is also compounded by: (i) limitations inherent in the WTO dispute settlement system (e.g., prospective-only, remedial litigation; limited bilateral reach; etc.); and (ii) the role of the sui generis composition of Turkey's trade partners, most of which are either neighbors that have yet to become WTO Members, or are members of the European Union, to whom Turkey has surrendered trade sovereignty. Thus, in light of the limitations of trade litigation as a policy tool, Turkey must identify more promising alternatives for addressing its persistent current account and trade deficits. Any such alternative ought to account for Turkey's intermediate-good dependence and, more importantly, address its need for greater export diversification.

## V. WHY LITIGATION CANNOT ADDRESS TURKEY'S TRADE IMBALANCES

Two main reasons explain why litigation has not and cannot greatly help Turkey address its challenges: one systemic, the other, sui generis. We discuss each of them below.

### A. Systemic Limitations

Dispute settlement at the DSB has obvious, inherent limitations associated with its bilateral nature and type of remedies it offers. In a Member-to-Member[109] (i.e., bilateral) adjudicatory system, a Member can only protect its bargained-for concessions if it can establish that another Member's trade measures have nullified or impaired its benefits. This means that an aggrieved member can only vindicate its interest if it prevails upon the other to change its conduct either through consultations, or as a result of successful litigation. Yet, the scope of what can be offered in settlement during the consultations stage can be quite limited. Operation of the MFN principle

107. *See* Turkish Statistical Institute, Foreign Trade Statistics, Foreign Trade by Country Group and Year, New Exports by Country Group and Year, https://data.tuik.gov.tr/Kategori/GetKategori?p=dis-ticaret-104&dil=1 (last visited Jan. 30, 2021). We made the percentage calculations above based on data from this table.

108. *See* Appendix I.

109. Although "state-to-state" is the more intuitive phrase, technically, only states who are WTO Members can sue each other, hence the term "Member-to-Member." *But see* Joost Pauwelyn, *The Limits of Litigation: "Americanization" and Negotiation in the Settlement of WTO Disputes*, 19 Ohio St. J. Disp. Resol. 121, 129 (2003).

limits what potential Respondents can offer as settlement to induce potential Complainants to forgo litigation, because concessions made in settlement might trigger the obligation to extend similar concessions to non-litigant, third countries. That being the case, outright litigation is perhaps more likely in the WTO system than in other adjudicatory systems.

In addition to the *settlement constraints* imposed by the MFN principle, the *range of remedies* obtained through WTO litigation is also restricted, for successful litigation can only offer forward-looking remedies.[110] A harmed Member can only obtain relief, if eventually successful, and only against the Member that infringed its obligations. In fact, in some cases, such remedies come too little, too late. For instance, by the time the Complainant wins, the violating measure may have already entrenched the unlawful advantage the Respondent Member's industry obtained. In such cases, removal of the violating measure becomes a Pyrrhic victory. To wit, the flagrantly WTO-inconsistent Ontario Feed-in Tariffs ("FIT"), a program that provided subsidies to local producers of equipment associated with generating renewable energy in Canada. FIT hurt Japanese exports in that sector, but, more significantly, once adjudicated WTO-inconsistent, Japanese exports never recovered.[111] Thus, law-breaking first and removing offending measures later "paid off," rendering Japan's victory nearly meaningless.

Finally, the *duration of disputes* constitutes another major systemic limitation that reduces the value of WTO litigation. According to Reich (2017), the average duration of disputes (i.e., from the request of consultations to the adoption of a panel/AB report) was 28 months between 2007 and 2011.[112] Of course, many disputes do not end with the voluntary adoption of the resulting DSB report by the losing Member.[113] Such Member also benefits from the right to implement WTO-consistent measures within a reasonable time.[114] Although Members seem to have a very high compliance rate (i.e., 83 percent) overall, the on-time-compliance rate is only about 60 percent.[115] Thus, recalcitrance as well as built-in protections can result in delayed and ineffective justice.[116] This problem has also been noticed by other scholars.[117] To some, trade disputes could be more easily solved through trade diplomacy rather than trade litigation.

A recent example, involving Turkey, illustrates how limited and delayed remedies might affect potential Complainant's attitudes toward WTO litigation. In 2015, Russia imposed a number of sanctions, including trade sanctions, against Turkey. Most

110. *See* Colares, *supra* note 47, at 430.
111. *See* Appellate Body Report, *Canada–Measures Relating to the Feed-in Tariff Program*, WTO Doc. WT/DS412/AB/R (adopted May 6, 2013).
112. Arie Reich, *The Effectiveness of the WTO Dispute Settlement System: A Statistical Analysis* 23, 31 (European Univ. Inst., EUI Working Paper No. Law 2017/11).
113. *See* Pauwelyn, *supra* note 109, at 136.
114. *See DSU*, *supra* note 14, Art. 21.3.
115. William J. Davey, *Compliance Problems in WTO Dispute Settlement*, 42 CORNELL INT'L L. J. 119, 119-121 (2009).
116. *See id.* at 119; Bartosz Ziemblicki, *The Controversies over the WTO Dispute Settlement System*, EUROPEANA.EU 196, 199-201 (2009), https://www.europeana.eu/portal/en/record/09404/id_oai_www_bibliotekacyfrowa_pl_32203.html (last visited Jan. 30, 2021).
117. *See* Ziemblicki, *supra* note 116.

Turkish exports were embargoed following Turkey's shooting of a Russian jet that violated Turkey's airspace.[118] Bozkurt Aran, former Ambassador of Turkey at the WTO, posited that Turkey had a solid case and would bring the dispute against Russia before the DSB, because, according to him, Russian measures were inconsistent with Russia's WTO commitments.[119] Yet, Turkey never brought a dispute before the DSB. Turkey decided to solve the matter solely via direct diplomatic negotiation. Within less than two years, it settled the matter with Russia without going into protracted litigation.[120] Regardless of one's views on the desirability of Turkey's handling of this issue (i.e., directly) with Russia or the relative cost of the settlement, one has to wonder whether one could expect the WTO system to provide a more expedient outcome for Turkey.[121]

### B. Geographic Limitations

A non-systemic, notably geographical reason why litigation has not and could not have been an effective trade policy tool for Turkey has to do with Turkey's limited capability to use litigation against most of its sui generis, neighboring trade partners. The majority of Turkey's neighboring trade partners (i.e., Iraq, Syria, Iran, Azerbaijan, Algeria, etc.) are not WTO Members, and Russia, another important trade partner, only became a Member in 2012.[122] Hence, the prosecution of WTO disputes against these neighbors has been mostly impossible.

Turkey has also been severely constrained from litigating against its main Western neighbor, the European Union, because of their CU partnership. Indeed, since entering the CU (1996), the European Union and Turkey had never brought disputes against each other, until 2019.[123] As the junior partner in the CU, Turkey agreed to adopt EU trade laws and regulations[124] and has applied EU CETs on industrial products,[125] while it has been excluded from the trade decision-making process of the

118. *See* Kathrin Hille, *Russia Lifts Most Sanctions Imposed on Turkey after Downing of Jet*, FIN. TIMES (May 31, 2017), https://www.ft.com/content/38698b56-460c-11e7-8519-9f94ee97d996.
119. Hacer Boyacıoglu, *Russia's Sanctions on Turkey against World Trade Agreement*, HÜRRIYET DAILY NEWS (Dec. 2, 2015), http://www.hurriyetdailynews.com/russias-sanctions-on-turkey-against-world-trade-agreement-91975.
120. *See* Hille, *supra* note 118.
121. Determining whether this settlement led to a reasonable deal for Turkey in light of its relative cost is beyond the scope of this book.
122. ACCESSIONS: RUSSIAN FEDERATION, WTO, https://www.wto.org/english/thewto_e/acc_e/a1_russie_e.htm (last visited Jan. 30, 2021).
123. In 2019, the European Union filed a request for consultations in relation to Turkey's localization and technology transfer requirements for certain pharmaceutical products. As of January 2021, this dispute remains in the panel stage. *See Turkey–Certain Measures Concerning the Production, Importation and Marketing of Pharmaceutical Products*, WTO Doc. WT/DS583 (Mar. 17, 2020) (Complainant: European Union).
124. *See* Decision No. 1/95 of the EC-Turkey Association Council of 22 December 1995 on Implementing the Final Phase of the Customs Union 96/142, Art. 12, 1996 O.J. (L 035) (EC) [hereinafter *CU Decision*].
125. *See id.*, Art. 13.

European Union.[126] Presumably, Turkey's ambition to become a full member of the European Union operated as an important, litigation-constraining factor.[127] Turkey filed its first ever case against the European Union in 2020.[128]

In sum, trade litigation at the WTO has not and could not have been an effective trade policy tool for Turkey. Litigation-systemic and geographic constraints continue to affect its ability to resort to trade litigation as a main Complainant. That Turkey has occasionally become a Third-Party adjudicator against the European Union—hoping, presumably, to affect EU trade administration in one-off, discrete interventions—is likely to yield little tangible gain. Turkey's exports are not directly impacted by favorable outcomes in these disputes, however, because new opportunities from such (Third-Party) wins must be shared with a wide range of trade competitors; and eventual changes in EU measures might need to be implemented by Turkey itself, pursuant to the CU.[129] For these reasons, although Turkey's days of withholding from directly challenging EU trade policy before DSB are over, Turkey will have to adopt, inevitably, other trade policy tools to address its current account and trade deficits.

## VI. IMPLICATIONS

If Turkey were to regain its ability to pursue and forge additional trade ties, particularly with countries beyond its immediate European and Middle Eastern neighborhood, it would be better positioned to expand and diversify its exports, which, in turn, could help reducing its trade and current account deficits. In fact, current and evolving circumstances are increasingly favorable for such a move. Australia, Brazil, Japan, South Korea, the United Kingdom, and the United States are seeking to reduce their reliance on Chinese products and technology. Unfettered by CU constraints, Turkey could become a new, major hub in a more decentralized global supply network. Further, in light of the current stalemate over WTO Appellate Body replacements and the associated interruption of its operations, the opportunity to sign new FTAs would also allow Turkey and its new FTA partners to create new, more responsive and directly accountable dispute settlement systems that could help reduce eventual trade friction. Next, Chapter 6 discusses how such a plan can be put in place both legally and transactionally.

126. *See* Ufuk Alkan, *The Modernization of Turkey's Customs Union with the European Union: Reasons and Possible Outcomes*, C. of Eur. Dep't of EU Int'l Rel. & Dipl. Stud. EU Dipl. Paper 5-8 (September 2017), https://www.coleurope.eu/system/files_force/research-paper/edp-9-2017_ alkan.pdf?download = 1.
127. *See* Saribeyoglu, *supra* note 55.
128. *See* European Union–Safeguard Measures on Certain Steel Products, WTO Doc. WT/DS595 (Sept. 30, 2020) (Complainant: Turkey).
129. *See CU Decision*, *supra* note 124, Art. 12.

CHAPTER 6

# TURK-SWITCH: Turkey's Chance to Prosper Through Trade*

## I. OVERVIEW

After trying various policies (discussed in Chapter 4)—even the strategic use of WTO litigation (discussed in Chapter 5)—without much success in reducing its perennial trade and current account deficits, Turkey must consider other trade policy tools. Obviously, export growth is essential for Turkey to achieve these goals. To export a relatively higher share of GDP, Turkey will have to diversify exports and export destinations, while not ignoring the role of intermediate-good imports, which we also identified as a significant constraint on Turkey's trade-deficit reduction attempts (Chapter 4, Section II.A). If Turkey is indeed serious about attaining *above-trend* export growth, it has no alternative but to redeploy and leverage its significant tariff discretion under the WTO system.

As explained before (Chapter 4, Section II.B), Turkish negotiators succeeded in securing quite favorable tariff bindings in the Uruguay Round negotiations. Yet, only a couple of years later, Turkey relinquished much of its tariff discretion when the CU went into effect (1996). If Turkey expected the CU to be the ticket for EU membership, it stands to reason why it should carry on waiving its sizeable tariff discretion, when membership no longer seems attainable two decades later, *if it ever was*. Undoubtedly, with zero chance of EU accession, and facing stepped up EU FTA signings, Turkey's CU-related opportunity costs have increased appreciably. The reader will remember that, under CU rules, Turkey must offer the same concessions the European Union gives its new FTA partners, while extracting no similar concessions from those parties,

---

* An earlier version of this chapter was published in Oxford University Press's Journal of International Economic Law. *See* Juscelino F. Colares and Mustafa T. Durmuş, *TURK-SWITCH: The Tariff-Leverage and Legal Case for Turkey's Shift from Customs Union to FTA with the European Union and Beyond*, 22:1 J. INT'L ECON. L. 99-123 (2019) (peer reviewed).

so more EU FTA signings mean further erosion of Turkey's tariff leverage. Given Turkey's need to address economic challenges, the stalled (and hopeless) EU accession process, and the rising asymmetric effects of not having trade sovereignty, time has come for Turkey to revisit the CU question.

In this chapter, we seek to: (i) determine whether TURK-SWITCH—a combined exit from the CU with a transition to several FTAs, including a first with the European Union—could position Turkey closer to achieving significant export growth; and (ii) ascertain *how* Turkey might implement TURK-SWITCH both legally and transactionally. At first, we acknowledge that recovering trade sovereignty and restructuring a trade relationship will create risk and might introduce some uncertainty for the European Union and Turkey. Indeed, the protracted negotiations (2016-2020) between the European Union and the United Kingdom that followed the BREXIT-vote demonstrate that restructuring large relationships and their underlying legal frameworks are no trivial matter. Yet, those negotiations dealt with the severance of much *closer* ties: as an EU Member, the United Kingdom did adopt EU's trade policy—not unlike Turkey—but it was also *governed* by the same regulatory, financial, and foreign policy disciplines—Turkey is not. Although less complex negotiations will take place in case of TURK-SWITCH, they will reach a wide range of *trade* issues (e.g., antidiscrimination rules, ROOs, continued harmonization of rules on sanitary, phytosanitary, and other trade-related regulatory areas, etc.), and, there, cooler heads will need to focus on exploring opportunities for mutual gain under a restructured framework that maintains deeply integrated supply chains and economic policy convergence.

Because strong EU-Turkey ties and mutual interests (e.g., maintaining supply chains, financial interconnectedness, security, etc.) would be protected by *stability* in their overall relationship, should Turkey opt for TURK-SWITCH, EU-Turkey negotiations would likely take on aspects of the behavioral pattern known as *Coordination*. As explained in Chapter 1, when parties interact and perceive agreement restructuring as a positive-sum outcome (i.e., mutual gains are possible), they agree to coordinate, cooperate, or some combination of the two. Not unlike Cooperation, Coordination is premised on one party maintaining the ability to observe what the other does. When the benefit from one party's action depends on the action of the other, however, only Coordination can ensure that both actions are not in a collision course. In fact, in certain settings, change, as in restructuring a previous commitment, may only be possible when parties agree to coordinate their actions (e.g., in a two-lane road, one driver only benefits from driving on the lane right of the dividing line if the other, coming in the opposite direction, does the same). Take the EU-Turkey context, specifically: EU enthusiasm for greater FTA diplomacy—matched by TURK-SWITCH's aim of further trade liberalization—make it critical that both parties coordinate on assessing the impact of their FTAs on their existing supply chains and interconnected financial structure. This is no different than what Canadian, Mexican, and US trade diplomats do when they consider new FTAs in light of their remaining commitments under the North American Free Trade Agreement (NAFTA),[1] as well as under the United States-Mexico-Canada Free Trade Agreement, the successor to NAFTA.[2]

Lurking behind these initial concerns is also the undeniable fact that the one-sided deterioration of the original CU deal for Turkey is *unsustainable* in the long term (we discussed this issue in greater detail in Chapter 4, Section II.B and summarized it in Section II.A, below). Thus, even as EU negotiators initially may be tempted to resist any attempt by Turkey at restructuring away from the CU—an agreement that has been quite favorable to the European Union—a restructured relationship, on balance, would surely be preferable to rejecting Turkey's request and risking a future, major breakdown in EU-Turkey relations. Accordingly, a qualified argument for *cooperative action* can be also made in regard to TURK-SWITCH. In sum, negotiators will need to ensure existing supply chains remain largely untouched, while previous concessions are maintained, and those removed are traded off for others.

Finally, to quell domestic and international (i.e., particularly Western) anxieties about TURK-SWITCH, Turkey's leaders should stress, at the outset, that the very idea of Turkey leaving the CU in no way constitutes a departure from Turkey's century-old Republican commitment to further Westernization, but a fuller embrace of it.[3] As explained throughout this chapter, TURK-SWITCH is part of a *package* of policy initiatives that will further secure Turkey's Westernization by pushing the country toward the adoption of a more cosmopolitan trade stance, not unlike that proposed by the current Johnson Government in the United Kingdom.[4]

To determine whether TURK-SWITCH might be a feasible approach for Turkey, Section II provides a thorough analysis of Turkey's significant tariff discretion under

---

1. *See* North American Free Trade Agreement, U.S.-Can-Mex., Dec. 17, 1992, 32 I.L.M. 289 (1993) [hereinafter NAFTA].
2. The United States-Mexico-Canada Free Trade Agreement went into effect on Jul. 1, 2020. *United States-Mexico-Canada Agreement*, Office of the U.S. Trade Representative, https://ustr.gov/trade-agreements/free-trade-agreements/united-states-mexico-canada-agreement [https://perma.cc/7HCY-44G6] (last visited Feb. 24, 2021). Although the agreement replaced NAFTA on that day, it extends member consent to claims for investment arbitration under NAFTA for up to three years following NAFTA's termination, so long as those claims arise from investments "established or acquired" when NAFTA was in force and remained "in existence" on the date the new agreement went into effect. *Compare* Agreement between the United States of America, the United Mexican States, and Canada, Nov. 30, 2018, Preamble, https://ustr.gov/trade-agreements/free-trade-agreements/united-states-mexico-canada-agreement/agreement-between [hereinafter USMCA], *with* USMCA, Chapter 14, Annex 14-C, Arts. 3 & 6(a).
3. *See* Mine Eder, Becoming Western: Turkey and the European Union, *in Regionalism Across the North/South Divide: State Strategies and Globalization* 79, 79-95 (Jean Gruel & Wil Hout, eds., 1999); HARUN ARIKAN, TURKEY AND THE EU: AN AWKWARD CANDIDATE FOR EU MEMBERSHIP? 77-103 (2003).
4. *See, e.g., UK formally asks to join CPTPP*, INSIDE U.S. TRADE'S WORLD TRADE ONLINE (Feb. 2, 2021), *available at*: https://insidetrade.com/trade/uk-formally-asks-join-cptpp (quoting British Trade Secretary Liz Truss' statements that "the UK would like 'to formally request the commencement of negotiations on UK accession to [the Comprehensive and Progressive Agreement on the Trans-Pacific Partnership] CPTPP'," and that "Unlike EU membership, joining does not require the UK to cede control over our laws, borders, or money."); *accord* Jennifer Amur, *Full transcript: Theresa May's speech on Brexit*, WASH. POST (Jan. 17, 2017), *available at*: https://www.washingtonpost.com/news/worldviews/wp/2017/01/17/full-transcript-theresa-mays-speech-on-brexit/?noredirect=on&utm_term=.2241749f4d17 (quoting Prime Minister May's comment that "We want to get out into the wider world to trade and do business all around the globe.").

the WTO system, an essential source of *transactional* leverage on which Turkey could rely in a post-CU environment. CU withdrawal would restitute its tariff leverage, giving Turkey the necessary bargaining power to negotiate, first, a comprehensive FTA with the European Union and, later, other FTAs (i.e., this type of deal sequencing is another reason why Coordination might become the predominant behavioral pattern). Section III analyzes Turkish law to explore how TURK-SWITCH might be operationalized under the reformed constitution and discusses the legal hurdles Turkey will have to overcome under *international* law. After establishing the legal authority for the execution of TURK-SWITCH, Section IV discusses Turkey's negotiations with the European Union and, later, with other trade partners. It demonstrates how, through Coordination, a new FTA infrastructure would give Turkey the policy space it needs to pursue export growth (i.e., credibly, not just rhetorically) and, thus, have a chance to address its two historical trade challenges: trade and current account deficits. Section V concludes by explaining how, far from a departure, TURK-SWITCH's outward-looking trade approach would actually strengthen the Turkish Republic's historical commitment to Westernization.

## II. TURKEY'S TARIFF LEVERAGE UNDER THE WTO SYSTEM

As mentioned in Chapter 4, the conclusion of the Uruguay Round saw Turkey agree to bind 50.5 percent of all tariff lines (i.e., agricultural and nonagricultural goods).[5] While managing to limit tariff bindings to about slightly more than *one-third* (36.3 percent) of industrial goods at an average 42.6 percent a.v.,[6] Turkey bound *all* agricultural tariff lines at 61.8 percent a.v.[7] Should TURK-SWITCH be pursued, Turkey's reserve of tariff discretion could provide it negotiating power and flexibility.

### A. A Closer Look at CU Concessions and Loss of Trade Leverage

Since entering the CU, Turkey has had one of the *lowest* applied MFN[8] tariff levels on industrial goods[9] among developing countries, averaging 4.1 percent.[10] Turkey's tariffs on the larger *nonagricultural* goods category—which includes industrial, as well as fish

5. *See* Appendix II, Table II.1.
6. *See* Appendix II, Table II.1.
7. *See* Appendix II, Table II.2. Henceforth, unless otherwise indicated, all tariff percentages should be assumed to be a.v.
8. Generally, MFN tariffs refer to "most-favored nation" tariffs, meaning agreed-upon tariffs by parties to a trade agreement. MFN tariffs have become synonymous with the tariffs WTO Members have committed to applying to the goods they trade among each other. However, pursuant to GATT, Art. XXIV, countries that enter into certain types of trade arrangements can offer each other tariffs that are lower than MFN or WTO tariffs. This is the case with the EU-Turkey CU: Turkey and the countries in the European Union eliminated tariffs on industrial imports among them, yet charge MFN tariffs to non-EU Member industrial imports.
9. We focus the discussion largely on industrial good tariffs because the CU is restricted to these goods. *See* discussion *supra* Chapter 3, Section III.B.2.b.
10. *See* WTO Secretariat, *Trade Policy Review of Turkey*, WT/TPR/S/259/Rev.1, Table III.2 (Jan. 17, 2012) (using 2011 MFN tariff data on Harmonized Schedule Chapters 25-97, which cover all industrial products) [hereinafter Turkey TPR 2012].

and fishery products; minerals, metals and petroleum products; and leather and rubber, among other goods[11]—average 4.5 percent.[12] Such low MFN tariffs, particularly on industrial goods, largely reflect the CETs applied on these goods by all members of the single market.[13] By contrast, Argentina (14.0 percent), Brazil (13.9 percent), Egypt (11.6 percent), and Indonesia (8.0 percent) have higher average applied tariffs[14] on nonagricultural goods.[15] Turkey also has lower, average *bound* MFN tariffs (17.3 percent) on nonagricultural goods.[16] By contrast, Argentinean (31.7 percent), Brazilian (30.8 percent), Egyptian (27.4 percent), Mexican (34.8 percent) and Indonesian (35.5 percent) bound tariffs on such goods are nearly double.[17] Mexico, also a junior partner in another major trade block (USMCA) may impose up to 34.8 percent tariffs on nonagricultural goods from non-FTA countries—a discretion that, currently, Turkey lacks.[18]

As a middle-income country with developed-country-level tariffs on nonagricultural goods (5.5 percent average), Turkey should be in a position to obtain similar concessions from other middle-income countries that have FTAs with the European Union. That goods from Mexico or South Africa get zero tariffs when transshipped through an EU Member into Turkey—regardless of any concession they offer to Turkey (*see* discussion in Chapter 4, Section II.B)—amounts to a loss of substantial trade leverage.[19] Yet, this kind of asymmetry only partially captures the magnitude of Turkey's waived leverage on *industrial* goods trade: having only bound 36.3 percent of

---

11. *See* WTO Secretariat, *Trade Policy Review of Turkey*, WT/TPR/S/331, Table 3.3 (Feb. 9, 2016) [hereinafter Turkey TPR 2016].
12. *See* Appendix II, Table II.2 (providing WTO World Tariff Profiles data). Earlier data (2014) shows Turkey's applied tariffs on nonagricultural goods averaged 4.8 percent. *See* Chad P. Bown, *Trade Policy Flexibilities and Turkey: Tariffs, Anti-dumping, Safeguards and WTO Dispute Settlement*, The World Economy 193, 197 (2014) (providing data on "manufacturing products," a proxy for nonagricultural goods).
13. *See* Subidey Togan & Bartlomiej Kaminski, The Foreign Trade Regime and Trade Liberalization in Turkey, *in Economic Liberalization and Turkey* 13 (Subidey Togan ed., 2010).
14. *See* World Trade Organization, World Tariff Profiles 2020, at 20-24, https://www.wto.org/english/res_e/booksp_e/tariff_profiles20_e.pdf [hereinafter World Tariff Profiles 2020].
15. For the sake of comparability, we shall use nonagricultural tariffs as a "rough" proxy for industrial tariffs whenever country-to-country, industrial good-specific information for the *same* year is not available. We surmise the WTO stopped compiling *industrial* good tariffs by its Members in 2003 because of the Doha Round's focus on Non-Agricultural Market Access ("NAMA"), a broader, more ambitious negotiation agenda. To our knowledge, the last WTO document containing yearly, country-to-country comparisons on *industrial* goods—and the main source of such information for this book—remains Marc Bacchetta and Bijit Bora, *Industrial Tariff Liberalization and the Doha Development Agenda*, 15 World Trade Organization, Development and Economic Research Division (2003) (using 2001 data), *available at*: https://www.wto.org/english/res_e/booksp_e/discussion_papers_e.pdf. Because of the failure of the Doha Round and other negotiations on nonagricultural—and thus industrial—tariff reductions, we believe Bacchetta and Bora's data on bound industrial good tariffs remains accurate. For convenience, the portion of their data pertaining to the European Union and Turkey is summarized in Appendix II, Table II.1.
16. *See* Appendix II, Table II.2.
17. *See* World Tariff Profiles 2020, *supra* note 14.
18. *See id.*, at 22.
19. *See* World Bank, Evaluation of the EU-TURKEY Customs Union, at 24-25 and associated footnotes, Report No. 85830-TR (Mar. 28, 2014), http://www.worldbank.org/content/dam/Worldbank/document/eca/turkey/tr-eu-customs-union-eng.pdf [hereinafter World Bank Report].

its industrial tariffs in the WTO system, Turkey, under the CU, must apply CETs (i.e., 4.1 percent, the EU average bound rate) to 63.7 percent of such goods—goods on which it could impose *any* tariff.[20] Worse, with every new trade deal Brussels makes, Turkey's trade leverage is further eroded. Only a trading system *captured by multinational supply chain interests* could engineer such an exorbitant waiver of tariff leverage on the part of a sovereign nation.[21]

## B. Recovering Turkey's Industrial Tariff Leverage

As mentioned above, because bound EU MFN tariff rates on industrial goods are much lower than Turkey's—on average 4.1 versus 42.6 percent, respectively[22]—Turkey, by entering the CU, has effectively lowered tariffs on industrial imports from non-EU countries.[23] Moreover, the European Union bound *all* tariff lines in its WTO Schedule of Concessions, meaning that Turkey, a member of an industrial-goods-based CU, bound *all* industrial tariff lines as well; and at a much lower rate: 4.1 percent (on average).[24] With slightly more than one-third of its industrial tariff lines bound at more than ten times that rate (42.6 percent) and nearly two-thirds of such lines remaining unbound under the WTO system, leaving the CU would enable Turkey to recover much of its tariff leverage, thus allowing for generous concessions in an eventual EU-Turkey FTA. Such *residual* leverage—on industrial goods alone—would provide Turkey the opportunity to bargain lower industrial tariffs bindings and/or altogether new industrial tariff bindings in exchange for concessions from potential FTA counterparts. This

20. *See* Appendix II, Table II.1. *See also* International Trade Administration, Turkey-Import Tariff, *available at*: https://www.export.gov/article?id=Turkey-Import-Tariff (reporting Turkey as having left an even higher share unbound—66.5 percent—possibly resulting from compiling data on the broader nonagricultural category).
21. Note that, pursuant to the (EU) *acquis communautaire*, and, partly, to offset the revenue loss from CU implementation, the Turkish Parliament enacted Law No. 4760, creating a Special Consumption Tax ("ÖTV" or "SCT," its equivalent abbreviation in English) in 2002. *See* 4760 Numarali Özel Tuketim Kanunu, General Justification, 883, *available at:* http://www.gib.gov.tr/fileadmin/mevzuatek/gerekceler/KDV/tvk_4760_sayili_kanun.pdf. Since then, Turkish taxp ayers have been levied high internal consumption taxes on petroleum products (ranging from ₺2.15 to ₺2.29—per one-liter gasoline—almost 50 percent of the final consumer price), vehicles (up to 145 percent, a.v.), durable consumer goods (ranging between zero and 25), to name a few. SCT revenue amounted to 25.8 percent of total government tax revenue in 2014. *See* Turkey TPR 2016, *supra* note 11, at 60-64. Such revenue offset illustrates the monumental income transfer from the Turkish middle and lower classes to the export and banking sectors, the biggest winners from the CU.
22. *See* Appendix II, Table II.1.
23. *See* Appendix II, Table II.3 (providing tariff data on select industrial goods). A quick cross-reference to the fourth and sixth columns illustrates the point, but the reader should be mindful this Table II.3 does not include unbound industrial goods, where differentials should be much higher.
24. *See* Appendix II, Table II.1.

could also result in a non-negligible revenue gain by Turkey:[25] around 46 percent of Turkey's manufactured imports come from such third countries.[26]

## C. Leveraging Agricultural Tariffs

Of course, one would expect that agriculture—historically a politically sensitive sector in most countries and long-term recipient of government subsidies[27]—would be more protected than industrial sectors. Indeed, only with the establishment of the WTO did Members agree to a transition from nontariff import restrictions to tariffs, which are more transparent.[28] Not surprisingly, Turkey's WTO commitments on agricultural goods, particularly tariffs, stand in contrast to its commitments on industrial goods. For instance, Turkey's average bound MFN tariff rate for agricultural products is much higher, at 61.8 percent.[29] Reflecting this high level of protection, Turkey's simple average *applied* MFN tariff rate on agricultural goods was 42.3 percent in 2019.[30] Turkey's trade-weighted average tariff rate for such products was 20.4 percent in the same year—orders of magnitude higher than the comparable nonagricultural tariff rate, at 3.3 percent.[31]

Maintenance of the EU CAP—a set of subsidies and protections the European Union grants to its farmers—and subsidies the Turkish Government bestows to the agricultural sector explain, partly, why the CU does not cover agricultural goods. Accordingly, by not including agriculture in the CU, Turkey retained the significant tariff flexibility it reserved to itself under the Uruguay Round. In fact, Turkey has used its wider tariff discretion in agriculture to obtain trade concessions on industrial goods from other countries, including Iran.[32] Furthermore, in pursuit of its geopolitical interests, Turkey has granted agricultural goods from majority-Muslim Bosnia-Herzegovina near duty-free access.[33] That Turkey has exercised its remaining tariff discretion on agricultural goods to pursue wider, though, so far, mostly regional goals, reveals how a CU-free Turkey could become a dynamic dealmaker in international trade.

25. With this extra tariff revenue, the President stands a chance to decrease the above-mentioned, unpopular internal Special Consumption Tax. *See* discussion *supra* note 21.
26. *See* Turkish Statistical Institute, Statistics by Theme Foreign Trade Statistics, *available at*: http://www.turkstat.gov.tr/PreTablo.do?alt_id=1046 (follow "foreign trade Statistics" hyperlink; then click "Product/Product Groups-Partner Country"). Note that the authors arrived at the above number by using data on trade with countries Turkey has no preferential trade agreements or customs union.
27. *See* John H. Jackson, William J. Davey And Alan O. Sykes, Jr., Legal Problems of International Economic Relations Cases, Materials and Text 466 (6th ed. 2013).
28. *See id.*, at 465.
29. *See* Appendix II, Table II.2.
30. *See id.*
31. *See* World Tariff Profiles 2020, *supra* note 14, at 182.
32. Turkey and Iran signed a trade agreement in 2014, where Turkey used its agricultural tariff leverage to gain Iranian market access for 125 industrial products. *See* Turkey TPR 2016, *supra* note 11, at 36.
33. *Id.*, at 55-56.

### D. Tariff Flexibility and the Opportunity for TURK-SWITCH

Although withdrawal from the CU *alone* (i.e., without a negotiated replacement by an FTA) would be unwise, its immediate impact on Turkey's exports would not be profound. Initially, a no-deal scenario could lead to a relatively small increase in EU average tariffs. Under WTO rules and current commitments, EU tariffs on such goods—*all bound*—could rise from zero to 4.1 percent, the bound MFN tariff rate.[34] Turkey's industrial tariff increase could be much higher by comparison: tariffs could rise up to 42.6 percent and even infinity (i.e., no limit), for bound (one-third) and unbound (two-thirds) industrial goods, respectively.[35]

Obviously, the deep integration and complexity of EU-Turkey supply chains would strongly weigh against tariff hikes by either side. In today's complex and efficiently managed supply chains, tariff changes can be *profoundly* disruptive: marginal increases in cost structures might trigger consideration of new sourcing options. Yet, recognition of TURK-SWITCH's potential for supply-chain disruption must be weighed against Turkey's *costs* of maintaining the CU: (i) no voice in EU/CU trade policymaking; (ii) tariff erosion with respect to growing numbers of EU FTA partners; (iii) continued loss of (WTO) tariff leverage with respect to other countries; and (iv) diminished chances of achieving EU membership, as Turkey finds itself immersed in a process that lacks clear and objective criteria for membership and, worse, has no firm deadlines. Thus, even if one acknowledges the possibility on supply-chain disruptions, a negotiated departure from the CU with concurrent transition to an EU-Turkey FTA, followed by the signing of FTAs with other partners appears, on balance, as a more compelling alternative for Turkey. In fact, an EU-Turkey FTA that secured zero tariff rates on industrial and, potentially, other goods would be politically palatable to both sides without triggering trade disruption. Given these parties' high level of economic interdependence and the political advantages each could extract from a restructured framework, it is likely that coordinated and, to some extent, cooperative action would prevail as the dominant behavioral pattern in any eventual post-CU, EU-Turkey negotiations.

For Turkey, specifically, only a restructured trade framework would allow it to leverage its favorable WTO tariff schedule on industrial and agricultural goods to obtain reciprocal or at least semi-reciprocal tariff reductions from other trade partners and, thus, pursue export growth, which would allow it to begin addressing its intermediate-good dependency challenge.[36] Freed from the CU, Turkey could use its recovered trade sovereignty—particularly, its tariff leverage—to find new trade partners beyond its immediate European and Middle Eastern neighborhood and, thus, begin dealing with its trade and current account deficits. The following section explains

34. *See* Appendix II, Table II.1.
35. *See id.*
36. Remarkably, Turkey's 73 percent of imports are mainly intermediate and energy products. In case of withdrawal from the CU, Turkey might apply higher tariff rates for these products, which may increase the cost of exportable production and also increase the domestic inflation. Yet, since its tariff revenue would increase with the TURK-SWITCH, Turkey should lower its domestically imposed SCT to abate inflation.

how TURK-SWITCH might be operationalized under Turkey's domestic law (and new presidential regime), as well as under international law.

## III. OPERATIONALIZING TURK-SWITCH

### A. First Step: Legal Authority under Domestic and International Law

#### 1. *The Ankara Agreement, CU Decision, and Foreign Commerce Power under Turkish Law*

As discussed in Chapter 3, the 1963 Ankara Agreement[37] provides the legal framework for the EU-Turkey commercial relationship.[38] Following parliamentary ratification (1964),[39] the Turkish Government pursued the Agreement's main objective (i.e., to strengthen and deepen the Parties' economic partnership) on the belief that it constituted a major step toward to full membership in the Community.[40] Article 2 provided for the incremental establishment of a customs union under the auspices of the EU-Turkey Association Council.[41] The Council[42] was entrusted with the task of "ensur[ing] the implementation and progressive development of the Association" (i.e., the Customs Union).[43] Thus, the Association Council became *the vehicle* by which both Parties would pursue economic integration into a customs union.

According to the European Court of Justice (ECJ), Council Decisions have direct, binding effect on Members of the European Union.[44] Thus, Council Decisions cannot have direct effect in Turkey, a nonmember.[45] Such measures do create binding international obligations on Turkey, however. In principle, Article 90 of the Constitution of the Republic of Turkey provides a specific mechanism for approving international obligations contracted by Turkey: parliamentary approval, presidential sanction

37. *See* Agreement Establishing an Association between the European Economic Community and Turkey of September 12, 1963, 1964 J.O. (L 217) [hereinafter Ankara Agreement or Agreement].
38. *See* TÜRKIYE-AB ILISKILERININ TARIHÇESI [THE HISTORY OF THE TURKEY-EU RELATIONS], REPUBLIC OF TURKEY MINISTRY OF FOREIGN AFFAIRS, DIRECTORATE FOR EU AFFAIRS, *available at:* https://www.ab.gov.tr/111.html (last visited Mar. 1, 2021).
39. *See* 4 Subat 1964 Tarihli 397 Nolu Türkiye ile Avrupa Ekonomik Toplulugu Arasında bir Ortaklık Yaratan Andlaşma ve Eklerinin Onaylanmasının Uygun Bulunduguna Dair Kanun [Law No. 397 Approving the Ratification of the Agreement Establishing an Association between the European Economic Community and Turkey and Its Additional Protocols], Türkiye Cumhuriyeti Resmi Gazete [the Official Gazette of the Republic of Turkey], February 12, 1964 No. 11631.
40. *See* Ankara Agreement, Art. 2, *supra* note 37.
41. *See id.*, Art. 2.
42. *See id.*, Art. 23 (providing that "The Council ... consist[s] of members of the Governments of the Member States ... and of members of the Turkish Government on the other").
43. *See id.*, Art. 6.
44. *See* Case C-192/89, *Sevince v. Staatssecretaris van Justitie*, E.C.R. I-3462 (holding that "[t]he provisions adopted for the implementation of an association agreement ... by [an] Association Council ... form an integral part of the Community legal system, in the same way as the [association] agreement itself ... and must be regarded as being directly applicable ... ").
45. *See* Ilke Göçmen, *Avrupa Birligi ile Turkiye Arasindaki Gümrük Birliginin Guncellenmesinin Yontemi ve Usulu: Avrupa Birligi Açisindan Bir Bakis* [An Evaluation of Procedural Methods for Updating the EU-Turkey Customs Union], 15:1 ANKARA AVRUPA ÇALIŞMALARI DERGISI [ANKARA J. OF THE EUR. STUD.] 85, 93 (2016).

and official publication.[46] The Constitution also provides that such agreements "have the force of law," meaning they not only bind Turkey as a matter of international law but are also self-executing within Turkey.[47]

Remarkably, the CU Decision—the CU foundational document—has never been submitted to the Article 90 process and, thus, at least *formally*, remains not domesticated.[48] Lack of formal, constitutional domestication has not kept the CU from producing legal effects in Turkey for the better part of the last 26 years, however. Successive governments have brought Turkey into conformity with the CU Decision and many subsequent EU-Turkey Association Council measures affecting trade by amending domestic regulations pursuant to the express power conferred to the Council of Ministers by Law No. 474 of 1964 (tariff measures), Law No. 2976 of 1984 (additional financial measures on foreign trade), and Law No. 4458 of 1999 (nontariff measures).[49] In fact, under such delegated powers, the Council of Ministers could raise tariffs up to 150 percent.[50]

Following the 2017 Constitutional Reform, and pursuant to Articles 73:4 and 167:2 of the amended Constitution,[51] the GNA[52] delegated these very powers[53] to

46. *See* CONSTITUTION OF THE REPUBLIC OF TURKEY, Nov. 7, 1982 (as amended) Arts. 90:1 & 104:5 [hereinafter TURKISH CONST.], *available at*: https://www.constituteproject.org/constitution/Turkey_2017.pdf?lang=en.
47. *See* TURKISH CONST. Art. 90:5.
48. Some scholars have argued that, as a matter of Turkish law, because the CU Decision is an international commitment pursuant to an international treaty, "resulting in amendments to Turkish law," the Turkish Parliament had to approve it; the President had to sign it; and publication in the Official Gazette was required before deeming the CU Decision domesticated. According to this view, the EU-Turkey CU "must be declared as null and void." Kemal Baslar, *Gümrük Birligi "Anlaşması"nın (1/95 sayılı Ortaklık Konseyi Kararı'nın) Hukuksal Niteligi* [Legal Status of the Customs Union (Decision No. 1/95 of the Association Council Agreement)], 4:1 ANKARA AVRUPA ÇALIŞMALARI DERGISI [ANKARA J. OF THE EUR. STUD.] 151, 151 (2004). We do not subscribe to this view.
49. *See, e.g.*, Turkey TPR 2012, *supra* note 10, at 11 and Table A.II.1; Turkey TPR 2016, *supra* note 11, at 28, 45, & 118; 23 Haziran 2003 Tarihli ve 2003/5930 Sayili Avrupa Birligi Müktesebatının Üstlenilmesine Ilişkin Türkiye Ulusal Programının Uygulanması, Koordinasyonu ve Izlenmesine Dair Bakanlar Kurulu Karari [Council of Minister's Decision No. 2003/5930 regarding the Application, Coordination and Observation of the Turkish National Program in order to Undertake the EU *Acquis Communautaire*], Türkiye Cumhuriyeti Resmi Gazete [the Official Gazette of the Republic of Turkey], July 24, 2003 No. 25178.
50. *See* Turkey TPR 2016, *supra* note 11, at 50.
51. Article 73:4 of the Turkish Constitution provides that "[t]he President of the Republic may be empowered [by the Grand National Assembly] to amend the percentages of exemption, exceptions and reductions in taxes, fees, duties, and other such financial obligations, within the minimum and maximum limits prescribed by law." Article 167:2 provides that "to regulate foreign trade ... the President of the Republic may be empowered by law to introduce *additional* financial impositions on imports, exports, and other foreign trade transactions, ... or to lift them" (emphasis added).
52. To reflect Turkey's switch from a parliamentary to a presidential system, and the amended Constitution, henceforth, we shall refer to Turkey's post-referendum legislative branch solely as the Grand National Assembly or Assembly. *See* TURKISH CONST. Art. 7.
53. *See* 21 Ocak 2018 Tarihli 6771 Nolu Turkiye Cumhuriyeti Anayasasinda Degisiklik Yapilmasina Dair Kanun [Law No. 6771 Amending the Constitution of the Republic of Turkey], Türkiye Cumhuriyeti Resmi Gazete [the Official Gazette of the Republic of Turkey], February 11, 2017 No. 29976, Arts. 16 & 17 [hereinafter Referendum Law] (stating that, as a result of the 2017 Constitutional Referendum, the term *Cumhurbaskani* (President) replaces *Bakanlar Kurulu*

Turkey's President—now also head of government and successor to the Council of Ministers.[54] Because these constitutional provisions expressly refer to the *possibility* of presidential "empower[ment]," which implies legislative action, the Assembly, as principal, may also rescind its broad delegations, by legislation.[55] Of course, this seems highly unlikely in present-day Turkey. Yet, should the Assembly decide to withdraw its broad trade authority delegations to the President, and should the President veto such a bill, the Assembly can overcome a presidential veto by a mere absolute majority vote (i.e., a vote by more than half of all its members).[56] Thus, the President must hold close consultations with the Assembly.

## 2. *Limits to Presidential Treaty-(Re)Negotiating Authority*

Besides bestowing on the Assembly original foreign commerce power, the Turkish Constitution also grants the Assembly the final say on treaty approval.[57] Ratification—a process essential for the domestication of treaties—is designed for approving agreements the President negotiates and signs pursuant to his/her original constitutional power.[58] This process does not leave room for amendments, for any such attempt would defeat the notion of finalized negotiations. Ratification is also inherently incompatible with any action related to agreement-termination or withdrawal. Rather, in many presidential constitutional republics, the task of terminating treaties falls to the President, the head of an entirely separate branch of government, who is uniquely positioned to define and implement *a unified national interest*, and on whom constitutions typically bestow original treaty-negotiating power.[59] Recognizing the President as the preeminent center of energy within the US Government, Hamilton explained that "[t]o have intrusted [*sic*] the power of making treaties to the Senate [i.e., the ratifying body in the United States] *alone*, would have been to relinquish the benefits of the constitutional agency of the President in the conduct of foreign negotiations."[60] Not

(Council of Ministers) in all relevant Articles of the Turkish Constitution (Art. 16), as well in all statutes and regulations (Art. 17)). *Cf.* TURKISH CONST. Art. 73:3 (providing that "[t]axes, fees, duties and other such financial obligations shall be imposed, amended, or revoked by law").

54. *See* TURKISH CONST. Art. 8.
55. *See supra* note 51.
56. *See* TURKISH CONST. Art. 89:3.
57. Article 90 of the Turkish Constitution provides that "treaties ... shall be subject to adoption by the ... Assembly ... by a law approving the ratification." The language that bestows treaty-negotiating power upon the President employs the term "ratification" seemingly as synonymous with presidential negotiating and signing of treaties: Art. 104 states that the President "ratifies and promulgates international treaties." Taken together, Arts. 90 and 104 indicate that, under Turkey's legal system, the President has treaty-negotiating power, while the Assembly has treaty-ratifying power, as these terms are commonly understood in the Western legal traditions.
58. *See* TURKISH CONST. Art. 104.
59. *See id.* ("Executive power is vested in the President of the Republic ... he/she shall represent the Republic of Turkey and the *unity* of the Turkish Nation ... ") (emphasis added). *Cf.* U.S. CONST. Art. II, §§ 1 ("The executive Power shall be vested in a President") & 2, cl. 3 ("He shall have Power, by and with the Advice and Consent of the Senate, to make Treaties ... .").
60. *See* THE FEDERALIST NO. 75 (Alexander Hamilton) (emphasis added), *available at*: https://guides.loc.gov/federalist-papers/full-text. Although Hamilton lauded the President's unique position among the nations as a negotiator, he did indicate that the "greater prospect of security" for the

unlike consultations that precede and follow presidential conclusion of agreement negotiations, agreement withdrawals and any subsequent launch of new negotiations also require close consultation between the executive and the legislative branches.

If constitutional separation of powers were not construed as requiring the President to consult with the Assembly prior to CU withdrawal, the legal status of the Ankara Agreement would provide a compelling reason for close executive-legislative coordination and cooperation. Ratified pursuant to Article 90 of the Turkish Constitution and "hav[ing] the force of law," internally, the Agreement is deeply ensconced in Turkish *domestic* law.[61] Arguably, any change in the Agreement's architecture, including its termination, would likely result in new tariffs. As discussed above, the power necessary for such domestically focused action currently lies with the President, but that authority could be taken back if the Assembly rescinded its broad delegation. In sum, although the President has the power to withdraw Turkey from the Ankara Agreement, any such termination will require: (a) immediate amendment of Turkey's border measures on EU imports; or (b) replacing the Agreement with another that, to be binding, would require Article 90 *domestication*. Either option requires Assembly acquiescence (i.e., leaving its tariff power delegation in place) or direct legislative action (i.e., ratification, in the traditional sense) to produce domestic effects. It would thus behoove the President to secure a clear mandate from the legislature, so he can credibly operate as a fully empowered TURK-SWITCH negotiator with EU officials.

### 3. ***TURK-SWITCH and Potential International Law Hurdles***

#### *a. Ankara Agreement Silence on Modification and Termination*

Because TURK-SWITCH's first step—a negotiated legal replacement of the CU by an FTA—requires either modification or termination of the Ankara Agreement, and because the latter and the CU Decision are silent on modification or termination, one must consider, preliminarily, whether the EU-Turkey Association Council, the bilateral body entrusted with the "implementation and progressive development of the Association"[62] would have the authority to conduct such major alteration. Could "Association," a term semantically broader than "customs union," be interpreted, elastically, to permit such a body to aid, assist or implement TURK-SWITCH under the Ankara Agreement?

Article 2.1 defines the aim of the Agreement to be "to promote the continuous and balanced strengthening of trade and economic relations between the Parties." CU replacement with an EU-Turkey FTA could be loosely viewed as a form of "strengthening" such relations. Yet, such broad reference to "relations" cannot trump the

---

country laid on a division of labor, where the President holds treaty-negotiating and signing power, and the Senate treaty-ratifying power. The drafters of the Turkish Constitution seem to have agreed with Hamilton when they prescribed that the President and the Assembly share treaty-making power on behalf of the Republic.

61. *See* discussion *supra* Chapter 6, Section III.A.1.
62. *See* Ankara Agreement, Art. 6, *supra* note 37.

precise meaning the Parties gave to the term "Association" under the Agreement. In fact, the text, structure, object, and purpose of the Ankara Agreement point *precisely* in the opposite direction. First, Article 2.2 identifies the "progressive[] establish[ment]" of the CU as *the* mechanism by which the objectives of the Agreement are to be attained. It provides no other means for securing the objectives identified in Article 2.1. Second, Article 2.3 employs the term "Association" quite narrowly, identifying it as a three-stage process leading to a *customs union*.[63] Next, Articles 3 and 4 define the "preparatory" and "transitional" stages of such Association, assigning them strict time limits, without any reference to potential alternatives.[64] Finally, Article 5 expressly identifies the customs union as "the final stage" of such an Association.[65] Thus, the text, structure, object, and purpose of the term "Association" in the Agreement forecloses broader interpretations. The Agreement envisaged solely the establishment of a customs union.[66]

The obvious textual hurdles that Articles 2-5 provide to a flexible, expansive interpretation of the term "Association" notwithstanding, whether an FTA would "strengthen" EU-Turkey trade and economic relations beyond current CU levels is an open question. Certainly, the reason for Turkey's reassertion of its trade sovereignty would be to pursue *other* partnerships as well, which, arguably, could come at the cost of some established relations with EU businesses.

More importantly, even a willing EU-Turkey Association Council would lack the requisite authority to entertain such negotiations. Article 6 establishes that the Council "shall act within the powers conferred upon it by this Agreement."[67] Nowhere in the Agreement can one find express or implicit authority that would allow the Council to preside over negotiations that would replace the CU with an EU-Turkey FTA.[68] That being the case, short of first securing an amendment to the Ankara Agreement providing for the creation of an FTA under its auspices, Turkey would have to pursue the early stages of TURK-SWITCH by grounding its actions under international law.

### b. *Ankara Agreement Modification or Termination under International Law*

The 1969 Vienna Convention on the Law of Treaties ("VCLT") codifies the customary international law on treaties, broadly defined to include international *agreements*,[69] such as the Ankara Agreement. Although not a signatory to VCLT,[70] Turkey is bound

63. Ankara Agreement, Art. 2.2 expressly states the "Association shall comprise" three stages. These stages are clearly identified in the Agreement's following articles.
64. *See* Ankara Agreement, Arts. 3 & 4, *supra* note 37.
65. *See id.*, Art. 5.
66. *See id.*
67. *Id.*, Art. 6.
68. *See generally id.*; *see also* Göçmen, *supra* note 45, at 88-93 (arguing that the legal authority of the EU-Turkey Association Council extends (only) to updating the CU).
69. Vienna Convention on the Law of Treaties, May 23, 1969, 1155 U.N.T.S. 331 [hereinafter VCLT], Art. 2.1(a).
70. *See* United Nation, Treaty Collection, Status as at Nov. 10, 2018, *available at*: https://treaties.un.org/pages/ViewDetailsIII.aspx?src=TREATY&mtdsg_no=XXIII-1&chapter=23&Temp=mtdsg3&clang=_en (last visited Nov. 10, 2018).

by most of its provisions, because they constitute widely accepted *customary* international law principles.[71] Research through Turkish diplomatic practice reveals no objection by Turkey to VCLT's customary principles regarding amendment or termination of agreements. For this reason, we apply the principles codified under VCLT to determine whether and how Turkey can amend or terminate the Ankara Agreement under international law.

VCLT Articles 39 and 54 allow countries to amend or terminate treaties even if a treaty does not have any modification or termination clause, which, as discussed, is the case with the Ankara Agreement. Both require *agreement between the parties*.[72] Article 59 also allows countries to terminate agreements by concluding a later treaty, which obviously presupposes mutual consent to terminate.[73] Thus, the European Union and Turkey may, under international law, amend and/or terminate the Ankara Agreement and, thus, the CU. To proceed under VCLT, Articles 39, 54, and 59, however, Turkey, the party interested in the change, would have to persuade the European Union.

Should Turkey fail to obtain EU consent for amending and/or terminating the Ankara Agreement, it could still pursue these changes *unilaterally*, and in accordance to international law, by proving either: (i) material breach of the Ankara Agreement by the European Union (the binding principle codified under VCLT, Article 60);[74] (ii) impossibility of performance of the Ankara Agreement (same, as codified under VCLT, Article 61);[75] or (iii) fundamental change of circumstances (*rebus sic stantibus*, as codified under VCLT, Article 62).[76,77] The first two non-consent-based options do not seem persuasive.

First, a charge of material breach grounded on the European Union's continued resistance to granting Turkey EU membership would be countered by the defense that, under Ankara Agreement, Article 28, the European Union only promised to "examine the *possibility*" of Turkey's accession, an evaluation the European Union may claim it has undertaken in "good faith," and, most importantly, a *possibility* it has kept open.[78] Second, Turkey's alternative claim of impossibility of performing the Ankara Agreement due to "the permanent disappearance or destruction of an object indispensable for the execution of the treaty,"[79]—namely Turkey's expectation of accession under Ankara Agreement, Article 28—would be met by a similar EU argument: the "possibility" of accession remains alive, so the "object indispensable for the execution of the

71. *See* William P. Johnson, *Turkey's Accession to the CISG: The Significance for Turkey and for Sales Transactions with U.S. Contracting Parties*, 8:1 ANKARA L. REV. 1 13 (2011).
72. *See* VCLT, Arts. 39 & 54, *supra* note 69.
73. *See id.*, Art. 59.
74. *See id.*, Art. 60.
75. *See id.*, Art. 61.
76. *See id.*, Art. 62.
77. For a detailed analysis of these articles, *see* MARK E. VILLEGER, COMMENTARY ON THE 1969 VIENNA CONVENTION ON THE LAW OF TREATIES 730-781 (2009).
78. *See* Ankara Agreement, Art. 28, *supra* note 37 (emphasis added). This Article requires analysis of Turkey's compliance with "the obligations arising out of the Treaty establishing the Community," formally known as the Treaty Establishing the European Economic Community, Mar. 25, 1957, 298 U.N.T.S. 11, or the Treaty of Rome.
79. VCLT, Art. 61.1, *supra* note 69.

Treaty," has not "disappeared," much less been destroyed, permanently, by the European Union.

Turkey's most persuasive, non-consent-based argument for suspending or terminating the Ankara Agreement in accordance with international law would be grounded on the "fundamental change of circumstances" doctrine, enshrined under the customary international law principle *rebus sic stantibus* (codified in VCLT, Article 62).[80] Generally, as a matter of international law, an unforeseeable, fundamental change of circumstances *alone* does not constitute a legitimate ground for terminating or withdrawing from a treaty. This doctrine, however, provides a two-part exception. Where an unforeseeable and fundamental change of circumstances: (1) alters the "essential basis" for the parties' consent to be bound by the treaty; and (2) "radically [] transform[s] the extent of" the parties' performances under the treaty, "a party may invoke" such "change ... as a ground for terminating[,] withdrawing from ... [or] suspending the operation of the treaty."[81]

As discussed in Section III.A, Turkey signed the Ankara Agreement, which contemplated the creation of the CU not only to strengthen its economic relations with a young, expanding European Community, but also with the *expectation* that greater economic integration would lead to eventual membership in the trade block. The Agreement's exchanged promises—Turkey's waiver of trade sovereignty upon CU formation for EU accession, following examination, at some point in the future—cannot be *objectively* construed to imply that examination of "the possibility" of accession by the European Union runs *indefinitely*. Surely, the European Union might point to divergence on political and civil rights as legitimate grounds for concluding that Turkey does not yet satisfy "the obligations arising out of the Treaty establishing the Community"[82] and, thus, has not earned the right to join the Union. Yet, Turkey has an equally *legitimate* right to suspend or terminate the Ankara Agreement and, thus, reassert its trade sovereignty because: (i) it has been under *perennial* EU blockage of 14 Accession Chapters—ten of which bear no relationship to current, or past political differences[83]—and (ii) due to EU conclusion of several new FTAs, it has faced significantly increased obligations. Together, these two developments constitute a subsequent, fundamental change of circumstances that have altered the "essential basis of the consent of the parties to be bound by the treaty."[84]

Moreover, "[t]he effect of the change"—namely Turkey's *indefinite* submission to perennial arbitrary barriers and increasing costs that alter the essential basis of the

80. *See* VILLEGER, *supra* note 77, at 762-781 (discussing the history and scope of the doctrine).
81. VCLT, Art. 62.1(a) & 62.1(b), *supra* note 69.
82. *See* Ankara Agreement, Art. 28, *supra* note 37.
83. *See, e.g.*, CURRENT SITUATION, THE MINISTRY OF EU AFFAIRS, *available at*: https://www.ab.gov.tr/65_en.html (last visited Jul. 18, 2018). (listing "Free Movement of Goods"; "Right of Establishment and Freedom to Provide Services"; "Financial Services"; "Agricultural and Rural Development"; "Fisheries"; "Transport Policy"; "Customs Union" (blocked by the General Affairs and External Relations Council ("GAERC")); "Free Movement of Workers"; "Energy" and "Education and Culture" (blocked by Southern Cyprus). Seven of the identified GAERC-blocked chapters have been blocked since 2006, and all identified Southern Cyprus-blocked chapters have been blocked since 2009.
84. VCLT, Art. 62.1(a), *supra* note 69.

bargain—"is radically to transform the *extent* of obligations still to be performed under the treaty."[85] As discussed in Chapter 4, a CU-bound Turkey, with diminished accession prospects, has had to: (i) align, repeatedly, its preferential trade regime with the European Union's whenever the latter enters into *new* FTAs; and (ii) grant duty-free treatment to products that are imported to the single market, regardless of origin. As the European Union has embarked on an ambitious pursuit of FTAs over the last two decades, Turkey's obligations have far exceeded the concessions it originally undertook 58 (Ankara Agreement signing) and 26 (CU signing) years ago. Without being matched by meaningful progress toward EU accession—these changed circumstances have not only altered the essential basis for the parties' consent to be bound *by*, but also "radical[ly] ... transform[ed] the extent of obligations still to be performed *under* the" Ankara Agreement.[86]

Thus, should Turkey and the European Union fail to agree on amending, suspending, or terminating the Ankara Agreement, Turkey's initial push for TURK-SWITCH might require deployment of the doctrine of fundamental change of circumstances, which would allow it to suspend or terminate the Agreement in accordance with international law. Of course, TURK-SWITCH cannot happen without EU-Turkey mutual consent, and every diplomatic effort should be employed to secure it. Yet, Turkey should know that maneuvering toward an FTA might require initial, *unilateral* suspension or termination of the Ankara Agreement, particularly because maintenance of the CU benefits EU interests, asymmetrically.

### i. Pre-negotiation Alternatives

To execute TURK-SWITCH, namely the transition from CU to FTA with the European Union, Turkey's President, may follow either of two approaches, each with its own trade-offs. In one, the President, pursuant to express trade-negotiating authority, would leave the CU in place while negotiating amendments to the Ankara Agreement that would replace the CU with an EU-Turkey FTA. Subsequently, the President would seek Assembly ratification of the new agreement (i.e., the FTA) under Article 90 (the Leave-in-Place-and-Ratification Approach ("LPR")). The other alternative would see the President consult with the Assembly prior to withdrawing from the Agreement and negotiating a new FTA. Under the latter approach, the President, anticipating the need for eventual Assembly ratification of the agreement that replaces the CU, could commit to maintaining the current tariff regime for a *limited*, reasonable length of time until the conclusion of the EU-Turkey FTA (i.e., the Repeal-Pause-and-Ratification Approach ("RPR")).

Under LPR, keeping the CU until completion of an FTA would reduce uncertainty and thus benefit businesses on both sides of the border. However, it would most certainly lead to protracted negotiations, as the European Union would continue benefiting from the CU while its Turkey-unfriendly members could attempt to extract

85. *Id.*, Art. 62.1(b) (emphasis added).
86. *Id.* (emphasis added).

EU and Turkey concessions by engaging in opportunistic blocking of negotiations. LPR's initial uncertainty-reducing properties could unravel in the long run, as Turkish and EU officials grow frustrated with dilatory tactics. RPR would not be free from disadvantages, either. While immediate withdrawal—even with assurances of maintaining CU tariffs for a limited time—would keep both parties "honest" (i.e., each would be aware of time constraints), it would create economic instability in the short term. Yet, because LPR's transaction costs might be high or even prohibitive, particularly among EU Members, RPR's repeal-freeze-and-replace design provides the better structure of incentives for Coordination to emerge. Of course, once the parties settle into rounds of negotiations, it is possible that aspects of Cooperation might influence the essentially coordinated transition from CU to FTA.

Accordingly, besides working closely with the Assembly (*see* Section III.A.2), the President should formally invoke his/her constitutional foreign relations power to withdraw Turkey from the CU (and, thus, from the Ankara Agreement), effective immediately. The Presidential Decision should provide for temporary maintenance of CU tariffs for a *reasonable* period of time until conclusion of an FTA.[87] Note that under the RPR scenario, one can safely rule out Coincidence of Interest and Coercion. The first is unlikely because any threat of (or eventual) new tariffs by either Turkey or the European Union would not be tacitly acquiesced by the other. They will engage with each other because they recognize each party's self-interest *depends* on what the other does. The second (i.e., Coercion) is also unlikely for, though the more economically powerful party, the European Union cannot impose its will on Turkey due to the legal (i.e., its maximum 4.1 percent a.v. bound tariff on industrial goods under the WTO system) and policy constraints (i.e., its interest in maintaining existing supply chains and regional coordination on a wide set of issues) it faces. Thus, Turkey's relatively greater tariff leverage, openness to making new concessions, and time-limited proposal, together, would operate as a credible threat against opportunistic holdouts or EU-wide attempts at maintaining current asymmetries through mere cosmetic CU reform.

## B. Turkey's FTA Negotiations *Following* CU Withdrawal

### 1. *Bargaining Toward an FTA with the European Union*

Upon notifying the EU-Turkey Association Council of Turkey's withdrawal from the EU-Turkey Customs Union, the Turkish President should request immediate negotiations toward an FTA. To entice EU officials, Turkish negotiators could provide assurances that EU industrial and processed agricultural goods—currently included in the CU—would continue to enjoy the same access (i.e., zero tariffs) into Turkey for a certain, reasonable period. Of course, Turkey would expect similar treatment. To the

87. *See* GATT, Art. XXIV:5 (allowing prospective CU or FTA Parties to sign an "interim agreement," providing them *reasonable period of time* to transition their trade policies and practices prior to their eventual CU or FTA).

extent possible, these initial assurances could contribute to an orderly transition, while reducing undesirable market disruption under the circumstances.

As discussed earlier, under an FTA, Turkey would no longer be required to apply the EU CETs. An FTA would require negotiations on ROOs; however, Turkey should be prepared to offer new concessions to its senior partner. The European Union should be prepared to make concessions, too: a CU-free Turkey would regain the discretion to increase its tariffs on EU goods from zero up to 42.6 percent—for one-third of industrial goods—and from zero to unlimited levels (for the remaining two-thirds of such goods).[88] Because the nature and scope of concessions on both sides would be determined in detailed negotiations, we deem the estimation of such concessions to be outside the scope of this book. Suffice it to say, one would expect the final commitments on tariffs *and* ROOs to reflect "complex" trade-offs made in other FTAs (e.g., USMCA, EU-Canada FTA, EU-Mexico FTA, etc.): the main idea being retaining trade sovereignty while preserving trade flows and supply chains, to the extent possible.[89]

Yet, the transition from CU to FTA could also be facilitated by opening heretofore closed areas for negotiation under the CU. Specifically, going beyond industrial products might present opportunities for further liberalization: a new EU-Turkey FTA could include commitments in agriculture, services, technical barriers to trade, investment, and public procurement.[90] In light of the current stalemate over WTO Appellate Body replacements and the associated slowing pace of rulings, the establishment of a more robust dispute settlement system could also help reduce eventual trade friction.

### 2. *Bargaining Toward FTAs with Third Countries*

As mentioned in Chapter 3, in addition to EU-Turkey industrial trade flows, the CU Decision also regulates Turkey's industrial trade relations with third (i.e., non-EU) countries. For instance, Article 13 of the Decision provides "Turkey shall, in relation to countries which are not members of the Community, align itself on the Common Customs Tariff [CET]."[91] Article 14 further limits Turkey's tariff discretion: "[U]nder no circumstances" can Turkey apply tariffs lower than the CET.[92] Moreover, Article 16 of the Decision requires Turkey to align itself with the EU preferential trade regime by negotiating FTAs on a "mutually advantageous basis" with countries with which the European Union has concluded such agreements.[93] Having retained significant tariff

88. *See* Appendix II, Table II.1.
89. For a detailed discussion on ROOs, particularly on the complex interaction between ROOs and intra-industry trade flows and the distribution of gains resulting from alternative input distribution flows, *see* Mark Wu, *Rethinking the Rise and Fall of the TPP—Why the Analysis of Trade Agreements Requires an Overhaul* 25-31 (Cambridge-INET Brexit Conference, 2017) (cited with permission), *available at*: https://www.inet.econ.cam.ac.uk/our-events/copy7_of_DraftonlyRethinkingtheRiseandFalloftheTPPWhytheAnalysisofTradeAgreementsRequiresanOverhaul.pdf.
90. *See* World Bank Report, *supra* note 19, at 57-85.
91. Decision No. 1/95 of the EC-Turkey Association Council of 22 December 1995 on implementing the final phase of the Customs Union, 96/142/EC, Art. 13, 1996 O.J. (L 035) [hereinafter CU Decision].
92. *Id.*, Art. 14.
93. *Id.*, Arts. 16 & 54.

discretion under the WTO system, Turkey drastically undercut its ability to effectively negotiate trade arrangements with third countries by virtue of binding itself to the CU-set *CETs*.[94] As the EU membership carrot shrinks or disappears, one is hard pressed to find a rationale for Turkey's continued relinquishment of tariff leverage on industrial goods at such scale.

By executing TURK-SWITCH, Turkey would regain not only its dormant WTO tariff discretion on industrial products, it would also recover the sovereign right to independently pursue trade arrangements according to its *own* trade objectives with diverse counterparts, across a much wider scope of goods and services. Since Turkey's main trade objective has been to reduce its long, uninterrupted trade deficit, which obviously requires a substantial increase in exports, a CU-free Turkey would position itself to open markets for its most consequential exporting sectors (e.g., automobiles, textile and clothing, iron and steel, household appliances, chemicals, agriculture, etc.) by offering new concessions based on the significant reserve of tariff discretion available in its WTO Schedule of Concessions.[95] Thus, specifically, TURK-SWITCH would allow Turkey to: (i) review its current FTAs and restructure those finalized under the unfavorable terms dictated by its CU commitments; and (ii) negotiate new FTAs with high-income Western countries, dynamic neighbors in the East (i.e., the GCC and Turkic countries), and growing economies in Asia and the Americas.

### a. *Reviewing and, if Necessary, Restructuring Current FTAs*

Since the establishment of the CU, Turkey has concluded FTAs with most EU-FTA counterparts,[96] invariably under diminished leverage conditions. For instance (and as mentioned in Chapter 4), following the conclusion of the EU-South Korean FTA, Turkey began FTA negotiations with South Korea. Yet, South Korea, noting Turkey's diminished leverage, offered less generous concessions than Turkey's WTO schedule of commitments would ordinarily command.[97] Meanwhile, Turkey had to grant South Korean industrial goods—either directly or indirectly—the same tariffs offered by the

94. *See, e.g.*, Appendix II, Table II.1 (reporting an average bound tariff for industrial goods of 42.6 percent) *and* Table II.3 (showing significant differentials between Turkey's MFN-bound (fourth column) and current applied (i.e., pursuant to the CU) tariffs (sixth column) on select industrial products) *infra*.
95. *See* Turkey TPR 2016, *supra* note 11, at 23 & 140.
96. As a result of the CU, Turkey signed FTAs with: Israel; Macedonia; Bosnia-Herzegovina; Egypt; the Palestinian Authority; Tunisia; Morocco; Syria (suspended in 2011); Albania; Georgia; Serbia; Montenegro; Chile; Jordan; South Korea; Moldova; Faroe Island; Kosovo; Venezuela; and the United Kingdom. Turkey only signed an FTA with the EFTA prior to its CU with the European Union. Turkey has also FTAs with Malaysia, Mauritius, and Singapore (the European Union also started negotiations with them). *See Serbest Ticaret Anlaşmaları* [Free Trade Agreements], Ticaret Bakanlıgı [Republic of Turkey Department of Commerce], https://www.ticaret.gov.tr/dis-iliskiler/serbest-ticaret-anlasmalari (last visited Feb. 6, 2021) [hereinafter Turkey's FTAs].
97. *See* Mahmut Tekçe, *The Future of the Customs Union Between Turkey and the EU in the Context of the EU Trade Policy Agenda of the EU*, XXXVII: II, Marmara Univ. IIB Dergisi 397, 403 (2015).

European Union. In fact, of Turkey's 21 FTAs, 20 were concluded after 1996; and, in each, the same discounted leverage brought Turkey less than ideal outcomes.[98]

In fairness, Turkey had no choice but to accept such conditions in all negotiations, for that is what the CU and WTO law require. Pursuant to GATT[99] Article XXIV, CU Members must apply "substantially the same duties" to outside countries or else they fail to qualify for the exemption from the general MFN obligation.[100] Freed from the CU, Turkey will be able to revisit more than 95 percent of its FTAs (i.e., 20 out of 21). In light of Turkey's significant tariff leverage and commitment to further liberalization, free-trading partners would likely agree to coordinate with Turkey to keep and/or expand trade levels by restructuring their current FTAs. These new, restructured trade deals would secure greater market access for Turkey's exporters, as well as provide them and their downstream partners greater sourcing flexibility. The latter possibility could result in a particularly positive outcome: Turkey's export sector is a *heavy* consumer of intermediate goods, which, if imported at tariffs lower than current CETs could make Turkish exports more competitive. Moreover, regained trade sovereignty should also help Turkey establish strategic trade partnerships, to which we now turn.

### b. *Negotiating New FTAs with Strategic Partners*

If one looks at Turkey's current FTA counterparts, one realizes the overwhelming majority of them are sovereign states in its wide neighborhood (e.g., Albania, Bosnia-Herzegovina, Egypt, Georgia, Israel, Jordan, Macedonia, Moldova, Montenegro, Morocco, Serbia, Syria (suspended in 2011), and Tunisia). Notably, many have had their share of internal conflict and/or economic turmoil, creating instability in their trade relations with Turkey. Hence, Turkey must pursue trade deals beyond traditional, neighboring trade partners. After regaining its tariff discretion and trade-negotiating sovereignty, Turkey will be able to expand trade relations with countries beyond its immediate neighborhood by temporarily abstaining from imposing unilateral tariff increases—subject to bound levels, of course—on products from countries interested in engaging in good faith negotiations. The following subsections explain some strategic choices Turkey must make as it contemplates priority partners.

#### i. High-Income Countries

Upon executing TURK-SWITCH, Turkey should prioritize concluding FTAs with high income, advanced industrialized countries (e.g., the United States, Canada, Japan, and

98. *See* Turkey's FTAs, *supra* note 96.
99. GATT 1994: General Agreement on Tariffs and Trade 1994, Apr. 15, 1994, Marrakesh Agreement Establishing the World Trade Organization, Annex 1A, 1867 U.N.T.S. 187, 33 I.L.M. 1153 (1994) [hereinafter GATT 1994].
100. *Id.*, Art. XXIV:8.

Australia).[101] These countries have dynamic markets and import relatively larger shares of low-and-medium-technology products, which, under new FTAs, could provide enhanced market access for Turkey's top export sectors. Yet, while their applied MFN tariff rates for manufacturing goods are quite low (e.g., 3.6 percent (US); 2.5 percent (Canada); 2.5 (Japan); and 3.0 percent (Australia)),[102] they tend to charge higher tariffs on low-and-medium-technology imports. To illustrate, in 2019, US average MFN tariffs on textile products and clothing are 8.0 and 11.6 percent, respectively.[103] Because textile and clothing goods make up about 18 percent of Turkey's total exports,[104] Turkey could benefit significantly from lower, preferential tariffs in these markets, particularly because its main competitors (e.g., India, Indonesia, Pakistan, and Vietnam) currently have no FTAs with these countries, excluding Japan.[105]

In return to lower tariffs on low-and-medium-technology products, Turkey could offer these countries concessions similar to those it currently offers the European Union (i.e., zero or close-to-zero tariffs) subject, of course, to the eventual EU-Turkey FTA rule-of-origin commitments. Turkey should also offer concessions on high-tech industrial products from these countries. Obviously, FTAs and expanded trade with large, stable economies would likely increase inbound FDI from these countries, whose capital, once deployed, would help increase the productivity of the relatively low-wage, well-trained Turkish workforce.[106]

### ii. Dynamic Regional Partners

The Turkic Republics (e.g., Azerbaijan, Kazakhstan, Kyrgyzstan, Turkmenistan, and Uzbekistan), with which Turkey has strong historical, cultural, and linguistic ties, but which remain under Russian influence, present another great opportunity for a CU-free Turkey to expand exports.[107] Ethnic ties create natural opportunities for cooperation and trade, and a shared religion can bring peoples together. The GCC Members (e.g., Bahrain, Kuwait, Oman, Qatar, Saudi Arabia, and the United Arab Emirates), traditionally significant importers of industrial and agricultural goods, have made economic diversification away from oil resources a strong priority and would seem natural partners to Turkey's developed manufacturing, services, and infrastructure sectors. Closer trade ties would mean more foreign direct and indirect investment from the GCC countries. Closer trade partnerships could also provide GCC partners with a secure and

101. *See* World Bank Country and Lending Groups—High-Income Countries, *available at*: https://datahelpdesk.worldbank.org/knowledgebase/articles/906519-world-bank-country-and-lending-groups (last visited Jul. 18, 2018).
102. *See* Tariff rate, Most Favored Nation, Simple Mean, Manufactured Products (%), *available at*: https://data.worldbank.org/indicator/TM.TAX.MANF.SM.FN.ZS (last visited Jul. 18, 2018).
103. *See* World Tariff Profiles 2020, *supra* note 14, at 186.
104. *See* Turkey TPR 2016, *supra* note 11, at 23.
105. Japan has FTAs with India, Indonesia, and Vietnam. *See* Japan Trade Agreements, *available at*: https://www.export.gov/article?id=Japan-Trade-Agreements (last visited Jul. 10, 2018).
106. *See* Turkey TPR 2016, *supra* note 11, at 12 & 23.
107. *See* Nilgün Önder, *The Turkish Project of Globalization and New Regionalism*, 7:2-3 Alternatives: Turkish J. of Int'l Rel. 86, 98 (2008).

convenient means to transfer oil and natural gas to Western markets through Turkey's secure, expanding pipeline network.

### iii. Mutual Interests in Farther Regions

In addition to high-income countries, Turkic Republics, the GCC, and countries in Turkey's extended periphery, growing South American (e.g., Colombia, MERCOSUR Members, Peru) and Asian (e.g., Malaysia, Indonesia, Pakistan, Thailand, Vietnam, etc.) economies can be approached in a third wave of FTAs.[108] Again, Turkey's regained tariff discretion would be key in these negotiations.

## IV. FURTHER TRADE LIBERALIZATION STRENGTHENS TURKEY'S WESTERNIZATION PROJECT

Because TURK-SWITCH—replacing the CU with an EU-Turkey FTA and negotiating subsequent FTAs with other countries—would mean jettisoning the pursuit of EU membership, it naturally raises questions on whether it comes at the cost of a retrenchment from Westernization. TURK-SWITCH would be far from a break from this principle, however. First, a well-functioning FTA would not be an obstacle to future discussions on membership. Stable economic ties and policy alignment is all that it should take. Second, if Westernization means building up modern-secular institutions, upholding the rule of law, and accepting market discipline, one wonders why only a customs union can do the trick—if it can at all. These Western ideas are much broader than and surely independent from the latter.

Third, the continued waiver of the independent exercise of trade authority in a customs union seems *less*—rather than more—compatible with the concept of Westernization that the Turkish founding leaders had in mind than entering into trade-liberalizing FTAs and exploring several new partnerships. Even in the Classical Westphalian connotation of restricted sovereignty, Westernization was more a *means* to strengthen a nascent Republic and building statehood than an end in itself. Further, Westernization cannot be exacted by keeping subservient ties to the European Union via the surrender of trade sovereignty. To wit, the UK's intention to sign FTAs with countries all around the world following the termination of its EU membership.[109] Why should Turkey be any different?

Since the 1990s, after major steps toward liberalizing trade, it was inevitable that newly assumed trade commitments would shape many of Turkey's policies, including

108. *See* Turkey's FTAs, *supra* note 96.

109. *See, e.g.*, Amur, *supra* note 4 (quoting Prime Minister May's comments that "We [the UK] want to get out into the wider world to trade and do business all around the globe. … I want Britain to be able to negotiate its own trade agreements. But I also want tariff-free trade with Europe and cross-border trade there to be as frictionless as possible. … I do not want Britain to … be bound by the Common External Tariff. These are the elements of the Customs Union that prevent us from striking our own comprehensive trade agreements with other countries.").

foreign relations.[110] Unsurprisingly, trade diplomacy, although limited by CU commitments, became an effective policy tool for Turkey to accomplish at least some of its trade objectives, following a long commitment to Westernization. Not by accident, by 2016 Turkey had accumulated 235 diplomatic missions, the world's sixth largest diplomatic core, only surpassed by the five permanent members of the United Nations Security Council (i.e., the United States, France, China, Russia, and the United Kingdom).[111] With TURK-SWITCH, this broad, *cosmopolitan* diplomatic network could be empowered to embrace closer, not weaker, ties to the West. That a portion of Turkey's technocratic elite might initially resist restructuring the current EU-Turkey trade framework—possibly, due to its close ties with the European Union—should be expected, yet need not deter leaders committed to deploying national sovereignty as a *means* of implementing Westernization beyond the confines of Europe.

Conceived thusly, beyond reducing the current asymmetric state of affairs between Turkey and the European Union, TURK-SWITCH would empower Turkey to begin addressing its secular, structural trade, and current account deficits. Recovery of significant dormant tariff discretion under the WTO—the currency in an eventual trade negotiation—would allow a CU-free Turkey to sign FTAs that much more closely match its own trade objectives, including *foremost* with the European Union. For Turkey to overcome perennial trade deficits and, more importantly, the middle-income trap, exporting a larger share of its GDP is absolutely critical. The road to higher exports requires the pursuit of more trade partnerships that *only* a TURK-SWITCH strategy can secure.

110. *See* Mustafa Kutlay, *Economy as the "Practical Hand" of "New Turkish Foreign Policy": A Political Economy Explanation*, 13:1 INSIGHT TURKEY 67, 76 (2011).
111. *See* Nazli Yuzbasioglu and Sultan Cogalan, *Turkey boasts no. 6 diplomatic network in the world*, ANADOLU AGENCY (Dec. 26, 2016), *available at:* http://aa.com.tr/en/todays-headlines/turkey-boasts-no-6-diplomatic-network-in-the-world/714459.

# Conclusion

Bad agreements exist, yet international law scholars have mostly ignored them, preferring to focus on examples of successful negotiations and treaty-making. While a preference for agreement stability and international organization-driven negotiations might be understandable in an increasingly interdependent world, the phenomenon of agreement restructuring between and among sovereign states deserves careful study, for even the most ardent, cosmopolitan expert would not deem all current agreements to be necessarily efficient, fair, or sustainable. Indeed, if states pursue new agreements on the basis of their own self-interest, it stands to reason why they would not also consider restructuring old ones on the same basis.

Recent "real world" events demonstrate a renewed interest on agreement restructuring on the part of *some* sovereigns. Both the restructure-"willing" May/Johnson Governments and the restructure-"enthusiastic" Trump Administration faced intense political pressure and bureaucratic resistance as they sought to restructure deals no longer in the "national interest." In the latter case, both Ambassador Lighthizer (USTR) and Secretary Ross (Commerce) invested significant time in media appearances designed to explain the suboptimality of NAFTA. Yet, the empirical reality of some deal-restructuring activity barely provides clues as to *how* the idea of revisiting agreements gains force, and, in some cases, becomes powerful enough to garner sufficient domestic support and even defeat cross-border resistance to restructuring.

As discussed in the Introduction and Chapter 1, rational choice theory credibly predicts that, invariably, restructuring initiatives face initial resistance from deeply integrated economic sectors, entrenched political elites, and the bureaucracy. Such resistance increases domestic transaction costs, using up valuable political capital, and, thus, might dissuade even a motivated national leader from pursuing agreements that would offer his/her country outcomes closer to the Pareto frontier. It follows that, more often than thought, national leaders rationally settle for legacy agreements that might fall below a country's wealth-maximizing potential. If that is true, the universe of net-negative-benefit agreements would be populated overwhelmingly by agreements that either: (i) remain operational (i.e., where one party, though dissatisfied, largely complies with the agreement, with deviations remaining well below a de facto termination threshold), or (ii) have been violated in such a fundamental way that they may exist only in paper (e.g., the Sino-British Joint Declaration of 1984).[1] Obviously, the latter type is not a target for restructuring, but only for eventual de lege abrogation. The first type provides the better case study, however. In these settings, the dissatisfied party may tolerate the losses incurred from keeping it either because it expects a greater payoff to materialize in the future (e.g., EU membership for Turkey), or because, so far, the total cost (i.e., domestic and external) of restructuring might exceed the expected benefit.

The ideas evoked by rational choice theory and in this book imply that a state will look to restructure such an agreement when its expected stream of benefits (or one-off, expected benefit) is deeply discounted (i.e., becomes ever less likely, or sharply decreases in absolute value), its cost rises, or both. In Part II of the book, we demonstrated why, as far as Turkey is concerned, the CU has become such a suboptimal agreement and, thus, constitutes a great target for restructuring. Over 26 years, Turkey's waiver of trade sovereignty, its application of EU-set CETs, and the European Union's commitment to signing multiple FTAs, taken together, have quite significantly eroded Turkey's substantial WTO-negotiated tariff leverage. Yet, during the same period, the prospect of Turkey's EU accession has only diminished. Worse, lack of independent tariff authority makes it impossible for Turkey to diversify and expand exports, which would help address its perennial trade deficits. In sum, the costs the CU imposes on Turkey have increased while the expected value of its benefits has sharply declined.

In Part III, we showed, first, how reliance on other mechanisms available in Turkey's current trade framework—particularly, WTO bilateral adjudication (Chapter 5)—is unlikely to bring Turkey any significant relief. Because a CU update (at least the ones reported, so far) would not change the major asymmetry in the deal nor provide objective criteria and a timetable for membership, TURK-SWITCH emerges as the only feasible alternative. In Chapter 6, we demonstrated the merits of TURK-SWITCH, and how it can be deployed legally and transactionally. Specifically, the deployment of Turkey's WTO (MFN) tariff leverage coupled with a robust diplomatic effort to restructure its trade relationship with the European Union and with new partners would offer Turkey its best chance for addressing its perennial trade issues. Considering the low likelihood of Turkey's accession in the coming years (i.e., a significant

1. *Compare* Joint Declaration of the Government of the United Kingdom of Great Britain and Northern Ireland and the Government of the People's Republic of China on the Question of Hong Kong, Art. 3(5), Dec. 19, 1984, 1399 U.N.T.S. 33, 23 I.L.M. 1366 (1985) (providing that "[t]he current social and economic systems in Hong Kong will remain unchanged, and so will [its] life-style," and stating that "[r]ights and freedoms, including those of the person, of speech, of the press, of assembly, of association, of travel, of movement, of correspondence, of strike, of choice of occupation, of academic research[,] and of religious belief will be ensured by law in the Hong Kong Special Administrative Region."), *with China says Sino-British Joint Declaration on Hong Kong no longer has meaning*, Reuters.com (Jun. 30, 2017), https://www.reuters.com/article/us-hongkong-anniversary-china/china-says-sino-british-joint-declaration-on-hong-kong-no-longer-has-meaning-idUSKBN19L1J1 (quoting Chinese Foreign Minister Lu Kang's statement that the agreement "no longer has any practical significance, and it is not at all binding for the central government's management over Hong Kong"). Arguably, after two decades, the Chinese Communist Party came to view this legally binding, yet significantly front-loaded agreement as a negative-benefit deal it could easily abrogate.

discount to the expected benefit), the continued and increasing erosion of Turkey's tariff leverage (i.e., the growing cost of the CU), and Turkey's substantial WTO (MFN) tariff leverage (i.e., the ability to credibly threaten higher tariffs by means of a *lawful* CU withdrawal), TURK-SWITCH's merit as a restructuring strategy comes into sharp focus.

Although trade wars rarely have winners and should be avoided by both parties, Turkey, if necessary, may counter any initial EU inflexibility or hard-bargaining tactics with tariff increases going up to its WTO-authorized (i.e., bound) levels. This is a form of leverage the United Kingdom *lacked* in the post-BREXIT negotiations, a setting in which one still observed coordinated and cooperative action emerge after a period of difficult negotiations. The convergence of EU and Turkish commercial interests (e.g., trade liberalization, supply-chain maintenance and resiliency) and their shared interests across a range of policy domains (e.g., public health, environment, security, immigration, etc.) indicates that Coordination (with possibly some aspects of Cooperation) is likely to emerge as the dominant behavioral pattern in post-CU negotiations.

Ultimately, the merit of TURK-SWITCH fully rests on its ability to help Turkey solve its perennial trade challenges while adhering to the major goals of its foundation as a *Republic*: modernization and improvement in the general welfare of the Turkish people. While this illustration does not exhaust the explanatory power of our model, it provides an ideal setting for evaluating (and, hopefully, testing) the prediction that coordinated and cooperative action will occur once Turkey stops delaying the decision it must make. Furthermore, this book's hypotheses—that: (i) net-negative-benefit agreements exist; (ii) provided certain conditions are met, states will seek to restructure them; and (iii) restructuring activity will be characterized by one (or a combination) of the four behavioral patterns—are all *falsifiable*. Certainly, these are questions that deserve more research, particularly empirical studies that should further refine the distinction between net-negative-benefit agreements that undergo restructuring and those that never do.

Hopefully, this effort to lay the foundation for a theory of agreement restructuring will draw the attention of international law scholars and government leaders, alike. Clearer thinking on the theoretical, legal, and transactional aspects of renegotiating bad deals should help both scholars and practitioners make better decisions about when to keep or how to restructure international agreements.

# Appendices

# APPENDIX I

*Table I.1 Historical GNP/GDP and Trade Data for Turkey*

| *Year (1923-2020)* | *Exports (X) (million $)* | *Imports (M) (million $)* | *X/M* | *Trade Surplus or (Deficit) (million $)* | *GNP (1923-1960) GDP (1961-2018) (million $)* |
|---|---|---|---|---|---|
| 1923 | 50 | 86 | 58.5 | -36 | 826 |
| 1924 | 82 | 100 | 82.1 | -18 | 932 |
| 1925 | 102 | 128 | 79.6 | -26 | 1,214 |
| 1926 | 96 | 121 | 79.4 | -24 | 1,258 |
| 1927 | 80 | 107 | 74.9 | -27 | 1,104 |
| 1928 | 88 | 113 | 77.6 | -25 | 1,291 |
| 1929 | 74 | 123 | 60.6 | -48 | 1,459 |
| 1930 | 71 | 69 | 102.6 | 1.8 | 1,061 |
| 1931 | 60 | 59 | 100.5 | 0.2 | 960 |
| 1932 | 47 | 40 | 117.8 | 7 | 808 |
| 1933 | 58 | 45 | 128.8 | 12 | 1,001 |
| 1934 | 73 | 68 | 106.2 | 4 | 1,406 |
| 1935 | 76 | 70 | 107.9 | 5 | 1,514 |
| 1936 | 93 | 73 | 127.2 | 20 | 1,959 |
| 1937 | 109 | 90 | 120.6 | 18 | 2,088 |
| 1938 | 115 | 118 | 96.7 | -3 | 2,157 |
| 1939 | 99 | 92 | 107.7 | 7 | 2,178 |
| 1940 | 80 | 50 | 161.7 | 30 | 2,537 |
| 1941 | 91 | 55 | 164.5 | 35 | 3,302 |
| 1942 | 126 | 112 | 111.7 | 13 | 6,890 |
| 1943 | 196 | 155 | 126.6 | 41 | 10,267 |
| 1944 | 177 | 126 | 141.0 | 51 | 7,434 |

| *Year (1923-2020)* | *Exports (X) (million $)* | *Imports (M) (million $)* | *X/M* | *Trade Surplus or (Deficit) (million $)* | *GNP (1923-1960) GDP (1961-2018) (million $)* |
|---|---|---|---|---|---|
| 1945 | 168 | 96 | 173.5 | 71 | 6,083 |
| 1946 | 214 | 118 | 180.5 | 95 | 5,519 |
| 1947 | 223 | 244 | 91.3 | -21 | 3,924 |
| 1948 | 196 | 275 | 71.5 | -78 | 4,939 |
| 1949 | 247 | 290 | 85.4 | -42 | 4,711 |
| 1950 | 263 | 285 | 92.2 | -22 | 5,044 |
| 1951 | 314 | 402 | 78.1 | -88 | 6,058 |
| 1952 | 362 | 555 | 65.3 | -193 | 6,966 |
| 1953 | 396 | 532 | 74.4 | -136 | 8,120 |
| 1954 | 334 | 478 | 70.0 | -143 | 8,280 |
| 1955 | 313 | 497 | 63.0 | -184 | 9,947 |
| 1956 | 304 | 407 | 74.9 | -102 | 11,471 |
| 1957 | 345 | 397 | 86.9 | -51 | 15,250 |
| 1958 | 247 | 315 | 78.5 | -67 | 18,211 |
| 1959 | 353 | 469 | 75.3 | -116 | 22,722 |
| 1960 | 320 | 468 | 68.5 | -147 | 13,995 |
| 1961 | 346 | 507 | 68.4 | -160 | 7,989 |
| 1962 | 381 | 619 | 61.5 | -238 | 8,922 |
| 1963 | 368 | 687 | 53.5 | -319 | 10,356 |
| 1964 | 410 | 537 | 76.5 | -126 | 11,178 |
| 1965 | 463 | 571 | 81.1 | -108 | 11,967 |
| 1966 | 490 | 718 | 68.3 | -227 | 14,100 |
| 1967 | 522 | 684 | 76.3 | -162 | 15,644 |
| 1968 | 496 | 763 | 65.0 | -267 | 17,500 |
| 1969 | 536 | 801 | 67.0 | -264 | 19,467 |
| 1970 | 588 | 947 | 62.1 | -359 | 17,087 |
| 1971 | 676 | 1,170 | 57.8 | -494 | 16,257 |
| 1972 | 884 | 1,562 | 56.6 | -677 | 20,431 |
| 1973 | 1,317 | 2,086 | 63.1 | -769 | 25,724 |
| 1974 | 1,532 | 3,777 | 40.6 | -2,245 | 35,600 |
| 1975 | 1,401 | 4,738 | 29.6 | -3,337 | 44,634 |
| 1976 | 1,960 | 5,128 | 38.2 | -3,168 | 51,280 |
| 1977 | 1,753 | 5,796 | 30.2 | -4,043 | 58,677 |
| 1978 | 2,288 | 4,599 | 49.8 | -2,310 | 65,147 |
| 1979 | 2,261 | 5,069 | 44.6 | -2,808 | 89,394 |
| 1980 | 2,910 | 7,909 | 36.8 | -4,999 | 68,789 |

| *Year (1923-2020)* | *Exports (X) (million $)* | *Imports (M) (million $)* | *X/M* | *Trade Surplus or (Deficit) (million $)* | *GNP (1923-1960) GDP (1961-2018) (million $)* |
|---|---|---|---|---|---|
| 1981 | 4,702 | 8,933 | 52.6 | -4,230 | 71,040 |
| 1982 | 5,745 | 8,842 | 65.0 | -3,096 | 64,546 |
| 1983 | 5,727 | 9,235 | 62.0 | -3,507 | 61,678 |
| 1984 | 7,133 | 10,757 | 66.3 | -3,623 | 59,990 |
| 1985 | 7,958 | 11,343 | 70.2 | -3,385 | 67,235 |
| 1986 | 7,456 | 11,104 | 67.1 | -3,648 | 75,728 |
| 1987 | 10,190 | 14,157 | 72.0 | -3,967 | 87,173 |
| 1988 | 11,662 | 14,335 | 81.4 | -2,673 | 90,853 |
| 1989 | 11,624 | 15,792 | 73.6 | -4,167 | 107,143 |
| 1990 | 12,959 | 22,302 | 58.1 | -9,342 | 150,676 |
| 1991 | 13,593 | 21,047 | 64.6 | -7,453 | 150,028 |
| 1992 | 14,714 | 22,871 | 64.3 | -8,156 | 158,459 |
| 1993 | 15,345 | 29,428 | 52.1 | -14,083 | 180,170 |
| 1994 | 18,105 | 23,270 | 77.8 | -5,164 | 130,690 |
| 1995 | 21,637 | 35,709 | 60.6 | -14,071 | 169,486 |
| 1996 | 23,224 | 43,626 | 53.2 | -20,402 | 181,676 |
| 1997 | 26,261 | 48,558 | 54.1 | -22,297 | 189,835 |
| 1998 | 26,973 | 45,921 | 58.7 | -18,947 | 275,967 |
| 1999 | 26,587 | 40,671 | 65.4 | -14,084 | 256,386 |
| 2000 | 27,774 | 54,502 | 51.0 | -26,727 | 274,303 |
| 2001 | 31,334 | 41,399 | 75.7 | -10,064 | 201,753 |
| 2002 | 36,059 | 51 553 | 69.9 | -15,494 | 240,249 |
| 2003 | 47,252 | 69,339 | 68.1 | -22,086 | 314,595 |
| 2004 | 63,167 | 97,539 | 64.8 | -34,372 | 408,865 |
| 2005 | 73,476 | 116,774 | 62.9 | -43,297 | 506,515 |
| 2006 | 85,534 | 139,576 | 61.3 | -54,041 | 557,076 |
| 2007 | 107,271 | 170,062 | 63.1 | -62,790 | 681,321 |
| 2008 | 132,027 | 201,963 | 65.4 | -69,936 | 770,449 |
| 2009 | 102,142 | 140,928 | 72.5 | -38,785 | 649,289 |
| 2010 | 113,883 | 185,544 | 61.4 | -71,661 | 776,968 |
| 2011 | 134,906 | 240,841 | 56.0 | -105,934 | 838,786 |
| 2012 | 152,461 | 236,545 | 64.5 | -84,083 | 880,556 |
| 2013 | 151,802 | 251,661 | 60.3 | -99,858 | 957,799 |
| 2014 | 157,610 | 242,177 | 65.1 | -84,566 | 938,934 |
| 2015 | 143,838 | 207,234 | 69.4 | -63,395 | 864,314 |
| 2016 | 142,529 | 198,618 | 71.8 | -56,088 | 869,683 |

| *Year (1923-2020)* | *Exports (X) (million $)* | *Imports (M) (million $)* | *X/M* | *Trade Surplus or (Deficit) (million $)* | *GNP (1923-1960) GDP (1961-2018) (million $)* |
|---|---|---|---|---|---|
| 2017 | 156,992 | 233,799 | 67.1 | -76,806 | 858,988 |
| 2018 | 167,933 | 223,047 | 75.3 | -55,113 | 778,382 |
| 2019 | 171,464 | 202,704 | 84,6 | -31,239 | 761,425 |

*Source*: *See* Foreign Trade by Years, Turkish Statistical Institute, *available at*: https://data.tuik.gov.tr/Kategori/GetKategori?p=dis-ticaret-104&dil=2 (search "Archive," click "Statistical Tables" and, then, click "Foreign Trade by Years") (last visited Feb. 10, 2021) (containing Turkey's 1923-2019 trade statistics—including export and import value, balance of foreign trade, total volume of foreign trade, and proportion of imports covered by exports); Hasan Saygin & Murat Çimen, Turkish Economic Policies and External Dependency 49, 56 & 63-67 (2013) (providing Turkey's 1923-1960 GNP statistics); GDP (current US$)—Turkey, the World Bank, https://data.worldbank.org/indicator/NY.GDP.MKTP.CD?locations=TR (last visited Feb. 10, 2021) (providing Turkey's GDP data between 1960-2019).

# APPENDIX II

*Table II.1 EU-Turkey Binding Coverage on Industrial Goods under the WTO System*

| | *Share of Bound Tariff Lines (Percent)* | *Simple Average for Bound Tariffs (Ad Valorem Percentage)* |
|---|---|---|
| Turkey | 36.3 | 42.6 |
| European Union | 100 | 4.1 |

*Source*: Marc Bacchetta and Bijit Bora, *Industrial Tariff Liberalization and the Doha Development Agenda*, 15 World Trade Organization, Development and Economic Research Division (2003) (using 2001 data), *available at*: https://www.wto.org/english/res_e/booksp_e/discussion_papers_e.pdf; *accord* World Trade Organization, Annual Report 2002, 42, *available at*: https://www.wto.org/English/res_e/booksp_e/anrep_e/anrep02_e.pdf.

*Table II.2 EU-Turkey Major WTO Tariff Categories*

| | *Binding Coverage (Percent)* | | *Simple Average for Bound Tariffs (Ad Valorem Percentage)* | | *Simple Average for Applied Tariffs (Ad Valorem Percentage)* | |
|---|---|---|---|---|---|---|
| | *Turkey* | *EU* | *Turkey* | *EU* | *Turkey* | *EU* |
| Agriculture | 100 | 100 | 61.8 | 12.7 | 42.3 | 11.4 |
| Nonagriculture | 43.0 | 100 | 17.3 | 3.9 | 4.5 | 4.2 |
| Total | 50.5 | 100 | 28.9 | 5.1 | 10.0 | 5.1 |

*Source*: World Trade Organization, World Tariff Profiles 2020, at 90, 182, https://www.wto.org/english/res_e/booksp_e/tariff_profiles20_e.pdf.

*Table II.3 Tariffs on Select Industrial Goods*

| | *Binding Coverage (Percent)* | | *Simple Average for Bound Tariffs (Ad Valorem Percentage)* | | *Simple Average for Applied Tariffs*[1] *(Ad Valorem Percentage)* | |
|---|---|---|---|---|---|---|
| | *Turkey*[2] | *EU* | *Turkey* | *EU* | *Turkey* | *EU* |
| Chemicals | 67.2 | 100 | 16.6 | 4.5 | 4.7 | 4.5 |
| Wood, paper, etc. | 42.5 | 100 | 26.9 | 0.9 | 0.9 | 0.9 |
| Textiles | 23.6 | 100 | 25.2 | 6.6 | 6.5 | 6.5 |
| Clothing | 3.7 | 100 | 27.3 | 11.5 | 11.5 | 11.5 |
| Leather, footwear, etc. | 49.1 | 100 | 22.9 | 4.2 | 4.1 | 4.1 |
| Nonelectrical machinery | 65.5 | 100 | 11.3 | 1.7 | 1.9 | 1.8 |
| Electrical Machinery | 64.8 | 100 | 11.7 | 2.4 | 2.8 | 2.3 |
| Transport equipment | 57.5 | 100 | 17.9 | 4.1 | 4.7 | 4.7 |

*Source*: World Trade Organization, World Tariff Profiles 2020, at 90, 182, https://www.wto.org/english/res_e/booksp_e/tariff_profiles20_e.pdf.

1. Pursuant to GATT, Article XIV(8)(a)(ii), duties "applied by each of the members of [a customs] union" shall be "substantially the same."
2. Despite binding more than 60% of tariff lines on machinery, precision equipment, chemicals, transport equipment, and plastics and rubber, Turkey did not bind tariffs in multiple (i.e., 11) HS Chapters. *See* WTO Secretariat, *Trade Policy Review of Turkey*, WT/TPR/S/259/Rev.1, Table III.2, (Jan. 17, 2012), at 28 (using 2011 MFN tariff data on Harmonized Schedule Chapters 25-97, which cover all industrial products) (hereinafter Turkey TPR 2012).

# APPENDIX III

## Table III.1 Turkey as Complainant

| | Dispute | Report No. | Respondent | Third Parties | Current Status | Filing Year | Product Involved | Agreement Involved | Winner |
|---|---|---|---|---|---|---|---|---|---|
| 1 | Egypt–Definitive Anti-Dumping Measures on Steel Rebar from Turkey | WT/DS211/R | Egypt | Chile; EC; Japan; and United States | Implementation notified by Respondent | 2000 | Steel Rebar | ADA, arts. 3, 4 & 6.8 | Complainant |
| 2 | South Africa–Definitive Anti-Dumping Measures on Blanketing from Turkey | WT/DS288 | South Africa | N/A | In consultations | 2003 | Blanket | ADA, arts. 5, 6 & 9; GATT arts. III & X | N/A |
| 3 | Morocco–Anti-Dumping Measures on Certain Hot-Rolled Steel from Turkey | WT/DS513/R | Morocco | China; Egypt; European Union; India; Japan; Kazakhstan; South Korea; Russia; Singapore; United Arab Emirates; and United States | Panel Report under Appeal | 2016 | Hot-Rolled Steel | ADA, arts. 3 & 6; GATT, arts. I, X & XI | N/A |
| 4 | United States–Countervailing Measures on Certain Pipe and Tube Products (Turkey) | WT/DS523/R | United States | Brazil; Canada; China; European Union; Japan; Kazakhstan; South Korea; Mexico; Russia; Saudi Arabia; and United Arab Emirates | Panel Report under Appeal | 2017 | Steel Pipe and Tube Products | SCM, arts. 1, 2, 10, 12, 14, 15, 19 & 32; GATT, arts.VI:3 | N/A |

| | *Dispute* | *Report No.* | *Respondent* | *Third Parties* | *Current Status* | *Filing Year* | *Product Involved* | *Agreement Involved* | *Winner* |
|---|---|---|---|---|---|---|---|---|---|
| 5 | United States–Certain Measures on Steel and Aluminum Products | WT/DS564 | United States | Bahrain; Brazil; Canada; China; Colombia; Egypt; European Union, Guatemala; Hong Kong; Iceland; India; Indonesia; Japan; Kazakhstan; New Zealand; Norway; Malaysia; Mexico; Qatar; Russia; Saudi Arabia; Singapore; Switzerland; Taiwan, Thailand; Ukraine; Venezuela; and Bolivia. | Panel Composed | 2018 | Steel and Aluminum Products | GATT, arts. I, II, X, XI, XIII & XIX; Safeguards, arts. 2, 3, 4, 5, 7, 8, 9, 11.1 & 12 | N/A |
| 6 | European Union–Safeguard Measures on Certain Steel Products | WT/DS595 | European Union | Argentina; Brazil; Canada; China; India; Japan; Norway; Russia; Korea, Switzerland; Taiwan; Ukraine; United Arab Emirates; United Kingdom; United States | Panel Composed | 2020 | Steel and Aluminum Products | GATT, arts. II, III & XX; Safeguards, arts. 2, 3, 4, 6, 7 & 9 | N/A |

*Source*: *See* Member Information, Turkey and the WTO, Dispute cases involving Turkey, World Trade Organization, https://www.wto.org/english/thewto_e/countries_e/turkey_e.htm (last visited Jan. 22, 2021).

*Table III.2 Turkey as Respondent*

| | *Dispute*[*] | *Report No.* | *Complainant* | *Third Parties* | *Current Status* | *Filing Year* | *Product involved* | *Agreement Involved* | *Winner* |
|---|---|---|---|---|---|---|---|---|---|
| 1 | Turkey–Restrictions on Imports of Textile and Clothing Products | WT/DS47 | Thailand | N/A | In consultations | 1996 | Textiles and Clothing | GATT, arts. I, II & XI | N/A |
| 1 | Turkey–Restrictions on Imports of Textile and Clothing Product | WT/DS29 | Hong Kong and China | N/A | In consultations | 1996 | Textiles and Clothing | GATT, arts. XI & XXIV | N/A |
| 1 | Turkey–Restrictions on Imports of Textile and Clothing Products | WT/DS34/AB/R | India | Hong Kong; China; Japan; Philippines; Thailand; and United States | Mutually acceptable solution on implementation notified | 1996 | Textiles and Clothing | GATT, arts. XI & XXIV | Complainant |
| 2 | Turkey–Taxation of Foreign Film Revenues | WT/DS43 | United States | Canada | Settled or terminated | 1996 | Showing of foreign films | GATT, art. III | N/A |
| 3 | Turkey–Anti-Dumping Duty on Steel and Iron Pipe Fittings | WT/DS208 | Brazil | N/A | In consultations | 2000 | Iron Pipe Fittings | GATT, art. VI; ADA, arts. 2, 3, 5 & 6 | N/A |
| 4 | Turkey–Certain Import Procedures for Fresh Fruit | WT/DS237 | Ecuador | Columbia; EC; and United States | Settled or terminated | 2001 | Banana | GATT, arts. III & XI; A.A., art. 4 | N/A |

* As discussed in Section II.A, to prevent double counting disputes, the first three disputes (i.e., WT/DS47, WT/DS29, and WT/DS34) were counted as one, because Hong Kong and Thailand also participated as Third-Party litigants in the dispute raised by India (WT/DS34).

| | *Dispute*[*] | *Report No.* | *Complainant* | *Third Parties* | *Current Status* | *Filing Year* | *Product involved* | *Agreement Involved* | *Winner* |
|---|---|---|---|---|---|---|---|---|---|
| 5 | Turkey–Import Ban on Pet Food from Hungary | WT/DS256 | Hungary | N/A | In consultations | 2002 | Pet Food | GATT, art. XI;<br>A.A., art. 14;<br>SPS, arts. 2, 5, 6 & 7 | N/A |
| 6 | Turkey–Measures Affecting the Importation of Rice | WT/DS334/R | United States | Argentina; Australia; China; Egypt; EC; South Korea;<br>Pakistan; and Thailand | Implementation notified by Respondent | 2005 | Rice | GATT, arts. III & XI;<br>A.A., art. 4.2;<br>Import Licensing, arts. 1, 3 & 5 | Complainant |
| 7 | Turkey–Safeguard Measures on Imports of Cotton Yarn (other than sewing thread) | WT/DS428 | India | N/A | In consultations | 2012 | Cotton Yarn | GATT, art. XIX:1(a);<br>Safeguards, arts. 4, 5, 6 & 7 | N/A |
| 8 | Turkey–Additional Duties on Certain Products from the United States | WT/DS561 | United States | Brazil; Canada; European Union; Guatemala; India; Indonesia; Japan; Kazakhstan; Mexico; New Zealand; Norway; Russia; Singapore; Switzerland; Taiwan; Thailand; Ukraine; Venezuela; and Bolivia | Panel composed | 2018 | Different Products | GATT, arts. I:1, II:1(a) & II:1(b) | N/A |

| | *Dispute*[*] | *Report No.* | *Complainant* | *Third Parties* | *Current Status* | *Filing Year* | *Product involved* | *Agreement Involved* | *Winner* |
|---|---|---|---|---|---|---|---|---|---|
| 9 | Turkey–Additional Duties on Imports of Air Conditioning Machines from Thailand | WT/DS573 | Thailand | Brazil; Canada; China; European Union; India; Japan; Russia; Singapore; Korea; Ukraine; and United States | Panel composed | 2018 | Air Conditioners | GATT, arts. I, II & XIX;<br>Safeguards, arts. 8.2 & 12.3 | N/A |
| 10 | Turkey–Certain Measures concerning the Production, Importation and Marketing of Pharmaceutical Products | WT/DS583 | European Union | N/A | Panel Composed | 2019 | Pharmaceutical Products | GATT, arts. III, X & XI;<br>TRIMs, arts. 2 & 3;<br>SCM, arts. 1 & 3 | N/A |

*Source*: *See* Member Information, Turkey and the WTO, Dispute cases involving Turkey, World Trade Organization, https://www.wto.org/english/thewto_e/countries_e/turkey_e.htm (last visited Jan. 22, 2021).

*Table III.3 Turkey as Third Party*

| | *Dispute*** | *Report No.* | *Complainant* | *Respondent* | *Third Party* | *Current Status* | *Filing Year* | *Product Involved* | *Agreement Involved* | *Winner* |
|---|---|---|---|---|---|---|---|---|---|---|
| 1 | United States–Measures Affecting Imports of Women's and Girls' Wool Coats | WT/DS32 | India | United States | Turkey; Canada; Costa Rica; EC; Norway; Pakistan | Settled or terminated (withdrawn, mutually agreed solution) | 1996 | Textiles (Wool Coats) (Safeguard Measure) | ATC, arts. 2, 6 & 8 | N/A |
| 2 | United States–Measures Affecting Imports of Woven Wool Shirts and Blouses from India | WT/DS33/AB/R | India | United States | Turkey; Canada; EC; Norway; Pakistan | Mutually acceptable solution on implementation notified | 1996 | Textiles (Woven Wool Shirts and Blouses) (Safeguard) | ATC, arts. 2, 6 & 8 | Complainant |
| 3 | European Communities–Protection of Trademarks and Geographical Indications for Agricultural Products and Foodstuffs | WT/DS174/R | United States | EC | Turkey; Argentina; Australia; Brazil; Taiwan; Columbia; Guatemala; India; Mexico; New Zealand | Implementation notified by Respondent | 1999 | Agricultural Products | GATT, arts. I & III:4 | Complainant |

** As discussed in Section II.A, to prevent double counting, disputes assigned the same number on the left margin were counted as one.

| | *Dispute*** | *Report No.* | *Complainant* | *Respondent* | *Third Party* | *Current Status* | *Filing Year* | *Product Involved* | *Agreement Involved* | *Winner* |
|---|---|---|---|---|---|---|---|---|---|---|
| 3 | European Communities–Protection of Trademarks and Geographical Indications for Agricultural Products and Foodstuffs | WT/DS290/R | Australia | EC | Turkey; Argentina; Brazil; Canada; China; Taiwan; Colombia; Guatemala India; Mexico; New Zealand; United States | Implementation notified by Respondent | 2003 | Agricultural Products | GATT, arts. I & III:4 | Complainant |
| 4 | Argentina–Definitive Anti-Dumping Measures on Carton-Board Imports from Germany and Definitive Anti-Dumping Measures on Imports of Ceramic Tiles from Italy | WT/DS189/R | EC | Argentina | Turkey; Japan; United States | Implementation notified by Respondent | 2000 | Ceramic Floor Tiles | ADA, arts. 2.4, 6, 8, 9 & 10 | Complainant |

| | *Dispute*** | *Report No.* | *Complainant* | *Respondent* | *Third Party* | *Current Status* | *Filing Year* | *Product Involved* | *Agreement Involved* | *Winner* |
|---|---|---|---|---|---|---|---|---|---|---|
| 5 | United States–Definitive Safeguard Measures on Imports of Certain Steel Products | WT/DS248/AB /R | EC | United States | Turkey; Brazil; Canada; China; Taiwan; Cuba; Japan; South Korea; New Zealand; Norway; Switzerland; Thailand; Venezuela | Report(s) adopted, no further action required | 2002 | Steel | GATT, Article XIX:1 (a) | Complainant |
| 5 | United States–Definitive Safeguard Measures on Imports of Certain Steel Products | WT/DS249 AB/R | Japan | United States | Turkey; Brazil; Canada; China; Taiwan; Cuba; EC; South Korea; New Zealand; Norway; Switzerland; Thailand; Venezuela | Report(s) adopted, no further action required | 2002 | Steel | GATT, arts. I:1 & XIX:1(a) | Complainant |

| | *Dispute*** | *Report No.* | *Complainant* | *Respondent* | *Third Party* | *Current Status* | *Filing Year* | *Product Involved* | *Agreement Involved* | *Winner* |
|---|---|---|---|---|---|---|---|---|---|---|
| 5 | United States–Definitive Safeguard Measures on Imports of Certain Steel Products | WT/DS251 AB/R | South Korea | United States | Turkey; Brazil; Canada; China; Taiwan; Cuba; Japan; EC; New Zealand; Norway; Switzerland; Thailand; Venezuela | Report(s) adopted, no further action required | 2002 | Steel | GATT, arts. I:1 & XIX:1(a) | Complainant |
| 5 | United States–Definitive Safeguard Measures on Imports of Certain Steel Products | WT/DS252 AB/R | China | United States | Turkey; Brazil; Canada; Taiwan; Cuba; EC; Japan; South Korea; New Zealand; Norway; Switzerland; Thailand; Venezuela | Report(s) adopted, no further action required | 2002 | Steel | GATT, arts. I:1 & XIX:1(a) | Complainant |

| | *Dispute*** | *Report No.* | *Complainant* | *Respondent* | *Third Party* | *Current Status* | *Filing Year* | *Product Involved* | *Agreement Involved* | *Winner* |
|---|---|---|---|---|---|---|---|---|---|---|
| 5 | United States–Definitive Safeguard Measures on Imports of Certain Steel Products | WT/DS253 AB/R | Switzerland | United States | Turkey; Brazil; Canada; China; Taiwan; Cuba; EC; Japan; South Korea; New Zealand; Norway; Thailand; Venezuela | Report(s) adopted, no further action required | 2002 | Steel | GATT, arts. I:1 & XIX:1(a) | Complainant |
| 5 | United States–Definitive Safeguard Measures on Imports of Certain Steel Products | WT/DS254 AB/R | Norway | United States | Turkey; Brazil; Canada; China; Taiwan; Cuba; EC; Japan; South Korea; New Zealand; Switzerland; Thailand; Venezuela | Report(s) adopted, no further action required | 2002 | Steel | GATT, arts. I:1 & XIX:1(a) | Complainant |

| | *Dispute*** | *Report No.* | *Complainant* | *Respondent* | *Third Party* | *Current Status* | *Filing Year* | *Product Involved* | *Agreement Involved* | *Winner* |
|---|---|---|---|---|---|---|---|---|---|---|
| 5 | United States–Definitive Safeguard Measures on Imports of Certain Steel Products | WT/DS258 AB/R | New Zealand | United States | Turkey; Brazil; Canada; China; Taiwan; Cuba; EC; Japan; South Korea; Norway; Switzerland; Thailand; Venezuela | Report(s) adopted, no further action required | 2002 | Steel | GATT, arts. I:1 & XIX:1(a) | Complainant |
| 5 | United States–Definitive Safeguard Measures on Imports of Certain Steel Products | WT/DS259 AB/R | Brazil | United States | Turkey; Canada; China; Taiwan; Cuba; EC; Japan; South Korea; New Zealand; Norway; Switzerland; Thailand; Venezuela | Report(s) adopted, no further action required | 2002 | Steel | GATT, arts. I:1 & XIX:1(a) | Complainant |
| 6 | European Communities–Provisional Safeguard Measures on Imports of Certain Steel Products | WT/DS260 | United States | EC | Turkey; Egypt; Japan; South Korea | Panel established, but not yet composed | 2002 | Steel | GATT, arts. I & XIX | N/A |

| | Dispute** | Report No. | Complainant | Respondent | Third Party | Current Status | Filing Year | Product Involved | Agreement Involved | Winner |
|---|---|---|---|---|---|---|---|---|---|---|
| 7 | United States–Laws, Regulations and Methodology for Calculating Dumping Margins (Zeroing) | WT/DS294/AB/R | EC | United States | Turkey; Argentina; Brazil; China; Taiwan; Hong Kong, China; India; Japan; South Korea; Mexico; Norway; Thailand; | Report(s) adopted, with recommendation to bring measure(s) into conformity | 2003 | N/A<br>All Products | GATT, art. VI:2<br>ADA, arts. 2.4.2 & 9.3 | Complainant |
| 8 | Mexico–Definitive Anti-Dumping Measures on Beef and Rice | WT/DS295/AB/R | United States | Mexico | Turkey; China; EC | Report(s) adopted, with recommendation to bring measure(s) into conformity | 2003 | Agriculture (Rice) | ADA, arts. 6.1, 6.10 & 12.1 | Complainant |
| 9 | United States–Subsidies and Other Domestic Support for Corn and Other Agricultural Products | WT/DS357 | Canada | United States | Turkey; Argentina; Australia; Chile; EU; India; Japan; Mexico; New Zealand; Nicaragua; South Africa; Taiwan; Thailand; Uruguay | Panel established, but not yet composed | 2007 | Corn and other primary agricultural products | GATT, art. XVI;<br>SCM, arts. 3.1(a) & 3.2 | N/A |

| | *Dispute*** | *Report No.* | *Complainant* | *Respondent* | *Third Party* | *Current Status* | *Filing Year* | *Product Involved* | *Agreement Involved* | *Winner* |
|---|---|---|---|---|---|---|---|---|---|---|
| 10 | China–Measures Affecting the Protection and Enforcement of Intellectual Property Rights | WT/DS362/R | United States | China | Turkey; Argentina; Australia; Brazil; Canada; European Communities; India; Japan; South Korea; Mexico; Taiwan; Thailand; | Implementation notified by Respondent | 2007 | Intellectual Property | TRIPS, arts. 9.1 & 41.1 | Complainant |
| 11 | United States–Domestic Support and Export Credit Guarantees for Agricultural Products | WT/DS365 | Brazil | United States | Turkey; Argentina; Australia; Chile; EU; India; Japan; Mexico; New Zealand; Nicaragua South Africa; Taiwan; Thailand; Uruguay | Panel established, but not yet compose | 2007 | Corn | SCM, arts. 3.1(a) & 3.2 | N/A |
| 12 | Colombia–Indicative Prices and Restrictions on Ports of Entry | WT/DS366/R | Panama | Columbia | Turkey; China; Ecuador; EC; Guatemala Honduras; India; Taiwan; United States | Implementation notified by Respondent | 2007 | Textile | GATT, arts. I:1, V & XI:1 | Complainant |

| | *Dispute*** | *Report No.* | *Complainant* | *Respondent* | *Third Party* | *Current Status* | *Filing Year* | *Product Involved* | *Agreement Involved* | *Winner* |
|---|---|---|---|---|---|---|---|---|---|---|
| 13 | European Communities and its Member States–Tariff Treatment of Certain Information Technology Products | WT/DS375/R | United States | EC | Turkey; Australia; Brazil; China; Costa Rica; Hong Kong, China; India; Japan; South Korea; Philippines; Singapore; Taiwan; Thailand; Viet Nam | Implementation notified by Respondent | 2008 | Flat Panel Displays (FPDs), Set-Top Boxes (STBs) and Multifunctional Digital Machines (MTMs) | GATT, arts. II:1(a), II:1(b), X:1 & X:2 | Complainant |
| 13 | European Communities and its Member States–Tariff Treatment of Certain Information Technology Products | WT/DS376/R | Japan | EC | Turkey; Australia; Brazil; China; Costa Rica; Hong Kong, China; India; South Korea; Philippines; Singapore; Taiwan; Thailand; United States; Viet Nam | Implementation notified by Respondent | 2008 | Flat panel display devices, multifunctional digital machines and set-top boxes | GATT, arts. II:1(a), II:1(b), X:1 & X:2 | Complainant |

| | Dispute** | Report No. | Complainant | Respondent | Third Party | Current Status | Filing Year | Product Involved | Agreement Involved | Winner |
|---|---|---|---|---|---|---|---|---|---|---|
| 13 | European Communities and its Member States–Tariff Treatment of Certain Information Technology Products | WT/DS377/R | Taiwan | EC | Turkey; Australia; Brazil; China; Costa Rica; Hong Kong, China; India; Japan; South Korea; Philippines; Singapore; Thailand; United States; Viet Nam | Implementation notified by Respondent | 2008 | Flat panel display devices, multifunctional digital machines and set-top boxes | GATT, arts. II:1(a), II:1(b), X:1 & X:2 | Complainant |
| 14 | United States–Definitive Anti-Dumping and Countervailing Duties on Certain Products from China | WT/DS379/AB/R | China | United States | Turkey; Argentina; Australia; Bahrain; Brazil; Canada; E C; India; Japan; Kuwait; Mexico; Norway; Saudi Arabia, Taiwan | Implementation notified by Respondent | 2008 | Steel; Textile and Auto (tire) | SCM, arts. 1.1(a)(1), 10, & 32.1 | Complainant |

| | *Dispute*** | *Report No.* | *Complainant* | *Respondent* | *Third Party* | *Current Status* | *Filing Year* | *Product Involved* | *Agreement Involved* | *Winner* |
|---|---|---|---|---|---|---|---|---|---|---|
| 15 | United States–Measures Concerning the Importation, Marketing and Sale of Tuna and Tuna Products[1] | WT/DS381/AB/R | Mexico | United States | Turkey; Argentina; Australia; Brazil; Canada; China; Ecuador; EC; Guatemala Japan; South Korea; New Zealand; Taiwan; Thailand; Venezuela; Norway | Report(s) adopted, with recommendation to bring measure(s) into conformity | 2008 | Tuna and Tuna Products | TBT, arts. 2.2 & 2.4 | Complainant |
| 16 | United States–Certain Measures Affecting Imports of Poultry from China | WT/DS392/R | China | United States | Turkey; Brazil; EC; Guatemala South Korea; Taiwan; | Report(s) adopted, no further action required | 2009 | Poultry Products | GATT, arts. I:1 & XI:1 SPA, arts. 1, 2 & 5 | Complainant |

1. Turkey participated in panel proceedings yet decided to withdraw its Third-Party involvement in the AB proceedings.

| | *Dispute*[**] | *Report No.* | *Complainant* | *Respondent* | *Third Party* | *Current Status* | *Filing Year* | *Product Involved* | *Agreement Involved* | *Winner* |
|---|---|---|---|---|---|---|---|---|---|---|
| 17 | China–Measures Related to the Exportation of Various Raw Materials | WT/DS394/AB/R | United States | China | Turkey; Argentina; Brazil; Canada; Chile; Colombia; Ecuador; EU; India; Japan; South Korea; Mexico; Norway; Taiwan; Saudi Arabia | Implementation notified by Respondent | 2009 | Raw Materials (bauxite, coke, fluorspar, magnesium, manganese, silicon carbide, silicon metal, yellow phosphorous, and zinc) | GATT, arts. VIII:1(a), X:1, X:3(a), XI:1 & XX | Complainant |
| 17 | China–Measures Related to the Exportation of Various Raw Materials | WT/DS395/AB/R | EU | China | Turkey; Argentina; Brazil; Canada; Chile; Colombia; Ecuador; India; Japan; South Korea; Mexico; Norway; Taiwan; Saudi Arabia; United States | Implementation notified by Respondent | 2009 | Raw Materials (bauxite, coke, fluorspar, magnesium, manganese, silicon carbide, silicon metal, yellow phosphorous, and zinc) | GATT, arts. VIII:1(a), X:1, X:3(a), XI:1 & XX | Complainant |

| | *Dispute*** | *Report No.* | *Complainant* | *Respondent* | *Third Party* | *Current Status* | *Filing Year* | *Product Involved* | *Agreement Involved* | *Winner* |
|---|---|---|---|---|---|---|---|---|---|---|
| 17 | China–Measures Related to the Exportation of Various Raw Materials | WT/DS398/ AB/R | Mexico | China | Turkey; Argentina; Brazil; Canada; Chile; Colombia; Ecuador; EU; India; Japan; South Korea; Norway; Taiwan; Saudi Arabia; United States | Implementation notified by Respondent | 2009 | Raw Materials (bauxite, coke, fluorspar, magnesium, manganese, silicon carbide, silicon metal, yellow phosphorous, and zinc) | GATT, arts. VIII:1(a), X:1, X:3(a), XI:1 & XX | Complainant |
| 18 | European Communities–Definitive Anti-Dumping Measures on Certain Iron or Steel Fasteners from China | WT/DS397/ AB/R | China | EC | Turkey; Brazil; Canada; Chile; Colombia; India; Japan; Norway; Taiwan; Thailand; United States | Report(s) adopted, with recommendation to bring measure(s) into conformity | 2009 | Iron or steel fasteners | GATT, art. VI; ADA, arts. 2.4, 4.1, 6.10 & 9.2 | Complainant |

| | *Dispute*[**] | *Report No.* | *Complainant* | *Respondent* | *Third Party* | *Current Status* | *Filing Year* | *Product Involved* | *Agreement Involved* | *Winner* |
|---|---|---|---|---|---|---|---|---|---|---|
| 19 | United States–Measures Affecting Imports of Certain Passenger Vehicle and Light Truck Tyres from China | WT/DS399/AB/R | China | United States | Turkey; EU; Japan; Taiwan; Viet Nam | Report(s) adopted, no further action required | 2009 | Autos and Tires | GATT, arts. I:1 II:1 & XIX | Respondent |
| 20 | European Union–Anti-Dumping Measures on Certain Footwear from China | WT/DS405/R | China | EU | Turkey; Australia; Brazil; Colombia; Japan; United States; Viet Nam | Implementation notified by Respondent | 2010 | Textile (footwear) | GATT, art. VI;<br>ADA, arts. 2.2.2(iii), 6.10 & 9.2 | Complainant |
| 21 | United States–Measures Affecting the Production and Sale of Clove Cigarettes | WT/DS406/AB/R | Indonesia | United States | Turkey; Brazil; Colombia; Dominican Republic; EU; Guatemala Mexico; Norway | Mutually acceptable solution on implementation notified | 2010 | Agriculture (Clove cigarettes) | GATT, art. III:4;<br>TBT, arts. 2.1 & 2.12 | Complainant |

| | *Dispute*** | *Report No.* | *Complainant* | *Respondent* | *Third Party* | *Current Status* | *Filing Year* | *Product Involved* | *Agreement Involved* | *Winner* |
|---|---|---|---|---|---|---|---|---|---|---|
| 22 | Dominican Republic–Safeguard Measures on Imports of Polypropylene Bags and Tubular Fabric | WT/DS415/R | Costa Rica | Dominican Republic | Turkey; Argentina; Brazil; Canada; Chile; Colombia; Ecuador; EU; India; Japan; South Korea; Mexico; Norway; Taiwan; Saudi Arabia | Implementation notified by Respondent | 2010 | Textile | GATT, arts. I:1, II:1(b) & XIX:1 (a); Safeguard, arts. 2.1 & 4.2(a) | Complainant |
| 22 | Dominican Republic–Safeguard Measures on Imports of Polypropylene Bags and Tubular Fabric | WT/DS416/R | Guatemala | Dominican Republic | Turkey; Argentina; Brazil; Canada; Chile; Colombia; Ecuador; EU; India; Japan; South Korea; Mexico; Norway; Taiwan; Saudi Arabia | Implementation notified by Respondent | 2010 | Textile | GATT, arts. I:1, II:1(b) & XIX:1 (a); Safeguard, arts. 2.1 & 4.2(a) | Complainant |

| | *Dispute*** | *Report No.* | *Complainant* | *Respondent* | *Third Party* | *Current Status* | *Filing Year* | *Product Involved* | *Agreement Involved* | *Winner* |
|---|---|---|---|---|---|---|---|---|---|---|
| 22 | Dominican Republic– Safeguard Measures on Imports of Polypropylene Bags and Tubular Fabric | WT/DS417/R | Honduras | Dominican Republic | Turkey; Argentina; Brazil; Canada; Chile; Colombia; Ecuador; EU; India; Japan; South Korea; Mexico; Norway; Taiwan; Saudi Arabia | Implementation notified by Respondent | 2010 | Textile | GATT, arts. I:1, II:1(b) & XIX:1 (a); Safeguard, arts. 2.1 & 4.2(a) | Complainant |
| 22 | Dominican Republic– Safeguard Measures on Imports of Polypropylene Bags and Tubular Fabric | WT/DS418/R | El Salvador | Dominican Republic | Turkey; Argentina; Brazil; Canada; Chile; Colombia; Ecuador; EU; India; Japan; South Korea; Mexico; Norway; Taiwan; Saudi Arabia | Implementation notified by Respondent | 2010 | Textile | GATT, arts. I:1, II:1(b) & XIX:1(a); Safeguard, arts. 2.1 & 4.2(a) | Complainant |

| | *Dispute*** | *Report No.* | *Complainant* | *Respondent* | *Third Party* | *Current Status* | *Filing Year* | *Product Involved* | *Agreement Involved* | *Winner* |
|---|---|---|---|---|---|---|---|---|---|---|
| 23 | Canada–Measures Relating to the Feed-in Tariff Program | WT/DS426/AB/R | EU | Canada | Turkey; United States; Japan; Australia; China; Taiwan; India; Saudi Arabia; Brazil; South Korea; Mexico; Norway; El Salvador | Implementation notified by Respondent | 2011 | Electricity generation equipment in the renewable energy sector | GATT, art. III:8(a); SCM, art. 1.1(a-b) | Complainant |
| 24 | China–Measures Related to the Exportation of Rare Earths, Tungsten and Molybdenum | WT/DS431/AB/R | United States | China | Turkey; Brazil; Canada; Colombia; EU; India; Japan; South Korea; Norway; Oman; Saudi Arabia; Taiwan; Viet Nam; Argentina; Australia; Indonesia; Peru; Russia | Implementation notified by Respondent | 2012 | Chemicals | GATT, arts. XI & XX(g) | Complainant |

| | *Dispute*** | *Report No.* | *Complainant* | *Respondent* | *Third Party* | *Current Status* | *Filing Year* | *Product Involved* | *Agreement Involved* | *Winner* |
|---|---|---|---|---|---|---|---|---|---|---|
| 24 | China–Measures Related to the Exportation of Rare Earths, Tungsten and Molybdenum | WT/DS432/ AB/R | EU | China | Turkey; Brazil; Canada; Colombia; India; Japan; South Korea; Norway; Oman; Saudi Arabia; Taiwan; Viet Nam; Argentina; Australia; Indonesia; Peru; Russia United States | Implementation notified by Respondent | 2012 | Chemicals | GATT, arts. XI & XX(g) | Complainant |
| 24 | China–Measures Related to the Exportation of Rare Earths, Tungsten and Molybdenum | WT/DS433/ AB/R | Japan | China | Turkey; Brazil; Canada; Colombia; EU; India; South Korea; Norway; Oman; Saudi Arabia; Taiwan; Viet Nam; Argentina; Australia; Indonesia; Peru; Russia; United States | Implementation notified by Respondent | 2012 | Chemicals | GATT, arts. XI & XX(g) | Complainant |

| | *Dispute*** | *Report No.* | *Complainant* | *Respondent* | *Third Party* | *Current Status* | *Filing Year* | *Product Involved* | *Agreement Involved* | *Winner* |
|---|---|---|---|---|---|---|---|---|---|---|
| 25 | Australia–Certain Measures Concerning Trademarks and Other Plain Packaging Requirements Applicable to Tobacco Products and Packaging[2] | WT/DS434 | Ukraine | Australia | Turkey; Argentina; Brazil; Canada; Dominican Republic; Ecuador; EU; Guatemala; Honduras; India; Indonesia; Japan; South Korea; New Zealand; Nicaragua; Norway; Oman; Philippines; Singapore; Taiwan; United States; Uruguay; Zambia; Zimbabwe; Chile; China; | Authority for panel lapsed | 2012 | Tobacco Plain Packaging | GATT, arts. I & III:4 | Respondent |

2. Although the authority for panel lapsed in WT/DS434, and the panel decided the following four cases (i.e., WT/DS435, WT/DS441, WT/DS458, and WT/DS467), excluding the WT/DS434, we count all these five cases as one.

| | *Dispute*** | *Report No.* | *Complainant* | *Respondent* | *Third Party* | *Current Status* | *Filing Year* | *Product Involved* | *Agreement Involved* | *Winner* |
|---|---|---|---|---|---|---|---|---|---|---|
| | | | | | Cuba; Egypt; Malaysia; Mexico; Moldova; Nigeria; Peru; Thailand; Malawi | | | | | |
| 25 | Australia–Certain Measures Concerning Trademarks, Geographical Indications and Other Plain Packaging Requirements Applicable to Tobacco Products and Packaging | WT/DS435/R | Honduras | Australia | Turkey; Argentina; Brazil; Canada; Dominican Republic; Ecuador; EU; Guatemala; India; Indonesia; Japan; South Korea; New Zealand; Nicaragua; Norway; Oman; Philippines; Singapore; Taiwan; United States; Uruguay; Zambia; Zimbabwe; | Report(s) adopted, no further action required | 2012 | Tobacco Plain Packaging | GATT, arts. I & III:4 | Respondent |

| | Dispute** | Report No. | Complainant | Respondent | Third Party | Current Status | Filing Year | Product Involved | Agreement Involved | Winner |
|---|---|---|---|---|---|---|---|---|---|---|
| | | | | | Chile; China; Cuba; Egypt; Malaysia; Mexico; Moldova; Nigeria; Peru; Thailand; Malawi; Ukraine | | | | | |
| 25 | Australia–Certain Measures Concerning Trademarks, Geographical Indications and Other Plain Packaging Requirements Applicable to Tobacco Products and Packaging | WT/DS441 | Dominican Republic | Australia | Turkey; Argentina; Brazil; Canada; Ecuador; EU; Guatemala; Honduras; India; Indonesia; Japan; South Korea; New Zealand; Nicaragua; Norway; Oman; Philippines; Singapore; Taiwan; United States; | Report(s) adopted, no further action required | 2012 | Tobacco Plain Packaging | GATT, arts. I & III:4 | Respondent |

| | *Dispute*[**] | *Report No.* | *Complainant* | *Respondent* | *Third Party* | *Current Status* | *Filing Year* | *Product Involved* | *Agreement Involved* | *Winner* |
|---|---|---|---|---|---|---|---|---|---|---|
| | | | | | Uruguay; Zambia; Zimbabwe; Chile; China; Cuba; Egypt; Malaysia; Mexico; Moldova, Republic of; Nigeria; Peru; Thailand; Malawi; Ukraine | | | | | |
| 25 | Australia–Certain Measures Concerning Trademarks, Geographical Indications and Other Plain Packaging Requirements Applicable to Tobacco Products and Packaging | WT/DS458 | Cuba | Australia | Turkey; Argentina; Brazil; Canada; Dominican Republic; Ecuador; EU; Guatemala; Honduras; India; Indonesia; Japan; South Korea; New Zealand; Nicaragua; Norway; Oman; | Reports adopted, no further action required | 2013 | Tobacco Plain Packaging | GATT, arts. I & III:4 | Respondent |

| | Dispute** | Report No. | Complainant | Respondent | Third Party | Current Status | Filing Year | Product Involved | Agreement Involved | Winner |
|---|---|---|---|---|---|---|---|---|---|---|
| | | | | | Philippines; Singapore; Taiwan; United States; Uruguay; Zambia; Zimbabwe; Chile; China; Egypt; Malaysia; Mexico; Moldova; Nigeria; Peru; Thailand; Malawi; Ukraine | | | | | |
| 25 | Australia–Certain Measures Concerning Trademarks, Geographical Indications and Other Plain Packaging Requirements Applicable to Tobacco Products and Packaging | WT/DS467 | Indonesia | Australia | Turkey; Argentina; Brazil; Canada; Dominican Republic; Ecuador; EU; Guatemala; Honduras; India; Japan; South Korea; New Zealand; Nicaragua; Norway; | Reports adopted, no further action required | 2013 | Tobacco Plain Packaging | GATT, arts. I & III:4 | Respondent |

| | *Dispute*** | *Report No.* | *Complainant* | *Respondent* | *Third Party* | *Current Status* | *Filing Year* | *Product Involved* | *Agreement Involved* | *Winner* |
|---|---|---|---|---|---|---|---|---|---|---|
| | | | | | Oman; Philippines; Singapore; Taiwan; United States; Uruguay; Zambia; Zimbabwe; Chile; China; Cuba; Egypt; Malaysia; Mexico; Moldova; Nigeria; Peru; Thailand; Malawi; Ukraine | | | | | |
| 26 | United States–Countervailing Measures on Certain Hot-Rolled Carbon Steel Flat Products from India | WT/DS436/AB/R | India | United States | Turkey; Australia; Canada; China; EU; Saudi Arabia | Compliance proceedings ongoing | 2012 | Steel | GATT, arts. I & VI; SCM, arts. 1.1(a)(1) & 2.1(c) | Complainant |

| | *Dispute*** | *Report No.* | *Complainant* | *Respondent* | *Third Party* | *Current Status* | *Filing Year* | *Product Involved* | *Agreement Involved* | *Winner* |
|---|---|---|---|---|---|---|---|---|---|---|
| 27 | United States–Countervailing Duty Measures on Certain Products from China | WT/DS437/AB/R | China | United States | Turkey; Australia; Brazil; Canada; EU; India; Japan; South Korea; Norway; Russia; Viet Nam; Saudi Arabia | Authorization to retaliate requested (including DSU art. 22.6 arbitration) | 2012 | Solar panels; wind towers; thermal paper; coated paper; tow behind lawn groomers; kitchen shelving; steel sinks; citric acid; magnesia carbon bricks; pressure pipe; line pipe; seamless pipe; steel cylinders; drill pipe; oil country tubular goods; wire strand; and aluminum extrusions | SCM, arts. 1 2 & 14(d) | Complainant |

| | *Dispute*[**] | *Report No.* | *Complainant* | *Respondent* | *Third Party* | *Current Status* | *Filing Year* | *Product Involved* | *Agreement Involved* | *Winner* |
|---|---|---|---|---|---|---|---|---|---|---|
| 28 | Argentina–Measures Affecting the Importation of Goods | WT/DS438/AB/R | EU | Argentina | Turkey; Australia; Canada; China; Ecuador; Guatemala; India; Israel; Japan; South Korea; Norway; Saudi Arabia; Switzerland; Taiwan; Thailand; United States | Report(s) adopted, with recommendation to bring measure(s) into conformity | 2012 | Most imports of goods | GATT, arts. III:4, X:1 & XI:1 | Complainant |
| 28 | Argentina–Measures Affecting the Importation of Goods | WT/DS444/AB/R | United States | Argentina | Turkey; Australia; Canada; China; Ecuador; EU; Guatemala; India; Israel; Japan; South Korea; Norway; Saudi Arabia; Switzerland; Taiwan; Thailand; | Report(s) adopted, with recommendation to bring measure(s) into conformity | 2012 | Most imports of goods | GATT, arts. III:4, X:1 & XI:1 | Complainant |

| | *Dispute*** | *Report No.* | *Complainant* | *Respondent* | *Third Party* | *Current Status* | *Filing Year* | *Product Involved* | *Agreement Involved* | *Winner* |
|---|---|---|---|---|---|---|---|---|---|---|
| 28 | Argentina–Measures Affecting the Importation of Goods | WT/DS445/AB/R | Japan | Argentina | Turkey; Australia; Canada; China; Ecuador; EU; Guatemala; India; Israel; South Korea; Norway; Saudi Arabia; Switzerland; Taiwan; Thailand; United States | Report(s) adopted, with recommendation to bring measure(s) into conformity | 2012 | Most imports of goods | GATT, arts. III:4, X:1 & XI:1 | Complainant |
| 29 | China–Anti-Dumping and Countervailing Duties on Certain Automobiles from the United States | WT/DS440/R | United States | China | Turkey; Colombia; EU; India; Japan; South Korea; Oman; Saudi Arabia, | Report(s) adopted, no further action required | 2012 | Automobile | ADA, arts. 6.8 & 6.9; SCM, art. 12.7 | Complainant |
| 30 | European Union–Anti-Dumping Measures on Imports of Certain Fatty Alcohols from Indonesia | WT/DS442/AB/R | Indonesia | EU | Turkey; India; South Korea; United States; Malaysia; Thailand | Report(s) adopted, with recommendation to bring measure(s) into conformity | 2012 | Fatty alcohols | GATT, art. X:3; ADA, arts. 2.3, 2.4, 3, 4 & 6 | Complainant |

| | *Dispute*[**] | *Report No.* | *Complainant* | *Respondent* | *Third Party* | *Current Status* | *Filing Year* | *Product Involved* | *Agreement Involved* | *Winner* |
|---|---|---|---|---|---|---|---|---|---|---|
| 31 | United States–Countervailing and Anti-Dumping Measures on Certain Products from China | WT/DS449/AB/R | China | United States | Turkey; Australia; Canada; European Union; Japan; Vietnam; India; Russia | Report(s) adopted, with recommendation to bring measure(s) into conformity | 2014 | 31 different products including iron pipe, tire, steel wheels | GATT, art. X:3; SCM, arts. 10, 19.3 & 32.1 | Respondent |
| 32 | China–Measures Imposing Anti-Dumping Duties on High-Performance Stainless Steel Seamless Tubes ("HP-SSST") from Japan | WT/DS454/AB/R | Japan | China | Turkey; EU; India; South Korea; Russia; United States; Saudi Arabia | Report(s) adopted, with recommendation to bring measure(s) into conformity | 2012 | Steel | ADA, arts. 3.1, 3.2 & 3.4 | Complainant |
| 32 | China–Measures Imposing Anti-Dumping Duties on High-Performance Stainless Steel Seamless Tubes ("HP-SSST") from the European Union | WT/DS460/AB/R | EU | China | Turkey; Japan; India; South Korea; United States; Saudi Arabia | Report(s) adopted, with recommendation to bring measure(s) into conformity | 2013 | Steel | ADA, arts. 3.1, 3.2 & 3.4 | Complainant |

| | Dispute** | Report No. | Complainant | Respondent | Third Party | Current Status | Filing Year | Product Involved | Agreement Involved | Winner |
|---|---|---|---|---|---|---|---|---|---|---|
| 33 | India–Certain Measures Relating to Solar Cells and Solar Modules | WT/DS456/AB/R | United States | India | Turkey; Brazil; Canada; China; EU; Japan; South Korea; Malaysia; Norway; Russia; Ecuador; Saudi Arabia; Taiwan | Authorization to retaliate requested (including 22.6 arbitration); Compliance Proceedings ongoing | 2013 | Solar Cells and Solar Modules | GATT, art. III:4; SCM, arts. 3.1(b), 5(c), 6.3(a), 6.3(c) & 25 | Complainant |
| 34 | Russian Federation–Recycling Fee on Motor Vehicles | WT/DS462 | EU | Russia | Turkey; Brazil; China; India; Japan; South Korea; Norway; Ukraine; United States | Panel established, but not yet composed | 2013 | Recycling fee imposed on motor vehicles | GATT, arts. I:1, II:1(a), II:1(b), III:2 & III:4 | N/A |
| 35 | United States–Anti-dumping and Countervailing Measures on large residential washers from Korea | WT/DS464/AB/R | South Korea | United States | Turkey; Brazil; Canada; China; EU; India; Japan; Norway; Thailand; Saudi Arabia; Viet Nam | Authorization to retaliate requested (including 22.6 arbitration) | 2013 | Large residential washers | ADA, arts. 2, 9.3, 9.4, 9.5 & 11 | Complainant |

| | *Dispute*** | *Report No.* | *Complainant* | *Respondent* | *Third Party* | *Current Status* | *Filing Year* | *Product Involved* | *Agreement Involved* | *Winner* |
|---|---|---|---|---|---|---|---|---|---|---|
| 36 | Ukraine–Definitive Safeguard Measures on Certain Passenger Cars | WT/DS468/R | Japan | Ukraine | Turkey; EU; India; South Korea; Russia; Australia; United States | Report(s) adopted, with recommendation to bring measure(s) into conformity | 2013 | Automobile | GATT, art. XI:1(a); Safeguard, arts. 2.1 & 4.2(a) | Complainant |
| 37 | European Union–Measures on Atlanto-Scandian Herring | WT/DS469 | Denmark | EU | Turkey; Australia; China; Guatemala; Honduras; Iceland; India; Japan; New Zealand; Panama; Russia; Taiwan; United States; Argentina; Brazil; Mexico; Norway; Peru; Thailand | Settled or terminated (withdrawn, mutually agreed solution) | 2013 | Herring and mackerel (Fish) | GATT, arts. I:1, V:2 & XI:1 | N/A |

| | *Dispute*** | *Report No.* | *Complainant* | *Respondent* | *Third Party* | *Current Status* | *Filing Year* | *Product Involved* | *Agreement Involved* | *Winner* |
|---|---|---|---|---|---|---|---|---|---|---|
| 38 | United States–Certain Methodologies and Their Application to Anti-Dumping Proceedings Involving China | WT/DS471/ AB/R | China | United States | Turkey; Brazil; Canada; EU; India; Japan; South Korea; Norway; Russia; Saudi Arabia; Ukraine; Vietnam; Taiwan | Authorization to retaliate requested (including 22.6 arbitration) | 2013 | Chinese Products | ADA, arts. 2.4.2, 9.2, 9.3 & 9.4 | Complainant |
| 39 | Brazil–Certain Measures Concerning Taxation and Charges | WT/DS472/ AB/R | EU | Brazil | Turkey; Argentina; Australia; Canada; China; Colombia; India; Japan; South Korea; Russia; South Africa; Taiwan; United States | Reports adopted, with recommendation to bring measures into conformity | 2013 | Automotive sector, the electronics and technology industry, and tax advantages for exporters | GATT, arts. I:1, II:1, III:2, III:4 & III:5 | Complainant |

| | *Dispute*** | *Report No.* | *Complainant* | *Respondent* | *Third Party* | *Current Status* | *Filing Year* | *Product Involved* | *Agreement Involved* | *Winner* |
|---|---|---|---|---|---|---|---|---|---|---|
| 39 | Brazil–Certain Measures Concerning Taxation and Charges | WT/DS497/AB/R | Japan | Brazil | Turkey; Argentina; Australia; Canada; China; Colombia; EU; India; South Korea; Russia; Singapore; Ukraine; United States | Reports adopted, with recommendation to bring measures into conformity | 2015 | Automotive sector, electronics and technology industry, and tax advantages for exporters | GATT, arts. I:1, II:1, III:2, III:4 & III:5 | Complainant |
| 40 | European Union–Anti-Dumping Measures on Biodiesel from Argentina | WT/DS473/AB/R | Argentina | EU | Turkey; Australia; China; Malaysia; Norway; Russia; Saudi Arabia; United States; Colombia; Indonesia; Mexico | Report(s) adopted, with recommendation to bring measure(s) into conformity | 2013 | Biodiesel | ADA, arts. 2, 3 & 9.3 | Complainant |

| | *Dispute*** | *Report No.* | *Complainant* | *Respondent* | *Third Party* | *Current Status* | *Filing Year* | *Product Involved* | *Agreement Involved* | *Winner* |
|---|---|---|---|---|---|---|---|---|---|---|
| 41 | European Union–Cost Adjustment Methodologies and Certain Anti-Dumping Measures on Imports from Russia | WT/DS474 | Russia | EU | Turkey; Argentina; Australia; Canada; China; Indonesia; Norway; Ukraine; United States; Saudi Arabia; Brazil; Mexico; Viet Nam | Panel established, but not yet composed | 2013 | Cost adjustment methodologies used by the EU for the calculation of dumping margins in anti-dumping investigations and reviews | ADA, arts. 2, 3, 9.2 & 9.3; SCM, arts. 10 & 32.1 | N/A |
| 42 | Russia–Anti-Dumping Duties on Light Commercial Vehicles from Germany and Italy | WT/DS479/ AB/R | EU | Russia | Turkey; China; India; Japan; South Korea; United States; Brazil; Ukraine | Report(s) adopted, with recommendation to bring measure(s) into conformity | 2014 | Automobile | ADA, arts. 2, 3, 4, 6, 9.2 & 9.3 | Complainant |
| 43 | European Union–Anti-Dumping Measures on Biodiesel from Indonesia | WT/DS480/R | Indonesia | EU | Turkey; United States; Japan; Singapore; India; China; Canada; Argentina; Australia; Norway; Russia; Brazil; Ukraine | Report(s) adopted, with recommendation to bring measure(s) into conformity | 2014 | Biodiesel | ADA, arts. 2, 3, 9.2 & 9.3 | Complainant |

| | Dispute** | Report No. | Complainant | Respondent | Third Party | Current Status | Filing Year | Product Involved | Agreement Involved | Winner |
|---|---|---|---|---|---|---|---|---|---|---|
| 44 | United States–Anti-Dumping Measures on Certain Oil Country Tubular Goods from Korea | WT/DS488/R | South Korea | United States | Turkey; Canada; China; EU; India; Russia; Mexico | Authorization to retaliate requested (including 22.6 arbitration) | 2014 | Iron and Steel | GATT, arts. I & X:3; ADA, arts. 2 & 6 | Complainant |
| 45 | United States–Anti-Dumping and Countervailing Measures on Certain Coated Paper from Indonesia | WT/DS491/R | Indonesia | United States | Turkey; EU; China; South Korea; Canada | Reports Adopted, no Further Action Required | 2015 | Coated paper products | SCM, arts. 2.1, 15.5 & 15.7; ADA, arts. 3.5, 3.7 & 3.8 | Respondent |
| 46 | Korea–Anti-Dumping Duties on Pneumatic Valves from Japan | WT/DS504/AB/R | Japan | South Korea | Brazil; China; Ecuador; European Union; Norway; Singapore; Turkey; United States; Viet Nam | Report(s) adopted, with recommendation to bring measure(s) into conformity | 2016 | Valve | ADA, arts. 1, 3, 6 & 12; GATT, art. VI | Complainant |
| 47 | United States–Countervailing Measures on Supercalendered Paper from Canada | WT/DS505/AB/R | Canada | United States | Brazil; China; European Union; India; Japan; South Korea; Mexico; Turkey | Report(s) adopted, with recommendation to bring measure(s) into conformity | 2016 | Supercalendered Paper | GATT, art. VI:3; SCM, arts. 1, 2, 10, 11, 12, 14, 19, 22 & 32 | Complainant |

| | Dispute** | Report No. | Complainant | Respondent | Third Party | Current Status | Filing Year | Product Involved | Agreement Involved | Winner |
|---|---|---|---|---|---|---|---|---|---|---|
| 48 | United States–Certain Measures Relating to the Renewable Energy Sector | WT/DS510 | India | United States | Brazil; China; Taiwan; European Union; Indonesia; Japan; South Korea; Norway; Russia; Saudi Arabia; Singapore; Turkey | Panel report under appeal | 2016 | Energy Sector | GATT, arts. III:4 & XVI; SCM, arts. 3, 5, 6 & 25; TRIMs, art. 2; Agr. Est. WTO, art. XVI:4 | N/A |
| 49 | China–Domestic Support for Agricultural Producers | WT/DS511/R | United States | China | Australia; Brazil; Canada; Colombia; Ecuador; Egypt; El Salvador; European Union; Guatemala; India; Indonesia; Israel; Japan; Kazakhstan; South Korea; Norway; Pakistan; Paraguay; | Authorization to retaliate requested (including 22.6 arbitration); Compliance proceedings ongoing | 2016 | Agriculture (wheat, rice, and corn) | AA, arts. 3, 6 & 7 | Complainant |

| | Dispute** | Report No. | Complainant | Respondent | Third Party | Current Status | Filing Year | Product Involved | Agreement Involved | Winner |
|---|---|---|---|---|---|---|---|---|---|---|
| | | | | | Philippines; Russia; Saudi Arabia; Singapore; Taiwan; Thailand; Turkey; Ukraine; Viet Nam | | | | | |
| 50 | Russia–Measures Concerning Traffic in Transit | WT/DS512/R | Ukraine | Russia | Australia; Bolivia; Brazil; Canada; Chile; China; European Union; India; Japan; South Korea; Moldova; Norway; Paraguay; Saudi Arabia; Singapore; Turkey; United States | Report(s) adopted, no further action required | 2016 | Transit Traffic | GATT, arts. V, X, XI & XVI<br>Prot. of Accession, art. VI:5 | Respondent |

| | Dispute** | Report No. | Complainant | Respondent | Third Party | Current Status | Filing Year | Product Involved | Agreement Involved | Winner |
|---|---|---|---|---|---|---|---|---|---|---|
| 51 | European Union–Measures Related to Price Comparison Methodologies | WT/516 | China | European Union | Australia; Bahrain; Brazil; Canada; Colombia; Ecuador; India; Indonesia; Japan; Kazakhstan; South Korea; Mexico; Norway; Russia; Taiwan; Turkey; United Arab Emirates; United States | Authority for panel lapsed | 2016 | N/A | ADA, art. 2; GATT, arts. I & VI | N/A |
| 52 | United Arab Emirates–Measures Relating to Trade in Goods and Services, and Trade-Related Aspects of Intellectual Property Rights | WT/DS526 | Qatar | United Arab Emirates | Afghanistan; Australia; Bahrain; Brazil; Canada; China; Egypt; European Union; Guatemala; Honduras; Japan; | Panel Composed | 2017 | N/A | GATT, arts. I, V, X, XI & XIII; GATS, arts. II, III, XVI & XXIII; TRIPS, arts. 3 & 4 | N/A |

| | *Dispute*** | *Report No.* | *Complainant* | *Respondent* | *Third Party* | *Current Status* | *Filing Year* | *Product Involved* | *Agreement Involved* | *Winner* |
|---|---|---|---|---|---|---|---|---|---|---|
| | | | | | Kazakhstan; South Korea; Malaysia; Mexico; Norway; Philippines; Russia; Saudi Arabia; Singapore; Taiwan; Turkey; Ukraine; United States; Yemen | | | | | |
| 53 | United States–Countervailing Measures on Softwood Lumber from Canada | WT/DS/533 | Canada | United States | Brazil; China; European Union; Japan; Kazakhstan; South Korea; Russia; Turkey; Viet Nam | Panel report under appeal | 2017 | Softwood Lumber | GATT, art. VI:3; SCM, arts. 1, 2, 10, 11, 14, 19, 21 & 32 | N/A |

| | *Dispute*** | *Report No.* | *Complainant* | *Respondent* | *Third Party* | *Current Status* | *Filing Year* | *Product Involved* | *Agreement Involved* | *Winner* |
|---|---|---|---|---|---|---|---|---|---|---|
| 54 | China–Certain Measures Concerning the Protection of Intellectual Property Rights | WT/DS/542 | United States | China | Australia; Brazil; Canada; Egypt; European Union; India; Japan; Kazakhstan; South Korea; New Zealand; Norway; Russia; Singapore; Switzerland; Taiwan; Turkey; Ukraine | Panel Composed | 2018 | N/A | TRIPS, arts. 3 & 28 | N/A |
| 55 | United States–Tariff Measures on Certain Goods from China | WT/DS/543 | China | United States | Australia; Brazil; Canada; European Union; India; Indonesia; Japan; Kazakhstan; South Korea; New Zealand; Norway; | Panel report under appeal | 2018 | N/A | GATT, arts. I & II; DSU, art. 23. | N/A |

| | *Dispute*[**] | *Report No.* | *Complainant* | *Respondent* | *Third Party* | *Current Status* | *Filing Year* | *Product Involved* | *Agreement Involved* | *Winner* |
|---|---|---|---|---|---|---|---|---|---|---|
| | | | | | Russia; Singapore; Taiwan; Turkey; Ukraine | | | | | |
| 56 | United States–Certain Measures on Steel and Aluminum Products | WT/DS/544 | China | United States | Bahrain; Bolivia; Brazil; Canada; Colombia; Egypt; European Union; Guatemala; Hong Kong, China; Iceland; India; Indonesia; Japan; Kazakhstan; Malaysia; Mexico; New Zealand; Norway; Qatar; Russia; Saudi Arabia; Singapore; South Africa; Switzerland; Taiwan; | Panel Composed | 2018 | Steel and Aluminum Products | GATT, arts. I, II, X & XIX; Safeguards, arts. 2, 4, 5, 7, 11 & 12 | N/A |

| | *Dispute*** | *Report No.* | *Complainant* | *Respondent* | *Third Party* | *Current Status* | *Filing Year* | *Product Involved* | *Agreement Involved* | *Winner* |
|---|---|---|---|---|---|---|---|---|---|---|
| | | | | | Thailand; Turkey; Ukraine; Venezuela, | | | | | |
| 56 | United States–Certain Measures on Steel and Aluminum Products | WT/DS/547 | India | United States | Bahrain; Bolivia; Brazil; Canada; China; Colombia; Egypt; European Union; Guatemala; Hong Kong, China; Iceland; India; Indonesia; Japan; Kazakhstan; Malaysia; Mexico; New Zealand; Norway; Qatar; Russia; Saudi Arabia; Singapore; South Africa; Switzerland; Taiwan; Thailand; | Panel Composed | 2018 | Steel and Aluminum Products | GATT, arts. I, II, X & XIX; Safeguards, arts. 2, 4, 5, 7, 11 & 12 | N/A |

| | *Dispute*[**] | *Report No.* | *Complainant* | *Respondent* | *Third Party* | *Current Status* | *Filing Year* | *Product Involved* | *Agreement Involved* | *Winner* |
|---|---|---|---|---|---|---|---|---|---|---|
| | | | | | Turkey; Ukraine; United Arab Emirates; Venezuela | | | | | |
| 56 | United States–Certain Measures on Steel and Aluminum Products | WT/DS/548 | European Union | United States | Bahrain; Bolivia; Brazil; Canada; China; Colombia; Egypt; Guatemala; Hong Kong, China; Iceland; India; Indonesia; Japan; Kazakhstan; New Zealand; Malaysia; Mexico; Norway; Qatar; Russia; Saudi Arabia; Singapore; South Africa; Switzerland; Taiwan; Thailand; | Panel Composed | 2018 | Steel and Aluminum Products | GATT, arts. I, II, X, XI & XIX; Safeguards, arts. 2, 4, 5, 7, 11 & 12; WTO Agreement, art. XVI:4 | N/A |

| | *Dispute*** | *Report No.* | *Complainant* | *Respondent* | *Third Party* | *Current Status* | *Filing Year* | *Product Involved* | *Agreement Involved* | *Winner* |
|---|---|---|---|---|---|---|---|---|---|---|
| | | | | | Turkey; Ukraine; Venezuela, | | | | | |
| 56 | United States–Certain Measures on Steel and Aluminum Products | WT/DS/550 | Canada | United States | Bahrain; Bolivia; Brazil; China; Colombia; Egypt; European Union; Guatemala; Hong Kong, China; Iceland; India; Indonesia; Japan; Kazakhstan; Malaysia; Mexico; New Zealand; Norway; Qatar; Russia; Saudi Arabia; Singapore; South Africa; Switzerland; Taiwan; Thailand; Turkey; Ukraine; Venezuela | Settled or terminated (withdrawn, mutually agreed solution) | 2018 | Steel and Aluminum Products | GATT, arts. I, II, X, XI & XIX; Safeguards, arts. 2, 4, 5, 7, 11 & 12; WTO Agreement, art. XVI:4 | N/A |

| | Dispute** | Report No. | Complainant | Respondent | Third Party | Current Status | Filing Year | Product Involved | Agreement Involved | Winner |
|---|---|---|---|---|---|---|---|---|---|---|
| 56 | United States–Certain Measures on Steel and Aluminum Products | WT/DS/551 | Mexico | United States | Bahrain, Bolivia; Brazil; Canada; China; Colombia; Egypt; European Union; Guatemala; Honduras; Hong Kong, China; Iceland; India; Indonesia; Japan; Kazakhstan; Malaysia; New Zealand; Norway; Qatar; Russia; Saudi Arabia; Singapore; South Africa; Switzerland; Taiwan; Thailand; Turkey; Ukraine; Venezuela | Settled or terminated (withdrawn, mutually agreed solution) | 2018 | Steel and Aluminum Products | GATT, arts. I, II, X, XI & XIX; Safeguards, arts. 2, 4, 5, 7, 11 & 12; WTO Agreement, art. XVI:4 | N/A |

| | *Dispute*** | *Report No.* | *Complainant* | *Respondent* | *Third Party* | *Current Status* | *Filing Year* | *Product Involved* | *Agreement Involved* | *Winner* |
|---|---|---|---|---|---|---|---|---|---|---|
| 56 | United States–Certain Measures on Steel and Aluminum Products | WT/DS/552 | Norway | United States | Bahrain; Brazil; Canada; China; Colombia; Egypt; European Union; Guatemala; Hong Kong, China; Iceland; India; Indonesia; Japan; Kazakhstan; Malaysia; Mexico; New Zealand; Qatar; Russia; Saudi Arabia; Singapore; South Africa; Switzerland; Taiwan; Thailand; Turkey; Ukraine; Venezuela, Bolivarian Republic of; | Panel Composed | 2018 | Steel and Aluminum Products | GATT, arts. I, II, X, XI & XIX; Safeguards, arts. 2, 4, 5, 7, 11 & 12 | N/A |

| | *Dispute*** | *Report No.* | *Complainant* | *Respondent* | *Third Party* | *Current Status* | *Filing Year* | *Product Involved* | *Agreement Involved* | *Winner* |
|---|---|---|---|---|---|---|---|---|---|---|
| 56 | United States–Certain Measures on Steel and Aluminum Products | WT/DS/554 | Russia | United States | Bahrain; Brazil; Canada; China; Colombia; Egypt; European Union; Guatemala; Hong Kong, China; Iceland; India; Indonesia; Japan; Kazakhstan; New Zealand; Norway; Malaysia; Mexico; Qatar; Saudi Arabia; Singapore; South Africa; Switzerland; Taiwan; Thailand; Turkey; Ukraine; Venezuela, Bolivarian Republic of; | Panel Composed | 2018 | Steel and Aluminum Products | GATT, arts. I, II, X, XI & XIX; Safeguards, arts. 2, 4, 5, 7, 11 & 12 | N/A |

| | *Dispute*** | *Report No.* | *Complainant* | *Respondent* | *Third Party* | *Current Status* | *Filing Year* | *Product Involved* | *Agreement Involved* | *Winner* |
|---|---|---|---|---|---|---|---|---|---|---|
| 56 | United States–Certain Measures on Steel and Aluminum Products | WT/DS/556 | Switzerland | United States | Bahrain; Brazil; Canada; China; Colombia; Egypt; European Union; Hong Kong, China; India; Indonesia; Japan; Kazakhstan; Malaysia; Mexico; New Zealand; Norway; Qatar; Russia; Saudi Arabia; Singapore; South Africa; Taiwan; Thailand; Turkey; Ukraine; United Arab Emirates; Venezuela, Bolivarian Republic of; | Panel Composed | 2018 | Steel and Aluminum Products | GATT, Articles I, II, X, XI & XIX; Safeguards, Articles 2, 4, 5, 7, 11 & 12; WTO Agreement, art. XVI:4 | N/A |

| | Dispute** | Report No. | Complainant | Respondent | Third Party | Current Status | Filing Year | Product Involved | Agreement Involved | Winner |
|---|---|---|---|---|---|---|---|---|---|---|
| 57 | Canada–Additional Duties on Certain Products from the United States | WT/DS/557 | United States | Canada | Brazil; China; Egypt; European Union; Guatemala; India; Indonesia; Japan; Kazakhstan; Mexico; New Zealand; Norway; Russia; Singapore; South Africa; Switzerland; Taiwan; Thailand; Turkey; Ukraine; Venezuela, Bolivarian Republic of; | Settled or terminated (withdrawn, mutually agreed solution) | 2018 | Different Products | GATT, arts. I & II | N/A |

| | Dispute[**] | Report No. | Complainant | Respondent | Third Party | Current Status | Filing Year | Product Involved | Agreement Involved | Winner |
|---|---|---|---|---|---|---|---|---|---|---|
| 57 | China–Additional Duties on Certain Products from the United States | WT/DS/558 | United States | China | Brazil; Canada; Egypt; European Union; Guatemala; India; Indonesia; Japan; Kazakhstan; Mexico; New Zealand; Norway; Russia; Singapore; South Africa; Switzerland; Taiwan; Thailand; Turkey; Ukraine; Venezuela, Bolivia | Panel composed | 2018 | Different Products | GATT, arts. I & II | N/A |

| | Dispute** | Report No. | Complainant | Respondent | Third Party | Current Status | Filing Year | Product Involved | Agreement Involved | Winner |
|---|---|---|---|---|---|---|---|---|---|---|
| 57 | European Union–Additional Duties on Certain Products from the United States | WT/DS/559 | United States | European Union[3] | Brazil; Canada; China; Egypt; Guatemala; India; Indonesia; Japan; Kazakhstan; Mexico; New Zealand; Norway; Russia; Singapore; South Africa; Switzerland; Taiwan; Thailand; Turkey; Ukraine; Venezuela, Bolivia | Panel composed | 2018 | Different Products | GATT, arts. I & II | N/A |

3. Note that Turkey has also participated as Third-Party litigant in *European Union–Additional Duties on Certain Products from the Unites States, WT/DS/559* (Complainant: the United States) (2018), we do not count this dispute, because Turkey was also sued by the United States in the same subject matter (i.e., *Turkey–Additional Duties on Certain Products from the Unites States, WT/DS/561* (2018)).

| | Dispute** | Report No. | Complainant | Respondent | Third Party | Current Status | Filing Year | Product Involved | Agreement Involved | Winner |
|---|---|---|---|---|---|---|---|---|---|---|
| 57 | Mexico–Additional Duties on Certain Products from the United States | WT/DS/560 | United States | Mexico | Brazil; China; Canada; Egypt; European Union; Guatemala; India; Indonesia; Japan; Kazakhstan; New Zealand; Norway; Russia; Singapore; Switzerland; Taiwan; Thailand; Turkey; Ukraine; Venezuela, Bolivia | Settled or terminated (withdrawn, mutually agreed solution) | 2018 | Different Products | GATT, arts. I & II | N/A |
| 57 | Russian Federation–Additional Duties on Certain Products from the United States | WT/DS/566 | United States | Russia | Brazil; Canada; China; European Union; Egypt; India; Indonesia; Japan; Kazakhstan; | Panel composed | | Different Products | GATT, arts. I & II | N/A |

| | *Dispute*** | *Report No.* | *Complainant* | *Respondent* | *Third Party* | *Current Status* | *Filing Year* | *Product Involved* | *Agreement Involved* | *Winner* |
|---|---|---|---|---|---|---|---|---|---|---|
| | | | | | Malaysia; Mexico; New Zealand; Norway; Qatar; Saudi Arabia; Singapore; Switzerland; Taiwan; Thailand; Turkey; Venezuela, Bolivia | | | | | |
| 58 | Saudi Arabia–Measures Concerning the Protection of Intellectual Property Rights | WT/DS/567 | Qatar | Saudi Arabia | Australia; Bahrain; Brazil; China; European Union; India; Japan; South Korea; Mexico; Norway; Russia; Singapore; Taiwan; Turkey; Ukraine; United Arab Emirates; United States; Yemen | Panel report under appeal | 2018 | N/A | TRIPS, arts. 3, 4, 9, 14, 16, 41, 42 & 61 | N/A |

| | *Dispute*** | *Report No.* | *Complainant* | *Respondent* | *Third Party* | *Current Status* | *Filing Year* | *Product Involved* | *Agreement Involved* | *Winner* |
|---|---|---|---|---|---|---|---|---|---|---|
| 59 | Qatar–Certain Measures Concerning Goods from the United Arab Emirates | WT/DS/576 | United Arab Emirates | Qatar | Afghanistan; Bahrain; Brazil; Canada; China; Egypt; European Union; India; Japan; Mexico; Norway; Russia; Saudi Arabia; Singapore; Taiwan; Turkey; Ukraine; United States | Panel established, but not yet composed | 2019 | N/A | DSU, art. 23; GATT, arts. I, III, X & XI | N/A |
| 60 | United States–Anti-dumping and Countervailing Duties on Ripe Olives from Spain | WT/DS/577 | European Union | United States | Australia; Brazil; Canada; China; India; Japan; Mexico; Russia; Saudi Arabia; Switzerland; Turkey | Panel composed | 2019 | Olives | SCM, arts. 1, 2, 10,14,15, 19 & 32; GATT, art. VI; ADA, art. 3 | N/A |

| | Dispute** | Report No. | Complainant | Respondent | Third Party | Current Status | Filing Year | Product Involved | Agreement Involved | Winner |
|---|---|---|---|---|---|---|---|---|---|---|
| 61 | India–Tariff Treatment on Certain Goods in the Information and Communications Technology Sector | WT/ DS/582 | European Union | India | Brazil; Canada; China; Indonesia; Japan; South Korea; Norway; Pakistan; Russian; Singapore; Taiwan; Thailand; Turkey; Ukraine; United States | Panel Composed | 2019 | Information and Communica-tions Technology Products | GATT, art. II | N/A |
| 61 | India–Tariff Treatment on Certain Goods | WT/ DS/584 | Japan | India | Brazil; Canada; China; European Union; Indonesia; Norway; Pakistan; Russia; Singapore; Republic of Korea; Taiwan; | Panel Composed | 2019 | Information and Communica-tions Technology Products | GATT, arts. II | N/A |

| | *Dispute*** | *Report No.* | *Complainant* | *Respondent* | *Third Party* | *Current Status* | *Filing Year* | *Product Involved* | *Agreement Involved* | *Winner* |
|---|---|---|---|---|---|---|---|---|---|---|
| | | | | | Thailand; Turkey; Ukraine; United Kingdom; United States | | | | | |
| 61 | India–Additional Duties on Certain Products from the United States | WT/DS585 | United States | India | Brazil; Canada; China; European Union; Guatemala; Indonesia; Japan; Malaysia; Mexico; Norway; Russia; Singapore; Switzerland; Taiwan; Turkey; Ukraine; Venezuela, Bolivarian Republic of; | Panel Composed | 2019 | Information and Communica-tions Technology Products | GATT, arts. II | N/A |

| | *Dispute*** | *Report No.* | *Complainant* | *Respondent* | *Third Party* | *Current Status* | *Filing Year* | *Product Involved* | *Agreement Involved* | *Winner* |
|---|---|---|---|---|---|---|---|---|---|---|
| 61 | India–Tariff Treatment on Certain Goods in the Information and Communications Technology Sector | WT/DS/588 | Taiwan | India | Brazil; Canada; China; European Union; Indonesia; Japan; Norway; Pakistan; Russia; Singapore; South Korea; Thailand; Turkey; Ukraine; United Kingdom; United States | Panel Composed | 2019 | Information and Communica-tions Technology Products | GATT, art. II | N/A |
| 62 | Japan–Measures Related to the Exportation of Products and Technology to Korea | WT/DS/590 | Republic of Korea | Japan | Brazil; Canada; China; Taiwan; European Union; India; Norway; Russia; Saudi Arabia; Singapore; Turkey; | Panel established, but not yet composed | 2019 | Fluorinated Polyimide, Resist Polymers and Hydrogen Fluoride, and Their Related Technologies. | GATT, arts. I, X, VIII, XI, XIII, & XXIII; TFA, arts. 2, 6, 7, & 8; TRIMs, art. 2; TRIPS arts. 3, 4, 28; GATS art. VI, VI WTO Agr. art. XVI | N/A |

| | Dispute** | Report No. | Complainant | Respondent | Third Party | Current Status | Filing Year | Product Involved | Agreement Involved | Winner |
|---|---|---|---|---|---|---|---|---|---|---|
| | | | | | Ukraine; United Kingdom; United States | | | | | |
| 63 | Colombia–Anti-Dumping Duties on Frozen Fries from Belgium, Germany and the Netherlands | WT/DS/591 | European Union | Colombia | Brazil; China; Honduras; India; Japan; Russia; Turkey; United States | Panel Composed | 2019 | Frozen Fries (potatoes, prepared or preserved (otherwise than by vinegar or acetic acid)) | GATT, art. IV; ADA, arts. 1, 2, 3, 5, 6, 9, 11, 12 & 18 | N/A |
| 64 | European Union–Certain Measures Concerning Palm Oil and Oil Palm Crop-Based Biofuels | WT/DS/593 | Indonesia | European Union | Argentina; Australia; Brazil; Canada; China; Colombia; Costa Rica; Ecuador; Guatemala; Honduras; India; Japan; Malaysia; Norway; Russia; | Panel Composed | 2019 | Palm Oil | GATT, arts. I, III, X, & XI; SCM, arts. 1, 3, & 5; TBT, arts. 2, 5, & 12 | N/A |

| | *Dispute*** | *Report No.* | *Complainant* | *Respondent* | *Third Party* | *Current Status* | *Filing Year* | *Product Involved* | *Agreement Involved* | *Winner* |
|---|---|---|---|---|---|---|---|---|---|---|
| | | | | | Singapore; South Korea; Thailand; Turkey; United States | | | | | |

*Source*: *See* Member Information, Turkey and the WTO, Dispute cases involving Turkey, World Trade Organization, https://www.wto.org/english/thewto_e/countries_e/turkey_e.htm (last visited Feb. 4, 2021).

# References

Agreement between the United States of America, the United Mexican States, and Canada, Nov. 30, 2018, https://ustr.gov/trade-agreements/free-trade-agreements/united-states-mexico-canada-agreement/agreement-between.

Aka, Halit Burç, and Bilge Gürsoy. 2014. Turkey's Objective of Full Membership in the EU with Reference to Maastricht Criteria. *Ataturk Universitesi Journal of Economics and Administrative Sciences* 28: 271.

Akman, M. Sait. 2012. Turkey in the World Trading System and the WTO: Activism under Global Challenges and the EU Process. *Afro Eurasian Studies* 1: 134.

Aktan, Coşkun C. 1993. Turkey: From Inward-Oriented Etatism to Outward-Looking Liberal Strategy. *Turkish Public Administration Annual* 17: 55.

Albright, Madeleine K., and Stephen J. Hadley. 2012. U.S.-Turkey Relations a New Partnership. *Project Director Independent Task Force Report* No. 69.

Alkan, Ufuk. 2017. The Modernization of Turkey's Customs Union with the European Union: Reasons and Possible Outcomes. *Department of EU International Relations and Diplomacy Studies EU Diplomacy Paper* No. 09.

Altun, Nurullah, and Hakan Yavuz. 2011. Türkiye'nin Avrupa Birliği Ülkeleri İle Olan Diş Ticaretinin Yapisal, Sektörel ve Ürün Gruplari İtibariyle Değerlendirilmesi (1990–2009 Dönemi). *Bilgi* 22: 13.

Argin, Nilüfer, and A. Can Bakkalci. 2011. *Türkiye'nin Diş Ticaret Tarihi* [*History of Turkish Foreign Trade*]. Bursa: Ekin Yayinevi.

Arikan, Harun. 2003. *Turkey and the EU: An Awkward Candidate for EU Membership?* Aldershot, U.K.: Ashgate Publishing.

Aydin, Levent. 2017. Economic Implications of Fethullahist Terrorist Organization and Parallel State Constitution on Turkish Economy. *Research in Applied Economics* 9: 31-44.

Babacan, Mehmet. 2011. Whither Axis Shift: A Perspective from Turkey's Foreign Trade. *Insight Turkey* 13: 129.

Bacchetta, Marc, and Bijit Bora. 2003. *Industrial Tariff Liberalization and the Doha Development Agenda*. Geneva: WTO Publications.

Bakkalci, Can, and Argin Nilüfer. 2013. Turk Dis Ticareti ve Ekonomi Politikaları Arasındaki Nedensellik Iliskileri [The Relationship Between Turkey's Trade and its Economy Policies]. *Yönetim Bilimleri Dergisi* 11: 49.

Bal, Harun, and Ali E. Alper. 2010. Baku-Tiflis-Ceyhan Petrol Boru Hatti ve Turkiye Ekonomisine Etkileri [The Effects of Baku-Tiblisi-Ceyhan Pipeline on Turkey's Economy]. *Çanakkale Üniversitesi Sosyal Bilimler Enstitüsü Dergisi* 19: 345.

Balim, Cigdem. 1999. The Political Economy of Export-Oriented Industrialization in Turkey. In *State and Market: The Political Economy of Turkey in Comparative Perspective*, ed. Ziya Öniş 435. İstanbul: Boğaziçi University Press.

Balkir, Canan. 2016. Europeanization of Trade Policy, An Asymmetric Track. In *The Europeanization of Turkish Public Policies: A Scorecard*, eds. Aylin Guney and Ali Tekin, 12. London: Routledge.

Başlar, Kemal. 2004 Gümrük Birliği "Anlaşmasi"nin (1/95 sayılı Ortaklik Konseyi Karari'nin) Hukuksal Niteliği [Legal Status of the Customs Union (Decision No. 1/95 of the Association Council) Agreement]. *Ankara Avrupa Çalişmalari Dergisi* 4: 151.

Bayraktar, Ali, and K. Sevgin Güngör. 2017. Countering Illicit Trade in Turkey's Free Zones. *Public Governance and Territorial Development Directorate Public Governance Committee reported by the Turkish Ministry of Economy.*

Baysan, Tercan, and Charles Blitzer. 1990. Turkey's Trade Liberalization in the 1980s and Prospects for Its Sustainability. In *The Political Economy of Turkey: Debt, Adjustment and Sustainability*, eds. Tosun Aricanli and Dani Rodrik 9. New York: Palgrave Macmillan.

Benlialper, Ahmet, Hasan Cömert, and Güney Düzçay. 2015. 2002 Sonrasi Türkiye Ekonomisinin Performansi: Karşilaştirmali Bir Analiz [Performance of Turkey's Economy After 2002: A Comparative Analysis]. *ERC Working Papers in Economics* No. 15/04.

Bhala, Raj. 1999. The Myth About Stare Decisis and International Trade Law (Part One of a Trilogy). *American University International Law Review* 14: 845.

Bhala, Raj. 2012. *Dictionary of International Trade Law.* 2d edition. New York: LexisNexis.

Blomström, Magnus, and Ari Kokko. 2003. The Economics of Foreign Direct Investment Incentives. *National Bureau of Economic Research Working Paper Series, Working Paper* No. 9489.

Bown, Chad P. 2014. Trade Policy Flexibilities and Turkey: Tariffs, Anti-dumping, Safeguards and WTO Dispute Settlement. *The World Economy* 37: 193.

Bown, Chad P., and Meredith A. Crowley. 2007. Trade Deflection and Trade Depression. *Journal of International Economics* 72: 176.

Bradford, Colin I., and William H. Branson. 1987. Patterns of Trade and Structural Change. In *Trade and Structural Change in Pacific Asia*, eds. Colin I. Bradford, Jr. and William H. Branson, 3. Chicago: University of Chicago Press.

Bülbül, Onur, and Asli Orhan. 2014. Beyond Turkey-EU Customs Union: Predictions for Key Regulatory Issues in a Potential Turkey-U.S. FTA Following TTIP. *Global Trade and Customs Journal* 9: 444.

Çağlar, Selda. 2015. Milletlerarasi Antlaşmalarin Onaylanmasina İlişkin İç Hukuk Rejimi. In Prof. Dr. Hüseyin Pazarci'ya Armağan [*A Festschrift for Prof. Dr. Hüseyin Pazarci*], ed. Erdem Denk, 631. Ankara: Ankara Üniversitesi Siyasal Bilgiler Fakültesi Kamu Yönetimi Araştirma ve Uygulama merkezi.

Cebeci, Tolga, and Ana M. Fernandes. 2013. Micro Dynamics of Turkey's Export Boom in the 2000s. *The World Bank Development Research Group, Trade and Integration Team Policy Research Working Paper* No. 6452.

Celasun, Merih, and Dani Rodrik. 1989. Trade Regime and an Anatomy of Export Performance, In *Developing Country Debt and Economic Performance, Country Studies—Indonesia, Korea, Philippines, Turkey*, eds. Jeffrey D. Sachs and Susan M. Collins, 716. Volume 3. Chicago: University of Chicago Press.

Colares, Juscelino F. 2009. A Theory of WTO Adjudication: From Empirical Analysis to Biased Rule Development. *Vanderbilt Journal of Transnational Law* 42: 383.

Colares, Juscelino F. 2011. The Limits of WTO Adjudication: Is Compliance the Problem? *Journal of International Economic Law* 14: 403.

Colares, Juscelino F., and Mustafa T. Durmuş. 2019. TURK-SWITCH: The Tariff-Leverage and Legal Case for Turkey's Shift from Customs Union to FTA with the European Union and Beyond. *Journal of International Economic Law* 22: 99.

Colares, Juscelino F., and Mustafa T. Durmuş. 2020. Turkey as a WTO Litigant: A Case of Waived Leverage and Mismatched Policy Ends and Means. *Georgetown Journal of International Law* 51: 867.

Council of the European Union, Enlargement and Stabilisation and Association Process—Council Conclusions. 2018. Online. *Available at*: http://www.consilium.europa.eu/media/35863/st10555-en18.pdf.

Davey, William J. 2009. Compliance Problems in WTO Dispute Settlement. *Cornell International Law Journal* 42: 119.

Davutoğlu, Ahmet. 2011. *Stratejik Derinlik* [*Strategic Depth*]. 109th edition. İstanbul: Küre Yayinlari.

Decision No. 1/95 of the EC-Turkey Association Council of 22 December 1995 on implementing the final phase of the Customs Union. 1995. 96/142/EC, 1996 O.J. (L 035).

Demir, Firat. 2004. A Failure Story: Politics and Financial Liberalization in Turkey, Revisiting the Revolving Door Hypothesis. *World Development* 32: 851.

Dudden, Lesley, and Kadir Üstün. 2017. EU-Turkey Refugee Agreement: Too Big to Fail. *SETA-Foundation for Political, Economic and Social Research* No. 34.

Economic Implication for Turkey of a Customs Union with the European Union. 1996. *The World Bank International Economics Department, International Trade Division Policy Research Working Paper* No. 1599.

Eder, Mine. 1999. Becoming Western: Turkey and the European Union. In *Regionalism across the North/South Divide: State Strategies and Globalization*, eds. Jean Gruel and Wil Hout, 79. London: Routledge.

Elwell, Craig K. 2012. The Depreciating Dollar: Economic Effects and Policy Response. *Congressional Research Service* No. RL34582.

Emrence, Cem. 2003. Turkey in Economic Crisis (1927-1930): A Panoramic Vision. *Middle Eastern Studies* 39: 67.

Erdogan, Eren, Osman Nuri Aras and Mustafa Öztürk. 2012. Does Overvalued Turkish Lira Affect Turkey's Foreign Trade Competitiveness? *International Journal of Social Sciences and Humanity Studies* 4:159.

European Parliament/Legislative Observatory, 2016 Commission Report on Turkey. 2017. Report No. 2016/2308(INI).

Evaluation of the EU-TURKEY Customs Union. 2014. *World Bank, Report* No. 85830-TR.

General Agreement on Tariffs and Trade 1994. 1994. (April 15). Marrakesh Agreement Establishing the World Trade Organization, Annex 1A, 1867 U.N.T.S. 187, 33.

Göçmen, Ilke. 2016. Avrupa Birliği ile Turkiye Arasindaki Gümrük Birliginin Guncellenmesinin Yontemi ve Usulu: Avrupa Birliği Açisindan Bir Bakis [An Evaluation of Procedural Methods for Updating the EU-Turkey Customs Union]. *Ankara Avrupa Çalişmalari Dergisi* 15: 85.

Goldsmith, Jack L., and Eric A. Posner. 2005. *The Limits of International Law.* New York: Oxford University Press.

Good, Kathryn. 1988. Institutional Reform Under the Single European Act. *American University International Law Review* 3: 299.

Gregory, Mankiw N. 2009. *Principals of Economics.* 5th edition. Mason, OH: South-Western Cengage Learning.

Guzman, Andrew T. 2008. *How International Law Works: A Rational Choice Theory.* New York: Oxford University Press.

Hale, William. 1981. *Political and Economic Development of Modern Turkey*. London: Routledge.

Hartler, Christina, and Sam Laird. 1999. The EU Model and Turkey a Case for Thanksgiving. *Journal of World Trade* 33: 147.

Hiç, Mükerrem. 2009. *Turkish Economy and Politics*. İstanbul: Beykent Üniversitesi.

Hudec, Robert E. 1993. *Enforcing International Trade Law: The Evolution of The Modern GATT Legal System*. Salem, N.H.: Butterworth Legal Publishers.

Jackson, John H., William J. Davey and Alan O. Sykes, Jr. 2013. *Legal Problems of International Economic Relations Cases, Materials and Text,* 6th edition. St. Paul, MN.: West Academic Publishing.

Johnson, William P. 2011. Turkey's Accession to the CISG: The Significance for Turkey and for Sales Transactions with U.S. Contracting Parties. *Ankara Law Review* 8: 1.

Joint Declaration of the Government of the United Kingdom of Great Britain and Northern Ireland and the Government of the People's Republic of China on the Question of Hong Kong. 1984. (December 19). 1399 U.N.T.S. 33, 23.

Kabaalioğlu, Haluk. 2010. Turkey-EU Customs Union: Problems and Prospects. *Dokuz Eylül Üniversitesi Sosyal Bilimler Enstitüsü Dergisi* 12: 47.

Karacaovali, Baybars. 2011. Turkey: Temporary Trade Barriers as Resistance to Trade Liberalization with the European Union? *Fordham University Department of Economics Discussion Paper* No. 2011-02.

Karli, Mehmet. 2008. Turkey, the UN and the WTO: The Emergence of a Trading Nation and a Good International Citizen. *Turkish Policy Quarterly* 6:58.

Kazgan, Gülten. 2013. *Tanzimattan 21. Yuzyila Turkiye Economisi* [*Turkish economy from Tanzimat to 21th Century*]. 5th edition. İstanbul: İstanbul Bilgi Üniversitesi Yayinlari.

Keating, William E. 2015. The Doha Round and Globalization: A Failure of World Economic Development? Unpublished B.A. dissertation. City University of New York.

Kirişçi, Kemal. 2013. Turkey and the Transatlantic Trade and Investment Partnership Boosting the Model Partnership with the United States. *Center on the United States and Europe at Brookings Turkey Project Policy Paper* No. 2.

Kirişçi, Kemal, and Neslihan Kaptanoglu. 2011. The Politics of Trade and Turkish Foreign Policy. *Middle Eastern Studies* 47: 705.

Kirişçi, Kemal. 2009. The Transformation of Turkish Foreign Policy: The Rise of the Trading State. *New Perspectives on Turkey* 40: 29.

Koh, Harold Hongju. 1997. Why Do Nations Obey International Law? *Yale Law Journal* 106: 2599.

Krueger, Anee O. *Economic Policy Reform in Brazil and Turkey* (Stanford Center for International Development Working Paper No. 445, 2011), *available at*: https://globalpoverty.stanford.edu/sites/default/files/publications/445wp.pdf.

Krueger, Anne O. 1974. *Foreign Trade Regimes and Economic Development: Turkey.* Cambridge Mass: National Bureau of Economic Research, Inc.

Krueger, Anne O., and Okan H. Aktan. 1992. *Swimming Against the Tide: Turkish Trade Reform in the 1980s*. New York: ICS Press.

Kutlay, Mustafa. 2011. Economy as the "Practical Hand" of "New Turkish Foreign Policy": A Political Economy Explanation. *Insight Turkey* 13: 67.

Landau, Jacob M. 1984. *Atatürk and the Modernization of Turkey*. Boulder, Colo.: Westview Press.

Lee, Eun Sup. 2012. *World Trade Regulation: International Trade Under The WTO Mechanism*. Berlin: Springer.

Macovei, Mihai. 2009. Growth and Economic Crises in Turkey: Leaving Behind a Turbulent Past? *Economic and Financial Affairs Directorate-General of the European Commission, Economic Papers* No. 386.

North American Free Trade Agreement, U.S.-Can-Mex. 1992. (December 17). 32 I.L.M. 289.

Önder, Gökhan, and Zeynep Karal Önder. 2013. Determinants of Foreign Direct Investments Outflow from a Developing Country: The Case of Turkey. *Business, Management and Education* 11: 241.

Önder, Nilgün. 2008. The Turkish Project of Globalization and New Regionalism. *Alternatives: Turkish Journal of International Relations* 7: 86.

Oral, Muhammed, and Ünal Özdemir. 2017. Küresel Enerji Jeopolitiğinde Türkiye: Firsatlar ve Riskler [Global Energy Geopolitics and Turkey: Opportunities and Risks]. *Journal of History Culture and Art Research* 6: 948.

Oran, Baskin. 2011. *Turk Dis Politikasi* [*Turkish Foreign Policy*]. İstanbul: İletişim Yayinlari.

Ozcan, Sebnem Kalemli, Miguel Eduardo Sánchez-Martín, and Gilles Thirion. 2016. A Difficult Relationship: Declining (but Productive) FDI Inflows in Turkey. *World Bank Group Macroeconomics and Fiscal Management Global Practice Group Policy Research Working Paper* No. 7918.

Pauwelyn, Joost. 2003. The Limits of Litigation: "Americanization" and Negotiation in the Settlement of WTO Disputes. *Ohio State Journal of Dispute Resolution* 19: 121.

Pazarci, Hüseyin. 2009. *Uluslararasi Hukuk* [*International Law*]. 8th edition. Ankara: Turhan Kitabevi.

Polat, Burcak, and Cem Payaslioğlu. 2014. Determinants of Foreign Direct Investment to Turkey: A Sectoral Approach. *Topics in Middle Eastern and African Economies* 17: 1.

Reich, Arie. 2017. The Effectiveness of the WTO Dispute Settlement System: A Statistical Analysis. *European University Institute Working Papers* No. Law 2017/11.

*Restatement (Third) of Foreign Relations Law*. 1987. Philadelphia: The American Law Institute.

Rittenberg, Libby. 1998. *The Political Economy of Turkey in the Post-Soviet Era: Going West and Looking East?* Westport C.T.: Praeger Publishers Inc.

Rodrik, Dani. 1990. Some Policy Dilemmas in Turkish Macroeconomic Management. In *The Political Economy of Turkey: Debt, Adjustment and Sustainability*, eds. Tosun Aricanli and Dani Rodrik 183. New York: Palgrave Macmillan.

Rodrik, Dani. 2005. Notes on Trade and Industrialization Policy, in Turkey and Elsewhere. *METU Studies in Development* 32: 259.

Rodrik, Dani. 2012. The Turkish Economy After the Global Financial Crisis. *Ekonomi-Tek* 1:41.

Saatçioğlu, Beken. 2013. Turkey-EU Relations from the 1960s to 2012: A Critical Overview. In *Turkey's Accession to the European Union: Political and Economic Challenges*, eds. Belgin Akçay and Bahri Yilmaz, 3. Minneapolis: Lexington Books.

Sahin, Hüseyin. 2014. *Turkiye Economisi* [*Turkish Economy*]. 14th edition. Bursa: Ezgi Kitabevi Yayinlari.

Sakallioglu, Umit Cizre, and Erinç Yeldan. 2000. Politics, Society and Financial Liberalization: Turkey in the 1990s. *Development and Change* 31: 481.

Saribeyoglu, Meltem. 2010. *Uluslararasi Ticaret Hukuku Açisindan Dunya Ticaret Orgutu, Gümrük Birliği ve Turkiye* [*World Trade Organization, Customs Union and Turkey in light of International Trade Law*]. İstanbul: Türkmen Kitabevi.

Saygin, Hasan, and Murat Çimen. 2013. *Turkish Economic Policies and External Dependency*. Newcastle, U.K.: Cambridge Scholars Publishing.

Şenses, Fikret. 1990. An Assessment of the Pattern of Turkish Manufactured Export Growth in the 1980s and Its Prospects. In *The Political Economy of Turkey: Debt, Adjustment and Sustainability*, eds. Tosun Aricanli and Dani Rodrik 60. New York: Palgrave Macmillan.

Takim, Abdullah, and Ensar Yilmaz. 2010. Economy Policy During Ataturk's Era in Turkey. *African Journal of Business Management* 4: 549.

Takım, Abdullah. 2012. Demokrat Parti Döneminde Uygulanan Ekonomi Politikalari ve Sonuçlari [Economic Policies Applied During Democrat Party Rule]. *Ankara Universitesi, SBF Dergisi* 67: 157.

Tasar, Izzet, Esma Gultekin, and Yunus Acci. 2015. Is Turkey in a Middle Income Trap? *Journal of Applied Research in Finance and Economics* 1: 36.

Taylar, Yildirim. 2010. Vergi Teorisi Açisindan Özel Tüketim Vergileri ve Türk Özel Tüketim Vergisi Uygulamasi [Special Consumption Taxes and Application of Turkey's Special Consumption Tax from the Perspective of Tax Theory]. *Dokuz Eylül Üniversitesi Hukuk Fakültesi Dergisi,* C12: 435.

Tekçe, Mahmut. 2015. The Future of the Customs Union Between Turkey and the EU in the Context of the EU Trade Policy Agenda of the EU. *Marmara Univ. IIB Dergisi* 37: 397.

*The Federalist No. 75* (Alexander Hamilton), *available at*: https://guides.loc.gov/federalist-papers/full-text.

Thornburg, Max Weston. 1949. *Turkey: An Economic Appraisal.* New York: The Twentieth Century Fund.

Togan, Subidey, and Bartlomiej Kaminski. 2010. The Foreign Trade Regime and Trade Liberalization in Turkey. In *Economic Liberalization and Turkey,* ed. Subidey Togan, 13. London: Routledge.

Torsten, Amelung. 1988. The Political Economy of Import Substitution and Consequent Trade Liberalization: The Case of Turkey. *Kiel Working Paper* No. 330.

Treaty Establishing the European Economic Community. 1957. (March 25). 298 U.N.T.S. 11.

Turkey: 2017 Article IV Consultation-Press Release, Staff Report, and Statement by the Executive Director for Turkey. 2017. *International Monetary Fund Country Report* No. 17/32.

*Turkish Exporters Assembly, Economy and Foreign Trade Report. 2016*. İstanbul: Küçük Mucizeler Yayincilik.

*Turkiye Ihracatcilar Meclisi* [*Turkish Exporters Assembly*], *Ekonomi ve Dis Ticaret Raporu 2017* [*Economy and Foreign Trade Report, 2017*]. 2017. İstanbul: Küçük Mucizeler Yayincilik.

Ünay, Sadik. 2006. *Neoliberal Globalization and Institutional Reform: The Political Economy of Development and Planning in Turkey.* New York: Nova Science Publishers.

Understanding on Rules and Procedures Governing the Settlement of Disputes, April 15, 1994, Marrakesh Agreement Establishing the World Trade Organization, Annex 2, 1869 U.N.T.S. 401.

United Nations, Conference on Trade and Development. 2021. Online. *Available at*: https://unctad.org/press-material/investment-flows-developing-asian-countries-fall-30-45-due-covid-19-says-un-report.

United Nations, Economic and Social Council, Draft Country Programme Document for Turkey. 2015. Online. *Available at*: http://www.unicef.org/about/execboard/files/2015-PL19-Turkey_CPD-ODS-EN.pdf.

United Nations, Key Statistics and Trends in Trade Policy 2014. 2015. Online. *Available at*: http://unctad.org/en/PublicationsLibrary/ditctab2014d3_en.pdf.

Uslu, Cennet. 2016. Why Did People Become Human Shields Against the Coup? *Bilig* 1: 197.

Utkulu, Utku, and Durmuş Özdemir. 2004. Does Trade Liberalization Cause a Long Run Economic Growth in Turkey. *Economics of Planning* 37: 245.

Vienna Convention on the Law of Treaties. 1969. (May 23) 1155 U.N.T.S. 331.

Villager, Mark E. 2009. *Commentary on the 1969 Vienna Convention on the Law of Treaties*. Leiden, the Netherlands: Martinus Nijhoff Publishers.

Voigt, Susanne. 2008. *The Customs Union Between Turkey and the EU: How Did It Affect Turkey?* Hamburg: Diplomica Verlag.

Webb, Steven. 1998. Turkey: Democratization and Adjustment from Above. In *State and Market: The Political Economy of Turkey in Comparative Perspective*, ed. Ziya Öniş 348. İstanbul: Boğazic,I University Press.

World Trade Organization Secretariat, Trade Policy Review of Turkey No. WT/TPR/S/44. 1998. Online. *Available at*: https://www.wto.org/english/tratop_e/tpr_e/tp83_e.htm.

World Trade Organization Secretariat, Trade Policy Review of Turkey No. WT/TPR/S/125. 2003. Online. *Available at*: https://www.wto.org/english/tratop_e/tpr_e/tp225_e.htm.

World Trade Organization Secretariat, Trade Policy Review of Turkey No. WT/TPR/S/259. 2012. Online. *Available at*: https://www.wto.org/english/tratop_e/tpr_e/tp359_e.htm.

World Trade Organization Secretariat, Trade Policy Review of Turkey No. WT/TPR/S/331. 2016. Online. *Available at*: https://www.wto.org/english/tratop_e/tpr_e/s331_e.pdf.

World Trade Organization Secretariat, Trade Policy Review of Turkey No. WT/TPR/S/192. 2007. Online. *Available at*: https://www.wto.org/english/tratop_e/tpr_e/tp292_e.htm.

World Trade Organization, *Annual Report 2002*, 2002. Geneva: WTO Publications.

World Trade Organization, Notification under Article 7.3 of the Agreement on Import Licensing Procedures for 2015 by Turkey. 2015. *Report* No. G/LIC/N/3/TUR/14.

World Trade Organization, Notification under Article 7.3 of the Agreement on Import Licensing Procedures for 2016 by Turkey. 2016. *Report* No. G/LIC/N/3/TUR/15.

World Trade Organization, Semi-Annual Report under Article 25.11 of the Agreement, 2018. *Report* No. G/SCM/N/334/TUR.

World Trade Organization, World Tariff Profiles 2017. 2017. Online. *Available at*: https://www.wto.org/english/res_e/booksp_e/tariff_profiles17_e.pdf.

World Trade Organization, World Tariff Profiles 2018. 2018. Online. *Available at*: https://www.wto.org/english/res_e/booksp_e/tariff_profiles18_e.pdf.

World Trade Organization, World Tariff Profiles 2020. 2020. Online. *Available at*: https://www.wto.org/english/res_e/booksp_e/tariff_profiles20_e.pdf.

Yenel, Selim. 2017. Resetting the Turkey-EU Relationship, *Turkish Policy Quarterly* 16: 29.

Yildiran, Mustafa. 2010. Foreign Trade Strategy in the Existence Area of Turkiye: Emerging Markets Originating from the East and the Economical Politics of New Orientations. *Süleyman Demirel University, The Journal of Faculty of Economics and Administrative Sciences* 15: 313.

Zamir, Eyal, and Doron Teichman. 2018. *Behavioral Law and Economics*. New York: Oxford University Press.

Zan, Tao. 2016. "Turkey Dream" and the China-Turkish Cooperation under "One Belt and One Road" Initiative. *Journal of Middle Eastern and Islamic Studies (in Asia)* 10:50.

Zurcher, Eric J. 1993. *Turkey: A Modern History*. London: I. B. Tauris.

# Table of Cases

# Table of Statutes

# Index

## C

**T**